W9-BKS-068

Africa and Africans

The Natural History Press, publisher for The American Museum of Natural History, is a division of Doubleday & Company, Inc. Directed by a joint editorial board made up of members of the staff of both the Museum and Doubleday, the Natural History Press publishes books and periodicals in all branches of the life and earth sciences, including anthropology and astronomy. The Natural History Press has its editorial offices at The American Museum of Natural History, Central Park West at Seventy-ninth Street, New York 24, New York, and its business offices at 501 Franklin Avenue, Garden City, New York.

Paul Bohannan is Professor of Anthropology at Northwestern University, where he is also associated with the Program of African Studies.

Born in Lincoln, Nebraska, he graduated from the University of Arizona and, a Rhodes Scholar, attended Oxford University where he received his B.Sc. and D. Phil. With his wife, Laura Bohannan, also an anthropologist, he spent a total of twenty-six months from 1949 to 1953 among the Tiv of central Nigeria and in 1955 he spent nine months with the Wanga of Kenya.

Before going to Northwestern in 1959, he taught at Oxford University and Princeton University. He is the author of numerous monographs, articles, and book reviews, and *Social Anthropology*, a textbook. He has edited *Homicide and Suicide in Africa*, and, with George Dalton, a symposium, *Markets in Africa*. He wrote the Encyclopedia Americana's article, "Africa: Peoples and Cultures."

Africa and Africans

PAUL BOHANNAN

Published for
The American Museum of Natural History

The Natural History Press
Garden City, New York

The line illustrations for this book were prepared by the Graphic Arts Division of The American Museum of Natural History.

Library of Congress Catalog Card Number 64-10025

Printed in the United States of America

Preface

The aim of this book is to put African culture in modern perspective for Western readers by the concomitant examination of the African facts and the Western myths that have obscured it.

I became interested in Africa through my teachers, E. E. Evans-Pritchard, Meyer Fortes, and Max Gluckman. I was, for almost four years, a colleague of the late M. J. Herskovits, some of whose passion for Africa I have absorbed. I worked on the continent as a social anthropologist for more than three years, on grants from the Social Science Research Council, The Wenner-Gren Foundation, and the East African Institute for Social Research. I am especially grateful to members of the committee of the Human Environments in Middle Africa Project—James S. Coleman, Leonard Doob, William O. Jones, G. P. Murdock, and Benjamin E. Thomas—for helping me to understand the views they and their disciplines took of the continent.

Nevertheless, the book remains "One Man's Africa," written at a time when Africa has just emerged as a world force, and African studies have reached maturity.

Paul Bohannan

Evanston, Illinois
August 3, 1963.

Contents

PART I THE NEW AFRICA

1 *The Myth and the Fact* 1

2 *Colonialism and the Seeds of Freedom* 11
The Working Misunderstanding 11
The Absentee Sovereign 13
Colonial Social Structure 14
Interpenetration of Cultures 21
The Seeds of Freedom 24
Nativism and Nationalism 25

PART II ANCIENT AFRICA

3 *The African Continent* 32
Size, Shape, and Geological Composition of the African Continent 32
Climates and Vegetation 35
Soils and Agriculture 39
Resources 42
Diseases 45

4 *The Peopling of Africa* 48
Early Man 48
Miocene Apes in Africa 51
Early Man in Africa 53
Genesis and Africa 56
Stone Age Man in Africa 57

5 *The Peoples of Africa* 60
Race 60
Seligman's Races of Africa 65

Changing European Views of Africans 68
Modern Population Problems 77

6 *Farms and Iron* 79
The Agricultural Revolution 80
Egypt in the History of Africa 85
Iron and Kingship 88
The Spread of Iron and Feudalism to the South 95

7 *Darkest Africa* 98
The Great Tradition and the Little Tradition 98
Prince Henry and the Beginnings of "Discovery" 103
Slavery and the Slave Trade 105
Abolition of the Slave Trade 110
The Explorers 111
The Scramble for Africa 116

PART III TRIBAL AFRICA

8 *Tribal Africa* 124
The Languages of Africa 128
Subsistence Areas of Africa 133

9 *African Arts* 140
Artistic Comment 141
The Forms and Techniques of African Art 142
The History of African Art 145
The Place of Art in African Society 148
The Aesthetics of African Art 150
African Art in the Western World 156

10 *African Families* 158
Family Life 159
Nonfamilial Kinship Groups 168

11 *African Land and Labor* 174
Space and Territoriality 174
Labor 182

12 *African Politics and Courts* 188
States 190
Stateless Societies 194
Law in African Societies 199

13 *African Markets* 206
Marketing and Trading 209
Market Places 212
Systems of Market Places 216
The Spread of the Market Principle 217

14 *African Religion* 222
A Rubric for African Religion 224
Dogma 227
Ritual 229
Witchcraft: the Parasite of Religion 232
Islam and Christianity 233

PART IV AFRICA AND THE MODERN WORLD

15 *The Scrambles for Africa* 238
The Newest Scramble 239
Africa and the United States 242
The New Africans 245
Envoi 248

Further Reading 250

Index 255

List of Maps

1. Africa in early 1965 — *Frontispiece*
2. Africa, with the United States superimposed 33
3. Climatic regions of Africa 36
4. Some of the old African empires 90
5. European toeholds in Africa, 1884 115
6. Europeans in Africa after the Berlin Conference, 1885 117
7. Africa in 1914 119
8. Language areas of Africa 130
9. Subsistence areas of Africa 134
10. Africa at the end of World War II 240

Part I
THE NEW AFRICA

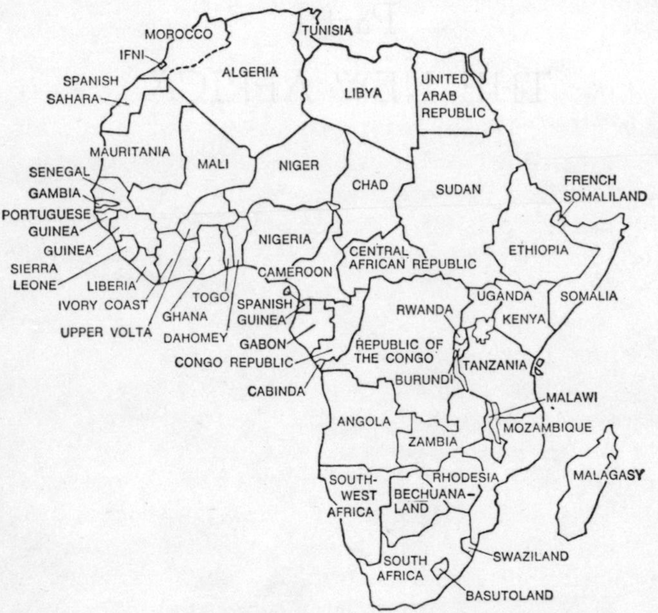

FIG. 1. Africa in early 1965.

Chapter 1

The Myth and the Fact

Africa has, for generations now, been viewed through a web of myth so pervasive and so glib that understanding it becomes a twofold task: the task of clarifying the myth and the separate task of examining whatever reality has been hidden behind it. Only as it is stated and told can the myth be stripped away. Only if the myth is stripped away can the reality of Africa emerge.

Africa splashed into the consciousness of the rest of the world in July of 1960 with the eruption of the newly independent Congo, all but forgotten since the days of the slave trade. In the century between 1860 and 1960 Africa had been the province of Africans, and of a few missionaries, colonial government officials, and scholars. Occasionally the isolation was pierced by travelers: yet men like André Gide, when they broke the dark barrier, admitted that they saw problems and moral questions of which they had sooner remain ignorant. For the rest, there was Dr. Schweitzer and there were the maunderings of moralistic and naïve romantics like Laurens van der Post to stand between Martin Johnson's *Lion* and today's New York *Times*. All of them, for one reason or another, had an interest in preserving the myths.

Africa was the "Dark Continent," but the darkness had much more to do with the European and American visitors to it, and workers in it, than it had to do with Africans. It was in the interests of officials to say, in their reports to their governments and indeed in their letters home, that Africa was peaceful and was progressing along predetermined lines. It was in the interests of missionaries, in emphasizing their undoubted victories, to exaggerate the depravity of the base line from which their ministrations had brought their converts. It was, on the other hand, in the interest of physical and biological scientists either to disregard Africans or to treat them as specimens. It was in the interests of many anthropologists who were studying alien cultures to look only at Africa's bright side.

It was, therefore, into a profoundly ignorant Western world that Africa was plunged in 1960. Some colonial governments had mountains of data—almost all of it the wrong kind to cope with the new situation. The professional association in America, the African Studies Association, had far fewer than three hundred fellows in that year and was nevertheless hailed as the largest national organization of its sort. The International African Institute was thirty years old—and it was almost the sole bastion of information and of facts about Africa: but it was run by a director, a librarian, an executive secretary, and a small editorial and office staff.

In the years since the Congo blew up, all this has changed drastically. But a new difficulty has been encountered: all the students who are going into African studies want to study the same thing. They follow the subjects and problems of pioneers like James S. Coleman in his study of Nigerian nationalism, and David Apter in his work on the political structure of the Gold Coast, which was soon to become Ghana, instead of following the pioneering spirit of inquiry that these men represent. Too many scholars follow the headlines, or else they follow the noble savage. Problems of Nigerian political parties; Mau Mau; the "emergence of elites" in eastern and central Africa or in Senegal; race in the Republic of South Africa. But less attention to French-speaking Africa, to Chad and Niger—indeed, the Central African Republic has never been studied (until a few months before the writing of these words, it had never even received a

UNESCO visitation. How backward and forgotten can a country get?)

Moreover, organizations like The Peace Corps, Cross-Roads Africa and many other smaller operations are suddenly providing us with a large number of Americans who know something about Africa, and perhaps more important, who know something about cross-cultural living. The business and industrial worlds, as well as the academic and artistic worlds, must make ready to receive these people and utilize their talents and their experience: not just as foreign representatives, but as analytical and constructive critics of world economy and world society.

There has, in fact, been a notable change in information about and attitudes toward Africa on the part of the general American public—led, perhaps, by high school students and their teachers. In 1956, when anyone heard I was interested in Africa he would say, "Oh, do you know Dr. Schweitzer?" By the end of 1960, the question had become, "Do you know Tom Mboya?" naming the American press's favorite African politician. By the fall of 1962, things had changed even further: a high school audience began a discussion session after a short preliminary lecture with, "What are the precise differences in the platforms of KANU and KADU?" We have come a long way.

Yet, our information is scattered and disorganized. Nobody has, as yet, found a way to bring together systematically what is known to scholars, what the missionaries have learned, and what business and industrial representatives know.

Although it is of a limited sort, missionaries have amassed a tremendous knowledge about Africa that should be utilized. Missionaries speak the languages of the peoples they missionize. They tend to stay in these places from three to twenty-five years (with breaks, of course, because one cannot stay away from one's own culture for too long without its becoming diluted). However, lack of utilization of missionaries by scholars is only part of the problem. Missionaries, with all of their knowledge, have garnered it for specific purposes. I do not question these purposes, but only state that they are not the purposes of statesmanship or scholarship.

Businessmen who have been in and out of Africa know an amazing amount about it—people in the copper companies, trading companies, and more recently the banks and the flour mills. Their knowledge is about very different subjects from that of the missionaries or the scientists, but they do have a tremendous fund of untapped information. There is little opportunity for businessmen, missionaries, and scholars to forgather and talk.

Because informed people were rare, and because those who did exist did not pool their knowledge, Americans and other Westerners became aware and conscious of Africa with all the myths intact.

Some of the most pervasive myths are the simplest: the myth of the lions in the jungles. Lions do not live in jungles. In the first place, only about 5 percent of the African continent can be called jungle in any case. What few lions there are live in the grasslands. But darkness goes with jungles and wild beasts, and the lions in the jungles persist as a symbol for the unrecognized fear that Americans have for Africa.

The myth that Africa is the dark continent is, actually, a subject-object confusion. Europe was certainly isolated—as isolated as Africa has ever been, and was much more so than Africa during the Middle Ages. Africans and Arabs and Indians, during this time, had an active trade across the Indian Ocean and across the Sahara—even across the Mediterranean. Morocco leather was made south of the Sahara—it was bought from the Moroccans by Europeans, who did not ask further where it came from. In the twelfth and thirteenth centuries the whole subcontinent of Africa south of the Sahara was flooded with cowrie shells, which became a currency—and they came from the Maldive Islands, via Venice and the Arabs.

Africa was in touch with the rest of the world while most of Europe slept. Africa was even in touch with the fringes of Europe. There are portraits of Africans on Greek vases; there are portrait busts of Negroes in Roman art. Europe must recognize the fact that it was *Europe* that woke up only in the fifteenth century.

The next myth—and it is one that will be met everywhere—is that Africa was "savage." The myth began in the seventeenth and eighteenth centuries when savages became a philosophical necessity for the emergence of Europe. Savages, both depraved and noble, explained historical as well as psychic problems—but the ideas concerning savages were buttressed with few facts. Savages were next to "missing links," mythical creatures of a cosmographic theory known as the "chain of being" outliving the theory that spawned them. Savages were clean, and unriddled by the problems of industrialization and vast (and vastly painful) social change. Savages, on the other hand, could not speak, knew not fire, and were at the mercy of the destructive forces of brute nature. Such savages were what we all might have been, except for the grace of God. It must also be admitted that missionaries, probably more than any other single group, kept the myth of savagery alive. The more "savage" a place, the greater the missionaries' mundane as well as supermundane rewards. Their undeniable fortitude and the hardships they bore were translated into the imagery of "savagery" by congregations and mission societies at home, even if they did not themselves write them so (and many were level-headed observers who did not). They knew better, as their papers show: yet the image they cast before them was that of heroes doing battle with cannibalism, lust, and depravity—the forces of "darkness."

Today, we can admit the facts on which such a myth was based, at the same time that we can be objective about them. African culture shares more of its traits, its history, its social organization with Europe than Asia shares with Europe and certainly more than the North American Indians and the Australian aborigines share with Europe. Economically, Africa and Europe are a single sphere. Methods of production of food in Africa are pretty much the same as they were in Europe a few centuries, and in some instances a few millennia, ago. Market organization was the same. The religions are variations on the same basic themes. Family organization—pretty much the same values, although Africans tend to be polygynous and Europeans tend to be monogamous. But the values are quite the same. Such could not be said of the Chinese or the Aztecs.

Moreover, there were in 1960 literally thousands of Africans who were trained and ready to take over the administration of their countries: not as many as they themselves would desire, but in most of British and French Africa—particularly those without European settlers—there were enough to start with. Along with their traditionalism, there is a very broad streak of modernism in all Africans. Unlike some peoples of the Pacific and the Americas, Africans have shown comparatively little resistance to change and so-called modernization. This again may stem largely from the fundamental similarity of African and European (including American) cultures. They share anciently a great common pool of culture, and although the African manifestations of it are different from those of Europeans, the differences are superficial when set beside the gulfs that separate either from Australian aborigines, Malays, or even the Japanese. Perhaps even more important, they share Europe's diseases and so were not decimated on contact.

But there are other myths to be exploded: one is the more generalized myth, in America, about race. Africans are "supposed" to be Negroes—but there are lots of Africans who are not. There are Caucasians and there are Bushmen.

The whole subject of race has been torn asunder and

"exposed" by modern genetics, yet the very term has encapsulated connotations from false scientific claims and ethical judgments of centuries. The word "race" means, to geneticists, an interbreeding population with distinct and heritable characteristics. The difficulty comes in properly delimiting the relevant characteristics. For a century and more, race and language were confused—race and culture are still confused. Language is often a characteristic of an interbreeding population, but it is not a biotic characteristic, and therefore has nothing to do with "race." The same is true of culture. In the guise of differential intelligence (whatever that may eventually come to mean) and therefore "cultural potential," the old problem is still with us, and is still given a false biological base. Like witchcraft to the Age of Reformation, the concept of race seems to be the non sequitur by which the modern world explains forces that it does not understand. Race as a social problem is still with us—and it is the social problem that must be dealt with.

The racial myth leads us to another: that is the myth among American Negroes about what Africa is and what its nature is. American Negroes came to this country, as we are all constantly aware, as slaves. The first Negro arrived in the New World in 1494. Negroes provided as much of the heritage of the American continent as any other group. They have been here just as long. American Negroes, toward the end of the nineteenth century, when they were being more systematically closed out from the dominant culture than they had ever been before, turned back to Africa in search of security. There were two reactions: one was to deny any kind of association with Africa. The other was to embrace it as a fatherland. Pan-Africanism started as a movement among American Negroes; they were its driving force from the late nineteenth century until the end of World War II. Since then, they have been grossly disappointed, because African aims are nationalistic and their own are equalitarian.

Today, none can any longer deny Africa, even culturally. Many Negroes have nevertheless turned against Africans. Yet they dare not deny them too loudly today, for to deny Africa is to deny the blackness of their skins, and to deny that is to be a traitor to the great force that French-speaking Africans call *negritude*, and that burns vibrantly in the Negro revolution in the United States. Educated and upper middle-class American Negroes are caught between Black Muslims and Africans—wishing to deny both, but able to deny neither.

American Negroes are as American as American Swedes, and their African heritage has made great contributions to American culture: from attitudes toward child care to southern cooking. Africanisms came into America the way that Polishisms came into it. People came in, and people always react to new situations according to the dictates of their old fundamental experience. If that experience was African or Swedish, this is "the way they do things." People bring up their children basically as they themselves were brought up. When one starts being a nursemaid or a mother or a father or an uncle, only a narrow part of the whole arc of culture is in Dr. Spock's book. The rest was learned in the social relationships in which one was involved when young. Therefore, there is a tendency for all basic values and ways of behavior to persist, even as they may be reinterpreted, or even superficially rejected.

The American Negro myth of Africa is one of the most dominant—and one of the most false, precisely because Negroes too were subject to the dominant myths about Africa. For many an American Negro, the myth that he has not contributed to American culture is compounded with—and confounded by—that other myth that Africans were "savages." The Negroes' problem was that cultural forces were at play making it necessary for them to subscribe to the myths about Africa at the same time that psychic forces of *amour-propre* forced them to dissociate from Africa. They had either to dissociate and give the lie to the first myth or turn their African background into a Golden Age. The contradiction was blatant, and often destructive.

Another wrongheaded myth, very like the ones we have already examined for all that the subject matter is different, is the myth of the 1960s: African nations must be either for us or against us in the Cold War. Since the Cold War is the major problem for Americans, as for Communists, it seems all but incredible that some peoples do not see the world as opposed camps. Africans are neither for nor against the West—neither for nor against the Communist bloc. They are *for Africa,* sometimes just for their own country or even their own tribe. If we are for Africa, they are for us, and if we are against Africa, they are against us.

And finally, one last position must be made clear. The West does not so much have an African problem, as Africa has a European problem. South Africa is enough a European country to appear to have a native problem, but the "natives" think of it as a European problem. East Africans have a European problem. So do the Katangese. It was only half in jest that Kwame Nkrumah suggested building a monument in Accra to the Anopheles mosquito, the carrier of the malaria that made Europeans reject West Africa as "unsuitable for colonization." In the long run, unless Europeans in Africa change their ways, their future there is a dim one.

The European nations began in the fourteenth and fifteenth centuries an expansion that is only now being reversed. This expansion against the rest of the world was intrinsic to Euro-American culture, an integral part of its growth. Europeans combined classical and Judaeo-Christian ideas to provide the basis of an emergent morality. Christianity made such demands after the Middle Ages that there was only one thing to do: to push outwards in all directions. The rest of the peoples of the world were hit from outside. With the settling of the Europeans in America and Australia and South Africa, the people who were already there either collapsed as the Australian aborigines did or turned themselves into dependent remnant tribes as the American Indians did in the face of white power. But Africans adapted and adopted.

After the West expanded and collided with all these people, the new society needed clerks and catechists and and laborers in order to carry on business and achieve its purposes. Europeans started teaching people to use shovels and pencils, to figure and to read. When a man learns to read, the door has been opened. People see culture that in a colonial situation they are by definition not allowed to have. They are perfectly capable of practicing it, but are not allowed it. In such a situation, colonial people become deprived people. Africans, when they were living a tribal life, were not deprived people. Lives of tremendous dignity and valued rewards can be lived away from the trappings of Western civilization. But once the consciousness of those trappings seeps into awareness, a new day has arrived, and a new struggle must ensue.

Chapter 2

Colonialism and the Seeds of Freedom

Since World War II most of the colonies of the world have been turned into independent nations. The exceptions are some small island communities of the Pacific, a few outliers such as the Portuguese colonies in Africa and Indonesia, and the vast reaches of Soviet central Asia. For Africa, the watershed year between colonialism and independence was 1960.

Colonialism is a political and economic form characterized by two major conditions: one can be called the principle of the working misunderstanding, the other the principle of the absentee sovereign. The interaction between these two principles leads always to basically the same form of social structure (even when its superficial decoration is very different) and, interestingly enough, to a single structure of events (even when the history in which they are played out seems totally diverse).

THE WORKING MISUNDERSTANDING

The essence of colonialism is that there are always two, often opposed, ways of looking at the power system and at the world in general: one is of the colonizing power and the other represents the views of the colonized peoples. The two viewpoints grow naturally and silently out of different cultural viewpoints and goals. The colonizers and the colonized, even when they are as generally similar as Africans and Europeans, have many cultural disparities. Thus, one group reacts to any given situation in a way quite at odds with the reaction of the other group.

Such a situation—the colonial condition—must not be confused with two-party government or other forms of regulating opposed views in government matters. Democrats and Republicans have different views and often different aims. They will usually disagree on means and often on ends and goals of the society. But, for all that, they usually understand one another—only too well. They share the major elements of their culture—particularly those unstated assumptions about the ultimate nature of God, society, the good life, and the value of the human being. All governments contain such opposed views, even if there is no recognized "opposition."

Colonialism presents a different picture from encapsulated opposition: in a colony the ruling group sees the local situation in terms of categories and problems—indeed, in terms of the very words—that they learned "at home" in quite a different polity and economy. Their schools, their families, their books and art galleries, plays and political associations all go toward shaping their opinions. And besides opinion, people absorb from these institutions basic axioms for viewing the world and thinking about life and about power that they do not even know they hold.

The members of the subject group, in the same way, look at the situation with eyes and ideas grown accustomed to the local scene. They do so in words, moral and ethical values, and expected responses that have been learned largely unconsciously and that have remained unconscious. The "ways" of nature and of the world are simply perceived and communicated differently by the two.

In an African colony, then, the political and economic situation was assessed by the European rulers in terms of European culture; the same situation was assessed by Africans in terms of their various African cultures. Their common heritage and their common humanity assured that for some matters the two evaluations were complementary. Just as surely, their separate histories led them to view other matters divergently. The result of their rubbing shoulders and ideas was not common understanding so much as it was a more or less fortuitous confluence of some aims and purposes, accompanied by a constant suspicion of tyranny, stupidity, or lack of good faith when things did not turn out as expected. Such is the nature of the "working misunderstanding."

In a situation such as African colonialism, the power system, as it would be seen by a social scientist, was not what it appeared to *anybody* on the ground. Communication was faulty—not merely incomplete, for communication is probably never total—but faulty. There were two sides and neither really knew the "codes"—the connotations of word and deed—in which the other group perceived the situation, valued it, communicated about it, and acted.

THE ABSENTEE SOVEREIGN

The second major characteristic of all colonial systems is that the most important decisions in the policy and economy of the colony are made by the ruling power (with more or less reference to the colonized peoples, and always subject to the working misunderstanding) primarily on the basis of factors operative in the metropolitan country rather than on the basis of factors operative in the colony itself.

The absentee sovereign leads inevitably to one of two possible outcomes: to tyranny on the one hand and to paternalism on the other. There is undoubtedly a continuum between tyranny and paternalism, and in some situations people find the one as distasteful as the other. If the rulers are "kind" (a very complex concept), or if they have "the interests of the people at heart" or consider their own "*mission civilisatrice*" as putting more "responsibility" on them than on the colonized peoples, one of the many forms of paternalism results. If, on the other hand, the rulers are selfish and exploitative the result can be labeled tyranny. Many a colonial official has been deeply hurt when, after thirty years of selfless service to a colony, he has been charged with tyranny by a subject people who do not distinguish tyranny from paternalism but see only the disjunction between their own cultural views and aims and those of the colonizing powers.

COLONIAL SOCIAL STRUCTURE

The result of these forces is a singularly static form of society in the midst of which great material and ideational changes can and do take place. The static quality emerges not from any inability on the part of the governed, or from any base desire by the governors to "keep a country backward," as has often been charged. Rather it arises from a desire on the part of the rulers to keep the situation predictable.

The British in Africa—and they are my target only because I know them better than I do the Belgians or the French or the Portuguese—made several revealing reversals in their own cultural attitudes in order to accommodate those greater "virtues" that they believed their culture had to offer Africans. One of the primary purposes of British administration was always to make the law "sure" or "certain"—this aim is based on the British idea that it is a virtue to maintain certain legal rights underlying democracy. Indeed, the "certainty of the law" was, in British eyes, one of the major virtues that they had to impart. They did not find the "law" to be "certain" in their African possessions, so they set about creating certainty: and in doing so, they of course used the tools and the institutions with which they were familiar and which they knew to "work." They established a hierarchy of responsible officials, and new systems of courts;

they began to write down those aspects of "native law and custom" with which they did not want to interfere.

"Responsibility" is a word that turns up, in some form, in all European languages with a predominantly Latin vocabulary; it has been translated into the languages with predominantly Germanic vocabularies (*Verantwortlichkeit*). It is, nevertheless, a concept that is very difficult to express in most African languages. African cultures, of course, recognize obligations toward kinsmen and toward officials that Europeans would call "responsibilities." But in the African view the obligation is toward people, not toward principles or a "system." One does not have "responsibility" toward an idea or to a position in a system; most of all, the African idea does not extend to the proposition: "*You* are responsible; *you* take the rap!"

When the European governments sought and found the politically "responsible" Africans, they did not extract only that part of the total meaning of "responsibility" which was in fact shared. Understandably enough, they brought the entire field of their connotation with them. The result was, of course, that they never considered African officials totally "responsible" in the context of colonial government.

The European colonial powers found in many parts of Africa a highly organized means of settling disputes that had much in common with the courts with which they were familiar—judges, witnesses, rules of evidence, and jural pomp and ceremony. Under the zeal of paternalism, and the philosophy of cultural evolution, they set about improving and "evolving" these courts into the more "efficient" mechanisms that they knew. In doing so, they credited Africans with understanding more of such intentions than was actually the case. The courts they established were not merely more "efficient," but in many cases they were different in kind—many disputes could no longer be heard, and the right of judicial compromise was denied.

Perhaps most important of all was the European fetish for writing down the law, which practice has still not run its course. Accompanying the writing of the law was a constant worry that the administrators were "freezing" the system so as actually to imperil the changes they themselves wanted to make—certainly a well-founded fear. Yet, there was widespread belief that it is possible to write down a law or set of laws without changing it significantly. The point was missed: "it" may not be changed, if the "it" is the particular rule itself. But the whole "it" is bigger: it included the substantive law, the way it is enforced, the attitude toward law and ultimately the social philosophy of justice and of the relationship between a man and his government.

The British case is particularly interesting, because the British so passionately defend their "unwritten" constitution at home, and so tease Americans about the difficulty of amending theirs. Having an unwritten constitution provides suppleness. Yet, in Africa, the British wrote down constitutions in order to supply certainty (the very while they were stating that they feared loss of suppleness to changing conditions).

The point is obvious: throughout, the British administrations were providing (so they thought) the very "security" of the law that they found in Britain and missed in Africa. They did not realize that the sureness and security in Britain came from a sureness of culture, not merely a sureness of the law. Where there is cultural security and predictability, an unwritten constitution is handy and easily adaptable. The British did not find the African system predictable—they did not sufficiently know the culture involved. So they wrote down the law, appointed "responsible" officials, and established "better organized" courts.

It is just this very procedure that gives to all British colonies, at any one time, the same type of formal social and political structure. The result is a "freezing" of social change, development, and growth. It takes place not merely at a slower rate, but at a pace and in a direction dictated from outside.

As a result, colonies in the nineteenth and twentieth centuries all have a fascinating similarity—and that similarity comes from the superficial (though sometimes powerful) institutions of the colonizers, implanted on peoples who do not fully comprehend the roles that have been assigned them. The British idea of "indirect rule" provides a ready example. This label applies to a method for trying to "maintain" the power system of an indigenous society, while hooking it to a supererogatory alien system of power. The fiction could then be maintained that the authorities continued to operate just as they always had. The result was, of course, uniform throughout the British Empire (in spite of local variations in detail). The British in Nigeria (say) established a colonial system with a governor, a lieutenant-governor, a series of provincial commissioners, and under them a number of district commissioners. The names and titles changed from one country to another—the hierarchical structure did not. Then, at a certain point, the "chiefs" fitted in, with their graduated subordinates. The "native administration" always linked in, via courts and council meetings, with the alien administration.

Precisely the same type of organization was to be found in Fiji, and indeed everywhere else there was British administration. The difference is that in Nigeria, the titles of the various officials were given in local languages such as Hausa, Yoruba, or Ibo whereas in Fiji, they were given Fijian names. In both cases it could be said by the aliens, "This is a traditional system." Yet from a longer view, British colonies form a single "type" society—and they differ only in detail from the French and the Belgian colonies.

In Africa, there are several characteristics of colonial

social structure to be examined. The societies within a colony are frozen not merely in time, but in space—in spite of the fact that mobility of *individuals* becomes vastly increased. Moreover, colonies are eternally at peace—there may be "uprisings" but there are no wars, except insofar as the colony takes the side of the metropolitan power in her wars. Colonies must have monetary systems that are congruent, in one way or another, with the monetary systems of the metropolitan power so that trade can be carried on, exports delivered, and—in recent decades—aid given from the metropole to the colony. Monetary systems both presuppose and create vast networks of contract. There are literally hundreds of other requisites, but these three will provide sufficient examples for our present purpose.

Africa was, before colonial days, full of people on the move. Because of the ways Africans provided for their own subsistence, and because of social, political, and even religious pressures, Africans moved and kept moving. The creation of colonial administration concomitantly created a need to know where everybody was. Moreover, the European background of the administrators told them that people should own their land, have rights in it against others and against the world, should be citizens of a stable and indeed of a fixed local community. And that meant boundaries.

Boundaries existed in Africa before the Europeans arrived there; but they are better thought of as "marches" than as "borders." They were cultural marches: the "adjoining places" of communities rather than legal dividing lines. Seldom were there, for any extended periods of time, marks on the land—although in a few areas of Africa they might be represented by streams or boulders, for short periods of time. One of the most important of all colonial activities was the splitting up of Africa, not just among nations, but among the Africans themselves, by means of legally enforceable boundaries. The whole basis of society was changed from what it had been—groups of people, held together by kingship, kinship, or religion, that occupied and exploited a more or less clearly defined area. It became vast numbers of areas, each occupied by people with citizenship rights in it. The difference may appear small, but the resultant misunderstanding was of staggering proportions.

Into what had been an extremely dynamic situation, of migrations, wars, and movement, peace was thrust by fiat. Africa became the homeland of the Pax Britannica, the Pax Gallica, the Pax Belgique. Thus, not only was the law changed and the political territories frozen in space, but the political units were not allowed to fight one another. To peoples accustomed to the nineteenth-century wars in Europe and South Africa and to World War I, such a situation appeared to be no more than the dawn of the new era. Whatever it may appear to Europeans in the second half of the twentieth century, it was considered by some Africans in the first half a serious deprivation—at the same time that they recognized its advantages. Certainly, however, it worked untold changes in the power and authority systems within African societies.

At the same time, the colonial peace created a situation in which individuals were safe far from home; colonial trade made available goods worth traveling to get. Therefore, as movement of social groups ceased, individuals began to travel far from home. Road and railroad networks began to appear—often excellent within a country, although the effects of colonialism are clearly visible on any railroad map of Africa, because the railroads of one colony do not connect with those of adjoining countries, but only link the "hinterland" with the seaports. The mode of movement within Africa thus changed fantastically; Africa is still a continent on the move, but the units of movement are now traveling individuals instead of migrating social groups.

Finally, the possibilities of travel and trade were given a fillip by the introduction of general purpose money. There were currencies of limited range in many parts of Africa before European impact. But with colonialism, the range of currency became total (that is, the same money could be used for any purpose that any money at all could be used for).

Trade, individual movement, currency, responsible officials, boundaries—it can all be summed up in another major, and all but unseen, development: the growth of contract. Modern Western society is based on contract—today in America, we even hire baby-sitters on contract. Economic growth and large-scale political organization functioning in the world as it is now organized, demand highly developed contract concepts and contract law. And the "sureness" of law comes to be even more an overt concern the greater the province of contract in the social fabric. In Africa the growth of "civil law" set in—a growth that is continuing at an even greater pace in the free nations of post-colonial Africa.

To repeat the leitmotiv: changes were made because the governors and the governed saw the problems differently, because the governors had the power to innovate regardless of the views of the governed, and because the misunderstanding could only grow. Nobody is to blame. There is no way in which guilt or innocence, good or bad, can be attached to these aspects of colonial activity. They exist and are part of it. I deplore the Africans who say that twentieth-century colonial officials were wicked as much as I deplore the colonial officials who claim that Africans are lazy or stupid. Both have failed to see the situation as it was: a janus, guarding the doors and entrances, without any possibility of unifying ideas about what is inside and what is outside the doors.

INTERPENETRATION OF CULTURES

In spite of the great apparent stability of colonial social and political structure, and its similarity the world over, there are points at which the two cultures interpenetrate and ultimately destroy the janus-faced system. These destroyers are in the world of things—the material items brought by trade—and in the world of ideas, the ideas brought by missionaries as well as by government officials and traders.

While the movement in time and space and the power structure remained more or less frozen in the colony, material culture flowed in both directions. Taxes were introduced. Africans are accustomed to paying tribute, but taxes are of a different nature: they require money, which is to be had in exchange for selling one's subsistence or new crops, one's labor or one's goods acquired in a cheaper market in order to provide money "income." Once income is achieved, it can be spent on imported cloth, enamelware, and tools, as well as on food itself and on prestige articles or activities. These imported items are usually cheaper and more durable than the craft items they replace. Revolutions of technical activity and striving for prestige take place—perhaps they are not as apparent to Europeans on the scene as they are to the Africans.

Obviously, with the introduction of cash crops and activities for labor and trade, social energy is deflected away from what has become traditional to call "traditional" activities. New values, new ideas, new demands have all been introduced. When labor entered the market, particularly in a situation in which it is not possible to sell labor near to home, the domestic structure was changed because as many as half the young men might be working in towns or mines at any given time. Here, old ideas were maintained in most cases—and the new situation was seen as undesirable even by the very Africans who knew that going out to work and having the things that laboring provided was desirable.

Ideas were as potent as things: ideas introduced purposefully by traders, by government officials and by missionaries. And even more telling were the ideas that these foreigners did not even know they were introducing.

Missionaries were, probably, the dominant importers of ideas, because their contact with Africans was of a broader social range and because the individual missionaries stayed in one area for much longer periods of time than did other foreigners. Missionaries brought not merely religious ideas; they brought economic and political ideas. And they brought the habits they had learned as children. Moreover, they had a very large role to play in the communication between the governors and the governed. Some of the Italian missionaries in the Sudan and eastern Africa, for example, settled down comfortably; insofar as they came from Italian peasant stock, they introduced less change than did the northern Europeans and the Americans. These latter were not peasants, and they did things in a different way and imported things of a different sort. Behind even their conversation lay ideas that were not totally overt, and hence were misunderstood by many of their hearers.

Whatever the religious impact of the missionary may have been, the initial impact was economic, and to a very real extent, political. Administrative officers were nominally at least of the same religious faith as the missionaries —they were certainly of the same cultures as the missionaries. There was constant discussion between them. The missionaries almost always knew quite a different aspect of the lives of Africans than did the administrative officers, and usually knew more. A sensible and sensitive administrative officer went to the missionaries for information. He could talk to people from his own country very much more easily; he could "pick up" his information. The result was that missionaries very often influenced policy profoundly.

At the same time, the missions were doing their jobs. What is a missionary's job? It turns out that, besides the purpose he goes over to achieve—the spread of his religion—he has an important secondary task. That secondary task is to hold the pieces of a society together when it smashes, and ultimately to put them back together again in a new pattern. No mission has ever been successful until the initial smashing of the culture made it necessary for new answers to be given to new questions. And then, in Africa and most other places, almost the only people who were in a position to teach, who were willing to explain new answers instead of declaring them, were the missionaries. In 1960, 96 percent of the schools in Nigeria were mission-operated schools; many of them were supported or assisted by government funds, but they were mission schools. It was the missionaries who taught Africans to read and write, and thereby supplied government clerks and traders' clerks and their own catechists, and ultimately the national leaders, the national businessmen. It was they who did the constructive job. Missionaries are very often blamed because they destroyed and misunderstood, and so they did. But so did everybody else. And missionaries are the only people who *built* below an institutional level. In many cases, I do not myself like what they built. That is beside the point. They did build and they are still building. Many of them are in even closer touch with citizens of new nations than they were with the colonized peoples of the first part of the twentieth century.

In spite of the duality of viewpoint that characterizes a colony, there is a strong flow of things and of ideas between the peoples who hold the viewpoints. Like unanimity of viewpoints, duality of viewpoints is probably never anything like complete. Nevertheless, it is sufficient to rip apart the very fabric of colonial social structure.

Life cannot change in the areas of polity and economy without tremendous concomitant changes in every other aspect of life. And here the ultimately destructive paradox of colonialism arises: in order to maintain the new power structure and the new economy, it becomes necessary for the colonizers either to move over and grant equality of opportunity to the colonized peoples (a painful process at best, because the duality of viewpoint has not been totally bridged), or else the colonizers must move toward tyranny along the paternalism-tyranny continuum. The basis of the polity is attacked by the very ideas and things which are encouraged by missions and schools and by the ordinary intercourse of trade.

THE SEEDS OF FREEDOM

European colonial powers intended to change the polity and the economy of African peoples. Missionaries intended to change their religions. And yet, equally great changes took place in all other aspects of life. The reason is simple: two (or more) cultures have come into contact in the process of achieving and working out the "working misunderstanding" that is characteristic of the colony. Cultural partitions cannot, however, be watertight. Ultimately the African peoples began to see and to understand—and to want—parts of those European cultures that they were, by the nature of the principle of the absentee sovereign, not able to have if the system was to be maintained. As that happened, Africans living in colonies became deprived people.

Tribal Africans were not and are not "deprived." They had the opportunity to run the whole gamut of their culture, or at least of their accepted place in it. Nothing deprived them of cultural experience which they did not choose to be deprived of in order to achieve some greater good. But in the colonial situation, such is not the case. More and more able people are produced—able in terms of and with the means of the ruling power. Yet, such people must be held in check—most often by being given limited opportunities, with different degrees of limitation being characteristic of different colonial powers.

From the African point of view, the limitation became tyrannous. And the dual nature of colonialism again reasserted itself. The existence of the working misunderstanding was discovered by those Africans who had penetrated European culture. Once that happened, the absentee sovereign could be challenged in a new and more effective way.

There are two major means of challenging the absentee sovereign: nationalistic revolutions and nativistic movements. Since World War II Africa has provided some notable examples of both, which bear close examination.

NATIVISM AND NATIONALISM

The presence of two cultures creates a particular kind of difficulty for the people living in the situation: if they want to do something prohibited by one culture, they escape into the other. They thus jump back and forth between the two cultural traditions, usually to their psychic cost. Their world, however, has widened; concomitant with a loosening of moral standards of behavior comes considerable realization of the provincialism of any single standard.

With the realization of provincialism comes the desire to change—to "improve." There are two paths that activities toward improvement may take in colonies; which is chosen depends on the strength and policy of the alien sovereign. To oversimplify, if the strength is weak and the policy paternalistic, the surging movements come out as nationalistic revolutions. If the strength is great and the policy tyrannical, the movements come out as "nativism." The nature of the particular African culture also brings obvious causal factors to bear.

Mau Mau was probably the most virulent of the modern nativistic movements in Africa. Nativistic movements occur when peoples are blocked from achieving what they have learned to want as goals and are not given adequate substitute goals. It is like repression and displacement in psychoanalytic theory.

Nativistic movements usually require two people to get off the ground: some sort of a prophet—a seer or mystic—and an impresario. There must be two personalities, two roles—the visionary and the organizer.

The visionary, through dreams or some other such means, divines that the ancestors or the spirits, God or some one of His agents, have made it known to him that the abyss into which the people have fallen was created when they abandoned such and such parts of the old culture. What they must do is go back and pick up that portion of belief or of culture, in order to achieve the cultural sureness that is longed for. He may also say that the new ways must be interpreted differently—most often in the light of traditional virtues. Thus, in nativism, Western culture traits may be equally predominant with traits from the traditional culture. The point is that there is a re-evaluation, with an emphasis on the traditional in an attempt to capture the capacity and the right to practice the full arc of the culture.

Nativistic movements, particularly in East and South Africa, often take the form of breakaway churches. This movement is the subject of a brilliant book by a Swedish missionary, Bengt Sundkler—*Bantu Prophets of South Africa.* He has made an exhaustive study of the details of breakaway sects and concludes that all of the various legitimate ways of getting ahead are blocked to all or some of the South African Bantu. They can go only so high in government, only so far in business. What they are searching for is an organization in which they can actually employ the totality of their talents. The only one from which they are not systematically barred is the breakaway church.

All this wealth of energy goes into trying to lure recruits away from one another and into arguing about small doctrinal points because they must argue about something in the search for followers and for salvation.

Literally thousands of such churches are formed. Most are short-lived. They occur from the Cape up to Kenya and into the regions of the Congo which had European settlers. Although they do occur in West Africa, breakaway churches are far more common in areas with European settlers, where Africans have been barred from offices in most other churches. In general, the greater the influence from European settlers, the greater the number of separatist churches. In West Africa, the people had much more opportunity. There were, in the colonial regime, definite limits set at the top, but those limits were far higher than those set in the areas of East Africa, the Congo, and South and Central Africa that were marked by settlers. Most important, in the non-settler areas, Africans of organizing ability had greater outlets for their energies in movements which led to nationalism thus weakening those which might have led to nativism.

With these facts in mind, we can examine Mau Mau. Many of the things that were done in Mau Mau can be found written in English reports on the Kikuyu as early as 1908. The difference lay in the fact that they were moral injunctions: you must *not* do this, you must *not* do that. They were also myth. The Kikuyu, moreover, are a driven people—driven in the same sense that eighteenth- and nineteenth-century capitalists were driven. What drives them we do not know—Kikuyu have never been adequately studied. The European stereotype of them is that they are "very intelligent." It is doubtful that there is more brain power among Kikuyu than among any other people. It is rather that because of Kikuyu personality traits their brain power could be harnessed in ways which Europeans approved.

When a driven people is "capped" the pressure mounts. If they are made to turn back to their old culture, they begin to relive their myths—this time in reality, for there are no safety valves. In the present society and culture, dominated as it is by Western traits and Kikuyu morals, the goal is toward greater achievement, wealth, and ease. Because of the "cap" the present society must be reinterpreted in quite different ways by the Kikuyu in order to have a reachable goal at all. What happened was Mau Mau.

Mau Mau was nasty—and nobody thinks so more than do the Kikuyu. It must be remembered that Mau Mau was not really an anti-European movement.[1] Although some ninety-five Europeans lost their lives in Mau Mau, that number compares with scores of thousands of murdered and lost Kikuyu.

Mau Mau was based on practices common in highland East Africa—a series of oaths. Most of the oaths for Mau Mau were new in detail, but the idea was traditional. The point of Mau Mau ritual was to put the oath-taker into an anti-social position from which no known ritual could cleanse him. He put himself beyond the pale of society and decent culture. Once such an oath was taken, a man is not just outside a society, but outside *the* society. Outlaw, outcaste—out everything. In such a condition people are more driven, more desperate than ever.

[1] Such a statement must be clarified. There is an anti-European sentiment that came out in Mau Mau, just as it comes out in the poetry of the Senegalese, the music of the South African Bantu, and the work songs of the Congolese. The main aim of Mau Mau was not anti-European so much as it was anti-establishment, and the establishment had an inordinately large number of Europeans in it. There were some of the oaths whose rituals demanded European body parts, and one in which a previously named European had to be killed in order to get them. It should be noted, however, that these anti-European elements are all ancillary to the main consideration.

What the so-called "loyal" Kikuyu had to do was to create a ritual that could cleanse these people so they could be made into decent citizens again. With the help of social scientists, these non-Mau Mau Kikuyu created such rituals. Working through the prisons, they began to cleanse the outcasts. Ultimately Mau Mau was brought under control: but the situation which led to Mau Mau was not greatly changed.

It doesn't much matter, for the analysis at any rate, what the rights on each side were in the Mau Mau conflict. This is only the worst example of a type of movement that constantly recurs in a colonial situation. It will continue to recur so long as the conditions leading to it persist.

Both nativism and nationalism are potentials in a colonial situation. It is impossible to educate clerks, policemen, and typists, and then stop with sixth grade typing and a little bookkeeping. Once people are taught to read, they will read about all the things and the ideas of Western cultures and they will not understand them, because their view of Western culture is necessarily curtailed by lack of direct experience of it.

At the other extreme are to be found people like Sekou Touré, the President of Guinea. Touré is a political and organizational genius; he cut his teeth on the leadership of one of the biggest trade unions in French Africa. He led his country to independence, and his energies are now being expended on creating a viable state in Guinea.

The nationalistic movements of Africa did not really get under way until after World War II. There were ground-breaking operations, but no more. When it did get started, it went very rapidly. The formation of political parties, of parliaments and electorates—it all happened with an amazing speed. When the largely bloodless African revolution did get under way, the European governments very quickly lost control. As Marjory Perham, one of the great scholars of Africa, has said, the only thing the governments could do was hang on and try to steer. Even that, in many cases, was not singularly successful.

The point is that it is impossible to limit arbitrarily the amount of culture that is given to anybody. Only his physical, intellectual, and emotional capacity and his choices make a sensible limiting mechanism (short, of course, of the criminal law—a related, but different, problem). Such a situation is found in flux, not merely in Africa, but in most of the rest of the world: with adolescents, with women, with Negroes, or with some other socially recognized category of people.

The duality of viewpoint inherent in colonialism breaks down, and either effectively or ineffectively, the absentee sovereign is rejected.

What is left? A desperate search for identity: an identity that has roots in many traditions and reaches for a unity with which to face a pleasant and honorable future.

Part II
ANCIENT AFRICA

Chapter 3

The African Continent

Africa is a part of the world about which Americans and Europeans can no longer afford to be ignorant. Realization is fast developing that to understand its present, one must understand something of the ecological environment, the history of both what has been called "traditional" Africa and colonial Africa, something of the cultural values and outlook with which Africans view the world, and something of African achievements and aspirations.

SIZE, SHAPE, AND GEOLOGICAL COMPOSITION OF THE AFRICAN CONTINENT

Perhaps the most staggering aspect of Africa is its sheer size, and its cultural and geographical diversity within a greater similarity. It is 5200 miles from Tangiers to Capetown—approximately the same distance as that from Panama City to Anchorage, Alaska. It is 4600 miles from Dakar to Cape Guardafui, the easternmost point of the African horn—only 65 miles less than the airline distance from New York to Moscow. Africa is a big place—over three times the size of the continental United States.

The African continent is a vast plateau: only 10 percent of its land area lies at less than five hundred feet above sea level, compared to 54 percent for Europe and 25 percent for North America. The African continental plateau is a vast shield of ancient hard rock. Except for a few incursions of the sea, it has been a land area since Pre-Cambrian times—for more than five hundred million

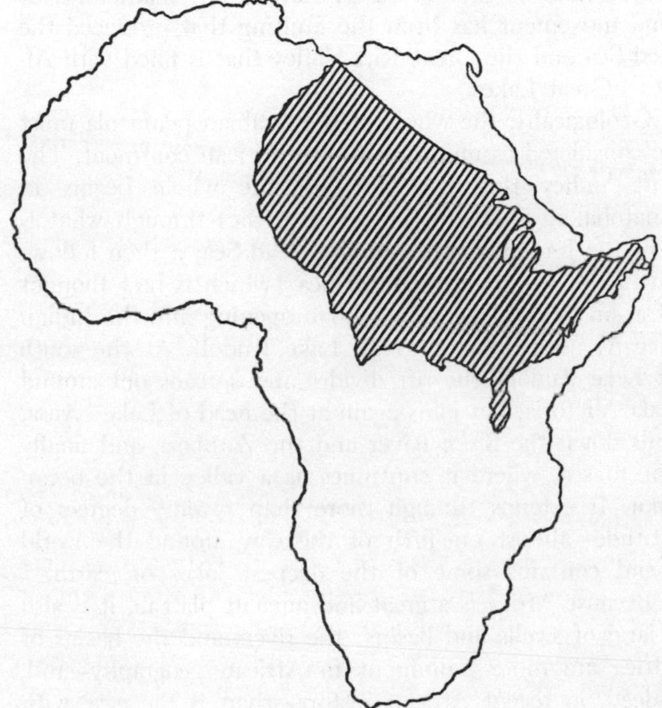

Fig. 2. Africa, with the United States superimposed.

years, give or take a few million. The entire continent has been raised and lowered at various times in geological history; but only in the extreme north and south has there been any building up of great folded mountains similar to the Rockies or the Caucasus. Rather, the main form of land movement has been the faulting that produced the Red Sea and the Great Rift Valley that is filled with Africa's Great Lakes.

Geologically, the whole of the Arabian peninsula must be considered as unitary with the African continent. The Rift Valley that cuts through the whole begins in Anatolia, in northern Turkey, stretches through what is now the Jordan Valley and the Dead Sea; it then follows down the length of the Red Sea (which is best thought of as an inland lake with a small opening into the Indian Ocean), and down through Lake Rudolf. At the south of Lake Rudolf, the rift divides and spreads out around Lake Victoria, but joins again at the head of Lake Nyasa, runs down the Shire River and the Zambezi, and finally out to sea, where it continues as a valley in the ocean floor. It extends through more than seventy degrees of latitude—almost one-fifth of the way around the world —and contains some of the deepest lakes on earth.

Because Africa is a great and ancient plateau, it is also a land of swells and basins: the rivers and the basins of Africa are more prominent in African geography—and, indeed, in recent African history—than is the case with any other continent. The vast basins of the Niger, the Nile, the Volta, the Zambezi, and the Congo empty into the sea, but those surrounding Lake Chad and the wastes of the Kalahari have no such outlets. The entire basin-dented plateau falls off, in steep escarpments, to the narrow coastal plain that surrounds the entire continent. The Niger-Benue and Zambezi-Shire, alone among the major rivers of Africa, do not somewhere plunge in falls and rapids over the scarps, making effective navigation from the sea an impossibility.

CLIMATES AND VEGETATION

If we oversimplify, Africa can be divided into five major physical and vegetational zones. At each end of the continent, and occupying only a small portion of its surface, there are equable Mediterranean and Mediterranean-type climates and vegetations. Coming inland, there are vast desiccated deserts and arid plains. Coming still closer to the equator are the wide savanna regions, covered with grass and widely spaced trees. Then along the equator there are humid and forested lands. Finally there are highland areas throughout the continent which respond to natural forces that override the climatic effects of latitude and of rainfall.

The humid forested lands straddle the equator in the Congo Basin and appear again in the coastal areas of western Africa that have the highest rainfall. Many of the most densely wooded areas take the form of gallery forests along streams and, at certain altitudes, surrounding the high hills. The forests vary from one extreme of dark tropical rain forest that might, with some justification, be called jungle; here little undergrowth can survive because the sun never seeps through to give the smaller plants light. At the other extreme, there are wooded areas open enough that only by scientific criteria can they be distinguished from savanna. Between the two extremes are many types of woodland.

North of and south of the humid zone lies the savanna. The savanna lands occupy by far the greatest number of square miles of Africa's surface. Their landscape is typically made up of rolling stretches of tall grasses, with intermittent bush and scattered trees. The inland valleys are broad and usually have gentle slopes at their sides, merging over large areas with the plateaus. Only where the streams descend rapidly over the scarps from the highland areas is that pattern broken.

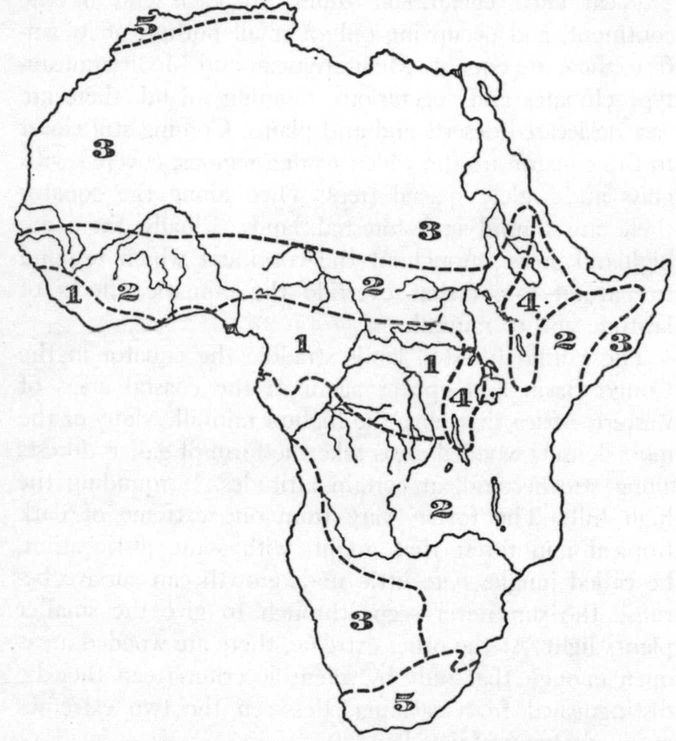

FIG. 3. Climatic regions of Africa: (1) Tropical Rain Forest; (2) Tropical Savanna and Summer Rain; (3) Low Latitude Dry Climates; (4) Undifferentiated Highlands; (5) Mediterranean.

Going farther from the equator in both directions, the dry lands of Africa are encountered. In the south is the Kalahari Desert, and in the north, the Sahara and the deserts along the coasts of the Red Sea and Somalia. They are marked by drought-resistant shrubs and a scant cover of grass. Some of the semi-arid African regions, where the desert and the savanna blend into one another, are reminiscent of the American Southwest. The deserts themselves—the center of the Kalahari and the several vast dry centers of the Sahara—are comparable to conditions found in Death Valley of North America.

Cities such as Algiers and Cape Town enjoy a climate much like that of southern France. The crops and cultures, where they have been subjected to European influence in these areas, are much the same: based on livestock, grain, and grapes.

The climatic areas of Africa might be seen as parallel belts stretching from east to west, a mirror image on either side of the equator, were it not for the fact that that pattern is seriously upset in the eastern part of the continent (and a few other small parts) by highland areas in which altitude overrides latitude. The highland areas of Africa are divided between steeply mountainous terrain like that found in Cameroun and the Ruwenzori, and the high rolling plateaus such as are found in Ethiopia and Kenya. Here the climate may be cool and temperate; Mt. Kilimanjaro and Mt. Ruwenzori bear permanent ice fields on their caps. Vegetation varies from humid forest or savanna at the foothills to Alpine mountains and tundra, adjoining barren glaciers.

One of the most distinctive aspects of the African landscape is that—once the scarp is climbed—it contains few impassable barriers, either for human beings, other animals, or plants. The climate therefore depends primarily on winds, the position of the sun, and altitude, more or less modified by the changes wrought by man. Because the terrain barriers are neither sudden nor insurmountable, the weather can "follow the sun." When the sun comes north in June, July, and August, it brings rain to the lands that lie between ten degrees and twenty degrees north of the equator. Similarly, during November, December, and January, rains come to the areas between ten degrees and twenty degrees south. Each enjoys a long dry season during the wet season of the other. In the humid forested lands, rain is often well distributed throughout the year, although short dry seasons may occur, depending primarily on the winds. The climates of eastern Africa are complicated by the monsoon winds coming in from the Indian Ocean, as well as by the high altitude. There are also parts of the west coast where the pattern is disturbed by winds created by the currents of the South Atlantic and the drought of the Sahara. As a general rule, rainfall throughout the continent tends to be heaviest when the sun is overhead.

Thus, the climate throughout the middle part of Africa exhibits an alternating wet and dry season, in a band crossing the continent; there is a stretch along the equator that has two wet seasons, and two dries, during the year; some areas show local variations, making it seem that there are no wet or dry seasons at all.

The amount of rain is usually far less important in determining the climatological variations within the African continent than is the number of months during which it falls. Rainfall maps have a way of hiding almost as much as they reveal about all of Africa: agriculture is possible only during the rainy months. It may be noted, nevertheless, that the savanna zones get from twenty-five to thirty-five inches per year. The high temperature and pronounced dry season lead to rapid evaporation and hence discourage the growth of forest and limit the types of agricultural activity that can profitably be pursued. The most typical trees are those that are drought-resistant, such as the acacia or the locust bean. On the other hand, the areas of heaviest rainfall along the equator have broad-leafed evergreen trees, but as one leaves the equator in either direction, or as one gains altitude, the trees give way to deciduous varieties. Along the equator, there is little range of variation in temperature from one season to the next, and temperatures drop only a few degrees at night. Rainfall may go to over one hundred inches.

The dry lands may receive less than five inches of rain a year, and sometimes the heart of the desert areas may go for years with no rainfall at all. When rain does fall, it may come in torrents that dump several inches within a few hours, creating floods and erosion that give way again almost immediately to desiccation.

SOILS AND AGRICULTURE

Most African soils are typical tropical soils and suffer from the disadvantages that all other tropical soils suffer from in greater or lesser degree: they are devoid of humus. Humus is the vegetable mold in the soil that results from slow decomposition of organic matter. In the so-called temperate zone there are at least some months during the year in which the oxidization of vegetable matter is slowed to a near standstill—winters enrich the soil not merely by the aeration that results from alternate freezing and thawing, but also from the fact that humus can decompose at a rapid rate only for half the year. The soil thus remains enriched in the sense that crops and other growing plants can live off a "current account" rather than off the "storage account" of fertility in the soil. Soils can, with much greater relative ease, be maintained by suitable farming practices. In tropical climates, humus oxidization goes on more or less at full speed the year round. That means that much of the fertility that might be used by plants is in fact "wasted" and that there is only a very small "storage account" in the soil in any case.

There is a further difficulty about tropical soils: they are easily leached. That is, the nutrients and minerals are washed out of them and flow away, either into the subsoil or into the sea. The lack of humus content and the ease of leaching interact with one another to ensure that tropical soils are thin, and that they never achieve the richness of the soils of the temperate zones. Tropical soils have a humus content of 1.8 percent of total volume, or less. The humus content of soils in upper New York State or in Ohio runs from 10–12 percent, and in the richest Iowa farmland, as high as 16 percent. African soils are indeed poor.

Since poor soils are easily exhausted, they can be worked only for short periods unless expensive and tedious steps are taken to maintain them. Few tropical peoples have ever had the technology or the knowledge to take the required steps. Rather, they have "mined" the soil of its nutrients by a method of farming known as "shifting cultivation."

Shifting cultivation is a method of farming in which land is cleared, either of the forest or of the grass that grows on it, and farmed without artificial fertilization. When the natural fertility of a farm so made has been exhausted, the farmer clears another patch and repeats the process, while the first patch is allowed to revert to fallow, and ultimately to regain fertility by natural means. The entire process may take as few as five or as many as thirty years, and some authorities (and some African farmers) claim that never again is the land as good as the first time it is cleared. This method of dry farming is found widespread in the tropical world: in the Philippines and Southeast Asia, in much of tribal India, and in tropical America. In Africa, farmers in some areas utilize the grass or tree limbs that they remove by burning them, and using the ash as fertilizer. Indeed, in parts of central Africa, notably in Northern Rhodesia and the surrounding areas, the process may amount to lopping branches off the large trees, burning them, and planting corn in the ash beds. The few exceptions in Africa are to be found in the Nile and Zambezi valleys and a few other areas in which there is a permanent, rich, alluvially deposited soil, maintained by seasonal flooding, and in those small areas in which European forms of agriculture are practiced, primarily in the extreme north and south and in some highland areas.

Shifting cultivation is, seen from the standpoint of modern technology and the needs of the modern world, a wasteful method of farming, and the agricultural experts of the world, including tropical Africa, are working on improvements in the system. But in most areas the method provides short-term security and, indeed, plenty for the African societies that practice it. Africans are willing to make changes, but those changes must be fully tested; the people must be convinced that the changes are for the better—that greater plenty and fuller security will result. Mere introduction of the plow, for example, is not sufficient: deeply plowed land leaches faster than does land which is merely scratched on the surface, and the oxidization of humus is speeded up by aeration. Fertilizer is expensive; green manure crops require as much labor as do crops from which a more immediately apparent return is reaped. Compost requires new and improved means of cartage in a continent accustomed to head-loading. Moreover, the cartage demands more and different animals, differently used, which in turn demands new types of roads and paths. Changing the pattern of African agriculture is a monumental task; many mistakes have been made, and many more will probably be made, before the job can be finished.

There are peoples in Africa who are primarily or even solely dependent on their herds. Such peoples always occupy the savanna areas, and most are nomadic or transhumant. Nomads do not merely wander; they proceed in more or less fixed patterns or routes that may take several years to complete. If the cycle of movement is one required by the seasons and is repeated in an annual cycle, it is called transhumance. There are some places in which mixed farming and herding is done by the same peoples, and others in which herders and farmers cooperate with one another to the point of mutual dependence. Herding is restricted for the most part to the savannas, and some of the highlands. The humid forests present conditions in which only goats can be kept; in a few places, even goats cannot thrive. Goats and donkeys can live in any parts of the desert that will support human populations, although a few of the human populations (particularly the Bushmen of the Kalahari Desert) do not keep them. Chickens are ubiquitous among the settled peoples of the continent, many of whom also keep ducks and pigeons.

In the past the major hazard for livestock has been endemic sleeping sickness. Although the problem has not been fully solved, there has probably been more research and effort expended on controlling sleeping sickness than on any other single health factor—certainly for animals.

RESOURCES

In Africa, as everywhere else, resources must be available in two senses: not only must they be physically present, but they must be culturally valued and utilized. This cultural availability may change rapidly in some instances, and so make possible new societies and new conditions in very quick time.

Mineral resources were, except for gold, not utilized by most African societies until well into the Christian era, it would seem. Gold is found and indeed produced in many different parts of Africa. The major areas are present-day Ghana, the northeastern Congo, in Southern Rhodesia, and of course the highly developed Rand area of the Republic of South Africa. African interest in gold is ancient: gold was apparently used in comparatively few places as anything except a trade commodity, although in some parts of the "Gold Coast" it was indeed used as a currency for limited purposes. Early Portuguese explorers looked for and found some of the sources of gold in Africa, but were never able to work them profitably; they lost interest when other sources of wealth in other parts of the world were found to be more readily tapped. It was not until the end of the nineteenth century that African gold was mined with anything like what metallurgical engineers would consider to be efficiency or on a large scale.

George H. T. Kimball has most cogently pointed out that metalworking in Africa was until comparatively modern times an art that was practiced in seclusion and one that was used to bolster the social position of certain social groups or of certain officials. It was only in the second half of the nineteenth century that African metals were discovered and only in the twentieth that the quantity and richness of the metallic deposits of the area have been recognized. The huge copper deposits of Katanga were discovered in 1892; two or three years later, the work of Cecil Rhodes and his associates led to the discovery of the area now known as the copper belt in Northern Rhodesia, adjoining Katanga. It was at the turn of the century that these areas were brought into production. The subsequent history of the mines in this area has fluctuated with conditions in Europe and America, and the demands for the metals that industrialization, wars, and peace have forced upon world economy. Conditions in Africa determined little, but reflected much.

Africa is almost a solid chunk of iron ore—most of it low-grade, obviously, though in some areas of Liberia and Guinea, the content runs as high as 84 percent. When mining in the Nimba Mountain area on the boundary between those two countries was begun in the early 1960s, the technique was merely to clear off the trees, let the thin topsoil wash away, and use surface mining methods on the naked, rusting hills.

Iron was used in many parts of Africa. The southern

fringes of the Sahara are littered with the remains of earthen furnaces in which pig iron was smelted—only in a few areas of northern Cameroun are these techniques still found in use in the 1960s: imported iron and steel is much cheaper in terms of time, labor, and even cash.

Diamonds are one of the continent's most important assets. In 1957, Africa accounted for more than 80 percent of the world's diamond production, both gem and industrial. Of this amount, almost three-quarters of the diamonds produced north of the Republic of South Africa come from the Congo, followed in order of importance by Ghana, Sierra Leone and Angola. Diamonds are to be found in Tanganyika, in Liberia, and Guinea, as well as in the Central African Republic and Southern Rhodesia.

It was only during World War II that any of the minor minerals in Africa began to be utilized. They include mica, quartz, tungsten, bauxite, uranium, tantalite, columbite, cobalt, zinc, and manganese.

Copper and tin were the major metals being produced in Africa at the time of the revolutions of independence. The copper deposits have considerable effect on the world market. The major copper mining areas of the continent are in Katanga and the Rhodesian copper belt, which produce about a fifth of the copper used in the world.

There is little doubt that the future of Africa is closely associated with her mineral resources. Extractive industries probably offer greater potential for rapid development than any other kind of industry. Whatever the development of technology and of the industrialized world brings, much will take place in Africa.

One of Africa's primary resource problems is water. Water shortage is an important problem in many parts of the continent, particularly in the tropical areas. Most African indigenous societies depend for their water on surface supplies, although a few do dig shallow wells, and others create devices by means of which the surface water can be better utilized—such devices as walk-in wells or terracing. It would seem, ironically enough, that although we have good and constantly improving knowledge about the mineral resources of the continent, there have been very few surveys that have concerned themselves with water supply, and the underground supply of water in Africa remains one of the large areas of ignorance.

DISEASES

Africa was long called "the white man's grave." For too long the climate has been the scapegoat. This in spite of the fact that we know it was the diseases rather than the climate itself that created the havoc among early explorers, settlers, and miners.

It is nevertheless true that tropical diseases are, today, curable diseases, once diagnosis has been achieved. Curing them, however, and keeping them stamped out, is an undertaking of gigantic proportions. Africa—like North America and most other continents—supports a formidable population of mosquitoes. Mosquitoes themselves are of nuisance value only unless they carry disease, and in Africa they carry two of the most debilitating, even deadly, diseases known to the modern world: malaria and yellow fever. It is not totally true to assume that malaria is solely a tropical disease; citizens' committees in North America as far north as central New Jersey concern themselves with the breeding grounds of the Anopheles mosquito and other carriers of malaria. In most areas of the United States, however, malaria has been largely stamped out, in part by mosquito control, and in part by seeing to it that the mosquitoes bite an uninfected populace and therefore do not act as carriers. Anti-malarial drugs today are quite efficient—and inexpensive, by the standards of the modern Western world. But they are expensive by the standards of African subsistence farmers, and large-scale mosquito clearance campaigns also cost phenomenal sums of money. Although some attempts at mosquito clearance have been made by colonial powers, few were on a broad enough scale to solve the problem. What steps the independent governments, assisted by world health bodies, will be able to take within the next decade may well be all but decisive in determining the extent and rate of African economic development. Malarial infection is all but total in those areas that harbor its carriers.

Greater efforts have been made to combat sleeping sickness or trypanosomiasis, both because the extent of the disease is more limited and hence more approachable, and because the successes are more apt to be startling.

There are several methods of reducing the sleeping sickness rates, each by tackling different vectors in the cycle of the trypanosome. It may be done by destroying the tsetse fly, which is the major (but not the sole) carrier; by preventive medication of the animal and human population, and even by the generally disapproved method of destroying the wild game which inhabits the general area, thereby making the medicated and hence presumably uninfected animals the only ones available to the flies, thereby stamping out the disease. Tsetse flies cannot live more than a few tens of yards from dense undergrowth of the sort usually found along streams. One of the ways of fighting the flies has been to cut out the undergrowth along the streams—though there have, of course, been side effects in other plant and animal life resulting from this course of action. It has also sometimes been considered desirable to use insecticides to clear out whole areas, although the degree to which one can justify killing off all insect life for the sake of getting rid of the tsetse flies is hotly argued. There were a few places, in fact, in which the most efficient way of getting rid of the flies was to have them captured by the local people—with a sort of "bounty" system of remuneration.

That the major diseases of Africa can be combated is

illustrated startlingly by the success of the UNICEF campaign to wipe out yaws—in most parts of the continent, the pain and embarrassment of yaws is a memory. Medical research and medical aid are of a sort that any country or organization that dispenses them can achieve stature in its own eyes and approval from the world community. It therefore seems highly probable that medical assistance will continue to be high on the priority of most assisting governments. Such an opinion can be underscored when it is realized that Africans themselves recognize the superiority of modern Western medicine and have an unalloyed desire to achieve health and physical well being.

Chapter 4

The Peopling of Africa

Africa, for all that it was the last continent to be "explored"—which means that it remained longest unknown to modern Western civilization—has nevertheless yielded the oldest "human" remains and artifacts yet discovered. According to our present information, the earliest anthropoid forms that could have begun the systematic invention of culture are indisputably associated with Africa.

To say that Africa is the "home" of mankind does not mean, however, that Africans as we know them today were the first human beings—indeed, it seems likely that except for a handful of "Boskopoids" or "Bushmanoids," the peopling of Africa has all been recent.

EARLY MAN

In any discussion of early man, the knotty question always emerges early: When is a man a man? In the apt phrase of Professor Raymond Dart, the earliest culture-creating anthropoid forms were "trembling on the verge of humanity." The question becomes: When did they topple over?

The usual answer to this question is made on the basis of an extension of activities rather than of the animal body. It is not the shape or the physique of the creature that defines man, but rather it is what he does. For decades, anthropologists have defined man as a tool-making animal, and said that every ape that makes a tool is human. If such a definition is maintained, both chimpanzees and gorillas are today "trembling on the verge of humanity," for both of them make tools of a crude sort. A tool is any creation, external to the physical body, that is made in order to accomplish something else. Elephants break off branches of trees in order to swish flies, but the branch is usually not considered to be a tool, for it is not worked specifically (although it is obvious that such a position can rapidly deteriorate into a quibble). Chimpanzees do alter the shape of the proto-tools that they create. They do not, however, shape them to a pattern and such students of early man as L. S. B. Leakey have preserved toolmaking as the criterion of the human—the point at which pithecus (ape) becomes anthropos (man)—by adding the criterion of tool pattern. A man is a hominid who shapes tools to a pattern.

Mankind, if such be the definition of him, shares a great many physical characteristics with the great apes, as well as the more general ones with all of the mammals or all of the animal world, and ultimately all the world of the living. The major blood types found among human beings are also found in the four great apes—gorilla, chimpanzee, orangutan, and gibbon. The body musculature is largely the same—the differences arise from such distinctive human features as the head being balanced more comfortably on the spine and so needing fewer heavy muscles to hold it up, and the fact that the bipedal locomotion has led to musculature development in the lower back, the legs, and the knot of muscle in the buttocks which none of the great apes shares with man. The great apes, some monkeys, and human beings are the only menstruating animals, showing again the closeness of their relationship. Other factors, such as the rhesus factor and the M-N factor in the blood, the shape of the skull, and the shape of the feet, are very different. The question emerges: What physical factor or combination of factors is correlated with the tool-making proclivities that define a beast as a man?

The argument rages, and it is this argument that lies

behind the difficulty in understanding the problems of early man. When we ask "Was he a man?" we usually mean "Was he like me?" And to answer that question demands extensive examination of the degree of self-knowledge and even of narcissism in the human outlook. It also brings up another problem: the only remains of early man that have ever been found are bone. When, in the course of reconstruction, the flesh and the external appearance is guessed at (and it is never anything but a more or less educated guess), the early man must be given features that resemble in one way or another at least some aspects of the presently existing races. What was the color of Java man? What was the hair texture? We do not know.

The only answer to these riddles is that we must begin to think of ourselves as part of a continuum of the living; we must also realize that the races we know are ephemeral and (a small minority of scholars to the contrary) that races change more rapidly than do species. We must also recognize the narcissism inherent in whatever reconstructions we make. Early man may be cast in the image of the man we most admire; he may, just as readily, be cast in the image of the man we least admire, in order that we can dissociate ourselves from the disadmired type.

What is true, however, is that man and the culture by which he lives evolved together. The development of one cannot be considered in the absence of the other. Man did not evolve a large brain and then discover culture, as the counterfeiter of the Piltdown "man" hoax would have had us believe. Neither did pre-man first discover culture and then evolve because of the benefits it conferred. Rather, the development of culture and the evolutionary changes in the beast counteraffected one another. Man and culture are indistinguishable historically—the distinction is valid only as a simplifying device for purposes of scientific study.

MIOCENE APES IN AFRICA

Although there have been two or three finds of apelike creatures in the Oligocene epoch—perhaps forty million years ago—the earliest apelike creatures of which there are adequate remains are those from the rainy and lush Miocene epoch of about twenty-five million years ago. Almost all of the early Miocene ape discoveries have been made in Africa, although by the late Miocene, these apes had spread widely into Europe and Asia.

It was long considered, and has been corrected only in the last two or three decades, that mankind was created in, or first evolved in, Asia, spreading from there to people the rest of the world. Most of the major civilizations of the world were committed to that view either because they themselves were located in Asia or because their myths of origin made that assumption feasible and comfortable. During the millennia before archaeology, and during the centuries in which Africa had disappeared from the purview of Europe, such seemed a sensible belief.

It was primarily a group of scientists working in Kenya with and around L. S. B. Leakey who have added immeasurably to our knowledge of Miocene apes and located the cradle of mankind in Africa.

Leakey, a Kenya-born archaeologist and anthropologist, and his wife Mary have made innumerable contributions to our knowledge of both early and contemporary man in Africa, but their two outstanding discoveries are Proconsul, a protohuman apelike creature, and the early man they named Zinjanthropus, or "the man from Zinj," the latter being the old Arabic term for the east coast of Africa. Both the Leakeys have a talent for discovering old bones—and it seems to be something that, like musical talent, you either have or do not have.

The creation of human palaeontologists and good prehistoric archaeologists takes so much time and such a peculiar array of talent that one can, on the fingers of the two hands, name the great human palaeontologists: there must be a sense of where to go, an exhaustive training in geology, biology, history, and anthropology, and a capacity to remain unhurried in a hurried world. It also takes money to do all this—money to travel, to hire assistants, to maintain museum connections. Leakey was on the spot and knew his East Africa; he was trained at Cambridge; he married the particular wife he married; he found assistance and money for his museum—on and on, through a combination of training, perspicacity, hard work, and luck, he was enabled to do his job.

In 1931 he found Proconsul on Rusinga Island, in Lake Victoria, where the ape remains bespeak a long and extremely dense habitation by apes. The geological stratum in which Proconsul was discovered can be dated to twenty-five million years ago—give or take a few million. Proconsul seems not to have been human, either on somatic grounds or on cultural grounds: physically, he was more generalized than either present-day man or the present-day apes, and it is amazing that he is called an "ape" when he is in fact as far removed from modern "apes" as he is from man. The word "ape" obviously has a residual meaning as well as a precise one, and anything which is hominoid but not human is often called an ape.

Proconsul exhibits only one specialty that is not shared by man—the enlarged and pointed canine teeth; this specialty, however, is shared by the modern great apes. Whereas man—like Proconsul—has remained largely unspecialized, modern apes have become much more specialized. As Robert Ardrey, American playwright and writer on Africa, has claimed, with truth but also with intent to shock, the human body is more "primitive" in the sense of being unspecialized than are the bodies of modern apes. There have been differences in development even in the areas in which specialization has occurred: whereas man added a chin to brace his jaw, apes added an internal wedge called the "simian shelf." Proconsul exhibits neither.

Proconsul's long bones indicate that he was much lighter in general bodily construction than are the modern apes. The animal was light and swift, and his feet were adapted to living on the ground. Proconsul was not a creature of the trees, although it would seem that some of his descendants (but, obviously, not man) took to the trees.

Miocene apes, of which Proconsul is the most significant, were plentiful. In the course of millennia, however, desiccation set in and the epoch gave way to that known as the Pliocene, which turned Africa almost completely into desert. We know that many of the species and genera that evolved during the late Miocene became extinct during the Pliocene, and that the turn of conditions again favored the least specialized of the animal forms.

EARLY MAN IN AFRICA

If the question "What is a man?" is bothersome in determining the relationship of Proconsul to ourselves, it becomes monumentally difficult when we begin to examine the finer distinctions among the various species of man and near-man that have been discovered or postulated for the Pleistocene epoch, which is to say the last million years or so.

Early Pleistocene primates have been found in East and in South Africa, and again the Leakeys are among the foremost in the discovery, a position that they share this time with two South Africans: Raymond Dart and Robert Broom. Dart was the first to report, in 1925, a part of a skull and an almost complete cast of the inside of the same skull, made naturally by limestone formation. Dart's name for this creature (and to this day, every new discoverer names his own discoveries) was Australopithecus —"southern ape." In the next few years, Broom and Dart discovered many more remains of these creatures in the various limestone caves and deposits of southeastern Africa.

The brain of Australopithecus was about half the size of modern man's brain, and the skull had some similarities to the skulls of modern apes, although the differences are far more commanding than the similarities. Most important of these differences is the position of the foramen magnum—the hole at the bottom of the skull through which the spinal cord enters. In Australopithecus, the foramen magnum is toward the bottom of the skull, rather than toward the back as in modern apes, indicating that the animal was better adapted to the upright posture than are modern apes, if not quite so well as is modern man. The teeth are distinctly more "human" than otherwise—in the sense that they resemble the dentition of modern man. Perhaps most telling of all is the position and shape of the pelvic bones, which resemble those of modern man and are far different from those of modern apes; they indicate without doubt adaptation to erect posture and bipedal locomotion. The following is the summary of the evidence made by the noted British anatomist, Sir Wilfred Le Gros Clark:

> [Australopithecines were] hominoids of small stature, with a brain not much larger in absolute size than those of the gorilla and chimpanzee, a massive jaw showing a number of human characters, a skull in which many of the structural details conform to the human rather than the ape pattern, a dentition fundamentally of human type . . . and lacking the tusk-like canines and large incisors of the modern anthropoid apes, and limbs approximating in their structure and proportions those of *Homo*. Undoubtedly the most surprising feature of their whole anatomy is the combination of a brain of simian dimensions with limbs which, in a number of details, are of human type, and it was this apparent contradiction which led

some anatomists in the first instance to doubt the validity of the evidence provided by these South African fossils. The most recent discoveries, however, have added so much more evidence of a confirmatory nature that any remaining doubts must now be removed.[2]

The question at stake, however, is whether or not the Australopithecines made tools—in a word, whether they "had culture." The problem is tied up with the fact that merely because stone is the earliest known cultural medium, it is not necessarily the oldest. Dart has claimed—in a particularly flamboyant manner, at times—that the Australopithecines did indeed have a culture based on bone, wood, and feathers; he and others assumed that the earliest chipped pebbles were used to work wood, bone, and skins. The difficulty is not that these ideas are wrong, for they may not be. However, they are not undeniably provable on the basis of present evidence.

The Leakeys reenter the picture in the late 1950s, finding in Olduvai gorge in Tanganyika a skull from a very early time—early Pleistocene, which Dr. Leakey at that time dated as 600,000 B.C.—and they named the creature Zinjanthropus—man from Zinj. Dr. Leakey unhesitatingly called this creature a man, because he was found in association with chipped "pebble tools" of the Lower Pleistocene—tools which had been known in vast quantities for some years. There were two confusing elements, however: most scientists agree that Zinjanthropus is one of the Australopithecines. Therefore, Australopithecine would be, by the tool-making definition, a "man." The matter was confounded when scientists from the University of California at Berkeley declared Zinjanthropus remains to be over one and a half million years old on the basis of potassium-argon tests.

In short, the "age" of mankind remains something of a

[2] W. E. Le Gros Clark, *History of the Primates*. Chicago: University of Chicago Press Phoenix Books, Fifth impression, 1960, p. 116.

mystery; whether or not Zinjanthropus-Australopithecus was "really" a "man" is a problem yet to be answered finally. Leakey faced some interesting problems in his reconstruction of Zinjanthropus—he felt he had to create a covering for the skeleton he had found. And Leakey could not know what Zinjanthropus really looked like: what color his skin was, how much hair there was on it, and what color that hair may have been. Leakey compromised, and indeed he could have done nothing else: he made the features more or less Caucasoid and issued the statement to the press that he probably did not look much like any living human race.

It would seem, then, that the first artifacts were made by a creature who resembles the modern apes almost as much as he does modern man.

GENESIS AND AFRICA

In a recent popular book, *African Genesis*, already introduced, Robert Ardrey has clothed some simple truths in flamboyant language and made remarks that seem calculated to prejudice his case. Yet, his basic point is well taken: indeed, it is a truism. Animals most fitted to survive are those that can best protect themselves. If protohuman beings developed weapons instead of somatic specializations (or, if the use of the brain which allowed weapons to be created is considered man's somatic specialization), then humanity as we know it becomes possible. The very animality of man—the necessity to protect oneself and to attack, and the necessity to eat at the cost of niceties—allows the "finer" aspects of human character to develop.

Modern science is, indeed, changing the myth on which present-day Westerners grew up. We are learning not to deny that human beings are animal in nature—that vast prejudice of European civilization. The argument of whether man is basically good or basically evil is coming to be considered a silly question. Man is man. He is not merely capable of both good and evil, but sets himself up to judge the matter. Man might even be defined as the only animal capable of formulating a moral dilemma. How many people who visit prisons discover that "criminals are not all bad"? How many people are shocked that demi-saints keep collections of pornography? Good and evil are culturally defined, even those points on which all men agree.

The forces of archaeology, social science, and zoology are converging in our own day in such a way as seriously to change man's view of himself and his myths of his origins. The forces of popularization in the form of Mr. Ardrey and his ilk are taking these ideas, just as they take all the other scientific ideas that are of any use, and forcing them into the popular attention so that ultimately man's view of himself will change drastically.

STONE AGE MAN IN AFRICA

The Old Stone Age, or Palaeolithic, cultures of Africa began with the well-known pebble tools that the Leakeys finally pinned down when they discovered them in association with the skeletal remains of Zinjanthropus, the prime Australopithecine. These rough stone tools were, in the course of aeons, supplanted by the so-called "hand-ax" type of cultures which developed as the human animal himself developed. Man and the cultures of the Stone Age developed one another just as, today, man and culture are still developing one another.

A hand-ax is now known not to have been an ax, but the name has been current for so long that changing it becomes as difficult as changing an image like "blood relative," simply because we now know it is genes rather than blood that carry biological relationship. It seems likely that the hand-ax was used for skinning and cutting up game, and perhaps for rough working of wooden implements: a general-purpose tool that was so easy to make that it was in all likelihood seldom carried from one place to another, but simply made anew on the spot where one was needed.

The hand-axes are of many styles and types, and they spread over most of the African continent, Europe, and Asia Minor, and into India, and over hundreds of thousands of years of time. While the type-sites, that is, the excavations which give the "culture" names to the types of implements, are those of Chelles and Acheul in France, hand-axes would seem (at least insofar as our knowledge at present allows us to generalize) to have come earliest into use in the highland area of present-day Kenya. These tools come to be mixed with, and finally superseded by, a whole series of more specialized and locally limited additions of scrapers, awls, points, barbs, and other stone tools in the very late Old Stone Age and the Middle Stone Age periods. In the most general of terms, it is to be seen that dry and highland Africa—that is, the north and the eastern spine—gave rise to cultures now called Levalloisian and Stillbay, with some special, later, and smaller ones called the Fauresmith and Capsian. The area which is today represented by the rain forest areas—the Congo Basin and the Guinea Coast—gave rise to another and significantly different set of stone tools called the Sangoan.

Recent discoveries concerning the Mesolithic or Middle Stone Age in Africa have upset some of the ideas held about it on the basis of archaeological findings in Europe, because the introduction of the defining culture traits came in a different order in Africa. Indeed, pottery is found in Kenya in what are, based on stone artifacts, typical Late Palaeolithic sites. Pottery had been, for Europe, one of the prime defining criteria of the Mesolithic.

Africa seems to have been the home not merely of mankind but also, and obviously, of human culture. It is not until the Neolithic period and the agricultural revolution that we must look outside of Africa for major contributions—and, indeed, only then if we follow the traditional but geologically debatable practice of throwing Asia Minor in with Asia instead of with Africa.

Chapter 5

The Peoples of Africa

In the last chapter the problem was "What is a man?" We discovered that distinguishing the genus *homo* from any other genus of the primates depended, ultimately, not on a physiological but rather on a cultural point: the capacity for making tools to a pattern. Similarly in the present chapter, the problem is a variant of the same question: "What is race?" The answer will be of the same sort: the differences between races cannot be specifically defined physiologically, but rather depend on a cultural point. The cultural point for defining race is a legal point. The continuity of physical types of modern man has no "natural" breaking points—there are only stereotypes from which all persons are removed in at least some degree. Only by fiat can the distinctions be made.

RACE

The trouble with "race," as a concept, is that it is two concepts. The two are hopelessly intertwined by our emotional and cultural notions into false unity on the basis of a mere word. "Race" has become the idiom in which the twentieth century has cast some of its practices of and ideas about persecution. It has, moreover, been utilized as a technical term by the biological sciences, and particularly by genetics. Then, it has been blandly—or, sometimes, aggressively—assumed by the Western world that the popular idiom and the scientific concept have some sort of bearing on one another.

"Race" as a social problem is what might be called a "cultural displacement." That is to say, just as some neurotics displace their difficulties into an idiom which ensures that they need do nothing to correct them, and which has little if anything to do with the "cause" of the neurosis, so the whole "race" question is created by something that is of quite a different order from the biologist's and geneticist's problems in which the term has scientific meaning and validity.

The task that this chapter must perform, then, is twofold: it must explain the biological definition of race, and it must review the European attitudes toward Africans that have culminated in the "race" concept as it is generally understood in the Western world, and as it affects Africa. It must, concomitantly, correct the "racial classifications" of Africans that have appeared in books that were at one time "authoritative" and that have colored all the accounts in all the major encyclopedias.

A race is, in biological science, a group of organisms, the members of which share a statistically significant proportion of their genes. The point at which "statistical significance" is reached is a matter for special determination in every problem before the scientist. In some situations, and for the purposes of some problems, the proportion can be rather small; in others, it must be defined as being much larger. In the latter case, the members of the "race" are fewer and are more nearly homogeneous than in the former. There is no point in nature, however, at which one race becomes another race—"race" is part of the analytical equipment of science, *not* part of the data.

Races are, therefore, interbreeding populations, and because the members of interbreeding populations are material and take up space, and further since they must meet in order to breed, every "race" has a geographical dimension: an area in which it is represented. Changes in the geographical dimension (which is the same thing as mobility of individuals) usually result in changes in the available genes, and hence ultimately in change of the "race."

To repeat, a race is (to a biologist) a group of plants or animals that share some of their genes, the proportions being dependent on definition.

It is wrong, however, to think of races as immutable or even as very old. The length of time that it takes to create a "race" depends (in addition to the definition, either social or scientific, of what characteristics make the difference) on how large, how homogeneous, and how isolated the group of interbreeding animals may be. All of the characteristics which mark the socially recognized, "phenotypical" races of today are (with the exception of the color of skin, hair and eyes, which are linked) determined by different and independent gene combinations. There is no genetic correlation between jaw shape and hair texture, between musculature and bone formation in the wrist and the presence or absence of epicanthic fold on the eye, all of which are among the criteria for determining the racial types with which we in the modern world are familiar. As the interbreeding of present-day "races" occurs with the breaking down of geographical and social barriers, the known "races" are changing. If, at a later date, new geographical isolation or new social barriers again create fairly small interbreeding populations, a new set of races may result.

In short, race is a scientific concept for congeners; it is also temporary, when seen in the sweep of geological and cultural time.

But race also means something else in the modern world, as a glance into any dictionary—or, indeed, into the newspaper—will show. The word is derived from the Latin term for "root," and it has been used in English, even within the last few decades, to refer to sex (the female race), to all of humanity (the human race), to members of a profession (writers are a peculiar race), to nationalities (the French race), to language groups (the Semitic race), and to religions (the Jewish race).

Moreover, in the Europe of the eighteenth and nineteenth centuries, "race" was the idiom in which democratic revolutions were organized, propagandized, carried out, and fought. In the Europe of the twentieth century, race has been one of the idioms in which the totalitarian revolution has been waged.

The first book on race with scientific pretensions is generally considered to have been that of a German named Blumenbach in 1806. To read it today is almost impossible—in fact, it leads to little except greater regard for the magnificent achievement of the Darwinian revolution of the 1850s and 1860s. Blumenbach still subscribed to the "degeneration" theory of race, based on the myth that man was created perfect but had everywhere degenerated to greater or lesser extent

Documents from the eighteenth century did, of course, recognize the physical differences that we today associate with race. But they did not consider them of telling significance.

Modern notions of racism developed out of the social revolutions of the late eighteenth and the nineteenth centuries. In France, the change from the feudal system to a modern industrial system was explained in terms of race—and Europe to this day means something quite different by "race" than does America. In the United States, the monumental social changes that followed the Civil War (which occurred within a few years of the Darwinian revolution, though the results collided only decades later) gave rise to many of the present-day beliefs about "race" in the United States. On both continents, a type of nobility and feudal or demi-feudal system was giving way to a new type of society, based on contract and the market. In Europe, the nobility under the tutelage of men like the Comte de Boulainvilliers and Gobineau began to think of themselves as "Teutonics" in contrast to the revolutionaries—their former serfs and yeomen—whom they called "Alpines" and "Mediterraneans." During the reign of National Socialism in Germany, "race" was again the idiom for social revolution, when "racial purity" was correlated with stamping out the people and institutions of one of the most progressive and powerful of Europe's minority groups. It was, in America, not until the social revolution created by the Civil War and Reconstruction had crippled old institutions that "race" was primarily a weapon to be used against Negroes; the "yellow peril" seemed of far greater moment even at the turn of the century, and may in fact again seem so before the turn of the next.

The facts of the matter are, of course, that heritable differences among human beings exist and can be seen with the naked eye; that scientific definitions of genetically interrelated groups of plants and animals exist and are pinned to words in the common language; that social problems exist that have, for almost two centuries now, been expressed in an idiom of "race." No one has as yet "proved" any verifiable association among the three meanings. Yet because words mean precisely what one intends them to mean, the racial attitudes of the modern Western world are so adamant that not a single study can be found to compare the ideas concerning such physical differences that might be held by peoples of cultures other than our own.

Race is, like "gravity," a concept, not a thing. But while gravity explains a great many empirically verifiable facts, nobody has ever shown scientifically that "race" explains anything—its unscientific use to "prove" points has never been more than special pleading. In short, it would seem that social scientists have hold of a wrong concept. Biologists can use the notion; social scientists cannot—except insofar as populations believe certain things and hence bring them about by cultural means.

SELIGMAN'S RACES OF AFRICA

Lists of the "races" of Africa, or of anywhere else, must be examined critically. The earliest of these classifications which still has an effect widespread enough to merit attention is that created by Charles Gabriel Seligman in 1930; although his book, *Races of Africa*, was revised in 1957, after his death, its basic out-of-dateness was unchanged. Seligman was a medical doctor, a pathologist, a physical anthropologist, and an ethnographer of great skill. His experience in Africa was firsthand.

Seligman divided the indigenous (that is, pre-colonial) inhabitants of Africa into five groups: 1) Hamites, 2) Semites, 3) Negroes, 4) Bushmen and Hottentots, sometimes combined and called Khoisan, and 5) Negrillos. Later and simpler classifications would refer to the first and second as Caucasoid, the third as Negroid, and the fourth and fifth as "Boskopoid" or "Bushmanoid." Some variant of this classification is almost universal. Insofar as any of these schemes have validity, it is a commonsense validity which has little if any scientific reference.

Separation of the Khoisan peoples from the Pygmy Negrillos is a procedure much debated: the information is not as yet available, or at least not as yet sufficiently analyzed, to determine whether or not the Bushmen and the Pygmies are descendants of a common stock—presumably the Boskopoid stock that inhabited Africa before the fairly recent infiltration of Negroes and Caucasoids—or whether they are quite different and the Pygmoids were created from Negroid stock by the same kind of dwarfing procedure that created pygmy hippos. Indeed, Pygmies and Negroes are so interbred today (perhaps they always were) as probably to leave the question moot for all time.

For the rest, Seligman divides the continent into two, with a line running from Dakar, to Timbuktu, to

Khartoum and to approximately the mouth of the Juba River. North of this line, he tells us, live the essentially Caucasoid Semites and Hamites; south of it live the Negroes. He then follows the questionable procedure of assigning all the recognized variations in either group to an intermixture of the two.

Throughout all parts of the continent except the western Africa area, Seligman claims on what is (to be honest, but not disrespectful) no evidence at all, that there has been some admixture of "Hamites" with the basically Negro peoples to form the "Bantu" on the one hand and the "Nilotes" on the other, leaving a residual category of "true Negroes" in West Africa. It should be noted that Bantu is a term of linguistic reference: *bantu* is the word for "men" in one of the most widespread of African language families—though later research has proved that even on linguistic grounds the "Bantu" and the languages spoken by some of the "true Negroes" are very closely related. "Nilote" is, furthermore, a geographical term. And it should be stressed again that "true Negro" is a residual category.

North of the line the situation was explained by the same device. "Semites" are the people who speak Semitic languages (mainly Arabic) and are Caucasoid in appearance. "Hamites" are people who speak broadly similar languages ("Hamitic languages" are no longer separated from the "Semitic" ones as they once were) but who are ostensibly *not* of the Caucasoid racial stereotype but also not of the Negroid racial stereotype.

The subdivisions and categories contained in the Seligman classifications are a mishmash, based on some head measurements (now known to be meaningless), language families (now outmoded by newer classifications based on far more extensive information and finer scholarship), geographical location, and a variant of Herbert Spencer's theory of the conquest origin of the state. At best they form a pseudo-scientific rationalization for a common sense, naked-eye view.

A recent, and more sensible, view is that of G. P. Murdock, the well-known American anthropologist, who in 1959 separated the Pygmoids from the Bushmanoids and noted the lack of agreement, and who then pointed out that there are Caucasoid and Negroid peoples throughout the rest of the continent. Murdock also notes what is surely true, that there is very little information available about the genetic attributes of Africans; that what we do have deals almost entirely with the blood, and that in the gross A, O, B, and AB types all of the races he recognizes in Africa seem to be much alike, although a certain percentage of Negroes are marked by the "sickle cell gene" which is adaptive in malarial climates, and which is almost absent in the rest of the world.

It is commonly said today, but the grounds for it are such as to make most authorities hedge in the opinion, that the Negro race is of recent origin. We are on firm ground that African Negroes are, so far as the little genetic information we have will take us, more closely related to the Caucasoids of Europe than they are to the Negroes of Melanesia. There are even some authorities who believe (but cannot prove) that the Negro race developed in the western sudan no more than ten thousand years ago, with a small, vigorous, interbreeding population, and has since spread eastward and southward, and indeed throughout the world.

What the true facts of the genetic races of Africa may be, it is certainly so that today we can say little more than this: if one stands at Suez and looks south and southwest, people tend to get darker the farther one goes. One must, even in this generalization, except the Bushmanoids. Just where one draws the line, and just how many subraces one wants to recognize, is a matter to be determined by the scientific problem in hand. The fact of the matter is that, empirically, Egyptians are more or less Mediterranean Caucasoids; that as one goes south and southwest, there is a gradual change; along the Guinea Coast or in the Congo forests, the Negroid stereotype is dominant. There is not, however, an undisputed "line" that can be drawn on a map, or distinctions that can be made between tribes (in other than statistical terms) with the claim that one is unequivocally Caucasoid and the other Negroid. In even the most dominantly Negroid tribe, there are to be found individuals with light skins and green eyes; in the northern regions of Africa, there are some people with dark skins and kinky hair.

Race is, in short, in the eye of the beholder.

CHANGING EUROPEAN VIEWS OF AFRICANS

Dogmas concerning the nature of the visible differences between Africans and Europeans have undergone many changes in Europe—and it is an amazing fact that we have almost no information whatever on ways in which African peoples look upon "racial" differences. Recently Professor Philip Curtin of the University of Wisconsin has done extensive historical research into European views of Africans. The following brief survey draws heavily on his accounts.

Great difficulty inheres in any attempt to explain to laymen that science can say nothing about the attitudes, endowments, capabilities, and inherent tendencies of different groups of human beings as they are determined by the stereotypes of race. The difficulty arises because in the early days of scientific discussion it was assumed, even by scientists, that such differences did exist. Race, indeed, appeared at one stage the major determinant of the course of human history. Twentieth-century science has recognized that its predecessors were mistaken. The twentieth-century populace has not quite caught up.

Racial doctrines of the eighteenth and nineteenth centuries contained much accepted "science," stated by men who were not themselves involved, at least overtly, in the racial struggle. Views current in the eighteenth century had been formed by several centuries of association of Europeans and Africans. There was a vague, unreasoned belief that Negro skin color, hair texture, and facial features were in some way associated with Africa, and ultimately with the status of slavery.

Culture prejudice was, throughout this period, expressed in terms of "racial" prejudice. Culture prejudice feeds on real or imagined superiority. Nineteenth-century European culture was admitted by all to be technologically superior—although technology was in the views of some writers not the whole of the matter. Because it is so difficult for any people to look back at their history, and especially at the situation which existed before they made certain key discoveries in morals, Europeans were not quick to see how recent the changes had been.

The problem was faced first by the Spanish in their American colonial empire; it was not until 1537 that a Papal Bull stated unequivocally that non-Westerners, specifically American Indians, were officially human beings. They were, by papal fiat, declared to have full spiritual equality with Christians. This position, be it noted, was very like the Mohammedan one as late as 1850. In the Protestant countries of northern Europe, the problem was postponed. The first real "native" problem that the English faced was with the Irish in the 1770s. The problems from America were of less virulence, and hence each American colony was left to its own devices.

It was not until the 1780s that the British began seriously to consider "the place in nature" of Africans. There were two conflicting traditions: the "noble savage," who was a well-established creation of the literati as a device for railing against the discontents of civilization, and the "natural varieties of mankind," as they were explained by biologists, most of them British or German.

The "noble savage" in the literature of the period is

little more than the standard hero decked out with anything that would represent the absence of the trappings of the modern world, therefore making the purest virtue easier of achievement. There was not then, and has not been since, much interplay between the ideas of the novelist and those of the biologists who were, at the very same time, denying the very nobility that the novelists were creating.

The work of the biologists must be considered in terms of the cosmographical background of the times: a central concept known as "the great chain of being." According to this dogma, all living beings could be fitted into a hierarchy, with apparent but very small differences between each. In this pre-Linnaean mode of classification, man took his place "naturally" at the highest point on the scale, while the smallest organisms were considered to be at the bottom—and therefore inferior.

Before the major revolutionary aspects of Linnaeus' work came to be understood—indeed, it would seem that he himself never grasped the point that his classifications would destroy the concept of the chain of being—his simple classification of the human races on the basis of skin color came to be adopted. Indeed, the classification of human beings by skin color goes back to the Egyptian papyri, though the concept of "race" almost surely does not.

In any case, Linnaeus named the four races to be the white, yellow, red, and black races. Narcissism, if nothing else, assured that Europeans would be at the top of the scale, for no two differentiated types in the great chain of being could be precisely equal. The hierarchy demanded ranking; ranking was carried out, in an idiom of "race," on the basis of subjective evaluations of the cultures that travel writers had associated with the various races. Voltaire, Rousseau, Hume—and most of their contemporaries—made the basic mistake of equating culture with race and ranking races on the basis of their attitudes toward various cultures. This error was perpetuated into the early twentieth century.

Linnaeus, still under the influence of the concept of the "great chain of being," changed his classification in 1758 so that the genus *homo* included the orangutan and several fabulous beasts of the "abominable snowman" variety. The philosophical concept—the great chain of being—was preserved, but the reputation of Africans in Europe sacrificed to it.

Both the noble savage and the "varieties of mankind" became embroiled in political issues. Colonial policy-makers took up positions; pressure groups such as the anti-slavery leagues took up theirs. Data, however, all came from a single source: travelers and planters. All, Curtin tells us, showed "a moderate xenophobia." It would seem that such moderate xenophobia rested on imperfect communication and ethnocentrism rather than on any conviction.

Throughout the debates about the abolition of the slave trade, the similarities between Caucasians and Negroes were minimized to the most basic in order to attract as many followers as possible to the cause—Christians claimed that Africans were "fellow creatures." Few would care to deny so minimal a claim. The initial issue of the slavery abolition movement had little to do with race, but it was very soon dragged into the matter, and in many cases argument proceeded on whether or not the "savages" were in fact "naturally" inferior. The equation of slavery with race was thereby more or less taken for granted; at least the question was begged by an assumption for the very most philanthropic of purposes. The stereotypes of "the Negro" began to appear, and qualities assigned to it that often could not be observed in individuals. Even Wilberforce argued that Africans, being men, were nevertheless "fallen men." They were degraded by their savagery. Throughout, there were some voices raised that "the Negro" was not a valid abstraction because of the very diversity within all African populations. Except for the philosophical background, which was changed radically in the nineteenth century, most of the argument remains with us today.

The "moderate xenophobia" of the written accounts, the position of the Negro in the "great chain of being" (echoes of which were still heard in the early twentieth century when the "missing link" was still being sought by some), the minimization of the similarities among all men in order to achieve philanthropic purposes—all these things came to influence the stereotype of the African that was being built up. The eighteenth-century position can be summed up as a change from the intellectual habit of looking for similarities in all men to the habit of looking for the differences among men in order to achieve scientific classification, to maintain self-images, and indeed to achieve moral distinction. It also ultimately led, in later days, to the simplistic doctrine of the physiological determinism of character.

The early decades of the nineteenth century were marked by two important advances: the idea of the "great chain of being" was giving way to the ideas that were ultimately to be organized by Darwin into evolutionary theory, and ideas of anatomy were becoming more and more precise with the development of scientific clinical medicine. In both spheres, questions began to emerge to challenge the stereotypes that had grown up. Men such as Winterbottom, a doctor who worked for years in Sierra Leone, began to question the old stereotypical myths: that African women could give birth without pain; that Negroes had better eyesight, but that in other matters they had less sensitive nervous systems than Europeans; that Negro brains and Negro bones were of a different color. Scientists such as James Pritchard even made claims that the usual classifications into races were conventional and arbitrary. Pritchard frankly admitted that he disliked African culture, but also claimed that there was no physical limitation to the potential achievement of African peoples—or any other. Another of Pritchard's achievements—but few noted it—was to notice that physical characteristics that had been used as classifiers: skin color, hair form and color, skull shape, facial features, all varied independently from one another.

Pritchard made, however, a mistake of exactly the same order as his predecessors. Instead of defining race by a general cultural criterion, he merely picked a precise one: language. In his effort, which we indeed know was right, to give up the determination of a "natural" division among the races, in which physiological differences "cause" other differences—he has the dubious honor of being the first anthropologist writing English to fall into the opposite trap and make a total overt confusion of race, language, and culture.

The science of phrenology was also instrumental in spreading the idea of linking physical traits with mental ability. Phrenology held the stage for some decades, only to be proved wrong on every point. Unfortunately it too left a residue of prejudice from which anthropology was long in freeing itself: the idea that head shape was meaningful did not disappear until well into the twentieth century.

There are many early nineteenth-century theories of racial origins that depend on natural selection, but the mechanisms by which they worked was not known until the *Origin of Species*. The main point is that it was during the decades from 1820 to 1860 that the change in philosophical background was made, and a vast array of knowledge added. The interesting thing, however, is that in this whole period there was no change in the cultural prejudices exhibited by Europeans. They merely began to justify them in terms of different theories. It was even held by one author that African physical features would change as they became more civilized. With the new ideas of the survival of the fittest, and stepping up of the anti-slavery activities, and further development of British humanitarianism, it became stylish to press the claims of the Africans *because* "they were inferior." We have some of the earliest suggestions of what was ultimately to become "the white man's burden."

Travel literature grew. Culture shock experienced by missionaries and other travelers was almost invariably reported in terms of the inferior qualities of the people who were being visited. Even the staunchest supporters of individual Africans said no more than that because some had become "civilized," all could become so. What we now know to have been the achievements of African culture were not recognized until well into the twentieth century.

During the early part of the nineteenth century, the most important single problem for British social theorists was human progress—by which they meant European progress. The forerunners of theories of cultural evolution kept pace with the forerunners of theories of physical evolution. The two constantly interaffected one another, and given the cultural chauvinism of the time, the African people came out with a very low ranking in the eyes of European moral historians. Historians of this period were also busy working out the comparative histories which were to culminate in Spengler and Toynbee. The claim was made by most that the human "race" developed in Mesopotamia and stayed there until after the flood, after which it moved out. Civilization went northwest. The Africans, obviously, had taken another direction.

At the same time, humanitarians began to lose what belief they had that the major cause of African "barbarism" was to be found in the chaos resulting from the slave trade. Against the commanding presence of the idea of the survival of the fittest, such a view seemed difficult to maintain. By the time that Mungo Park and other travelers actually penetrated the interior of Africa it became necessary—if the stereotype was to be maintained—

to deny that African Negroes could possibly have created any of the civilizations that were found. Curtin even found one writer (a phrenologist named Combe) who stated that the people of the western sudan could not be Negroes in spite of their black skins, because they had reached a state of comparative civilization higher than the inferior Negro race could possibly have achieved. The stereotype was working overtime.

In science, the Darwinian revolution corrected most of the errors of early nineteenth-century biology, but it allowed the racist error to stand. Indeed, it underwrote it without providing any confirmation of it. It made it possible to claim, with a new scientific "surety," that superior races were marked by their superiority—and to people interested in "progress," that meant technological proficiency.

As early as 1841, the old idea of the moving focus of history (one version of which was "westward the course of empire") was taken up by Thomas Arnold in his inaugural lecture as Regius Professor of History at Oxford. He set the old idea in terms of race. According to him, the force of world history came from a series of creative races; the Greeks, the Romans, the Germans, the English. Gustav Klemm, in 1843, distinguished between active and passive races; progress was seen as the result of the contributions of a monolithic succession of great races. Perhaps the first influential proponent was Dr. Robert Knox, the Edinburgh doctor who was supplied with corpses by Burke and Hare. Although he was not personally implicated in the murders that these two performed, his reputation was nonetheless ruined. He wrote a book called *The Races of Man*, and turned to lecturing about race, which he called "transcendental anatomy." Curtin lifted out his key statement, "Race is everything; literature, science, art—in a word, civilization depends on it."

In Knox's view, the dark-skinned peoples of the world were the first to evolve, but reached a maximum achievement possible to them and became stagnant. The light-skinned peoples evolved later and had to wage war to the death against the stagnant earlier "races," who would eventually become extinct, because they were "incapable" of civilization. Knox, like so many of his contemporaries, included under the dark races the southern Europeans or Mediterraneans. By the light races he meant the Saxons—the people that latter-day dictators have called Aryans. Soon the theory of racial determination of history became all but general—only The Ethnological Society and a few individuals held out against it.

As historians began to use racial explanation, other commentators introduced the factor of race into almost every other aspect of contemporary affairs. Every failure of European work in Africa became a further sign of the basic inferiority of Africans.

Thus, just as the eighteenth century had reduced the common elements of the races to a minimum, the middle of the nineteenth was able to destroy the intellectual foundation of racial egalitarianism.

It is hard today for us to understand that in the middle of the nineteenth century the study of language and the study of race were considered to be approximately the same thing. Gobineau claimed, and most of the authorities of the age agreed with him, that the hierarchy of languages was precisely the same as the hierarchy of races and that some languages were superior to others in a hierarchal arrangement more or less reminiscent of the "great chain of being." Languages evolved very much as races had evolved. In an opposite view (but proving the same point) it could be said that God had given language to man in the Garden of Eden, and that all known languages were greater or lesser degenerations following Babel. Tonal languages, being harder for Europeans to learn, were placed lowest on the scale. Latin was "obviously" highest. Linguistic studies also went into African oral literature and smashed once for all the theory that Africans had no myth and no tradition of the past. History began to be reconstructed from linguistic similarities.

The climatic theory was still very commonly subscribed to, however, and was reinforced by the high mortality rate of Europeans in West Africa. Diet, ecology, and sexuality all came in for examination as being effective differentia among races and among the levels of civilization achieved. Missionaries also began to enter the field in force at this point, and it was they who pointed out that African religion was not merely the absence of religious truth but was "a positive evil." These men in their writings very often equated their own "worst passions" with the deified forms in African religions.

It was not until late in the nineteenth century that historical and ethnographic data in any quantity began to be collected in Africa and brought to bear on the problems at hand. It was not, in fact, until the 1920s that any large amount of ethnographic data became available, and it was only after World War II that African history emerged as not merely a recognized branch of the subject, but indeed one that might ultimately change the nature of historiography. Indeed, it was not until the revolutions of independence in 1960 that it became possible for Europe, for the first time in centuries, to examine Africa with uncommitted eyes. The stereotypes are in the way, but it is beginning to be possible to see beyond some of them.

MODERN POPULATION PROBLEMS

Africa is, except for Australia (and Antarctica, which hardly counts), among the least peopled of the world's continents. The African census data are extremely foggy —ranging from fairly accurate counts in Ghana to total lack of census data in Ethiopia (estimated at perhaps twenty million). Census counts are for the most part poor, a fact which also casts doubt on growth rates. However, the people are probably less thick on the ground than anywhere in the world save the Amazon basin and the Australian outback. Information on birth and death rates is even sketchier than is census information. About all that can be said is that African birth rates are probably not high in comparison with other underdeveloped areas, and that death rates are being lowered because of improvements in sanitation, medical services, and the reduction of epidemic diseases, as well as improved food production and transportation. In spite of these facts, it would seem, however, that there is a high proportion of the population that are children—perhaps as much as 40 percent. But even assuming the correctness of this figure, Africa would seem not to be in the midst of a population explosion of the sort that is happening in other parts of the world—this statement, however, would be as widely disputed as it would be upheld, and the only sure statement is that our knowledge is fragmentary. In this matter, as in many others, knowledge about Africa is now being ardently sought by Africans.

Chapter 6

Farms and Iron

There have been many occasions in the history of human development when cultural steps were taken from which there was no return: steps which were so intrinsically simple and which so simplified the processes of living that to go without them thereafter would be quite literally unthinkable. Tool manufacture is such a step. Once the idea of a tool is present, men will make tools—particular techniques may be lost, and whole cultures may wither, but tools will be made, and the general direction of development will be toward efficiency. The discovery of use of fire is another such irreversible revolution. The comforts it provides—both for heating and for cooking—are so apparent and the idea so simple that men will put vast ingenuity into acquiring and maintaining a fire. To revert to fireless living would be quite literally unthinkable.

It is just such shatteringly simplifying discoveries as these that makes cultural evolution more than merely a faulty analogy to biological evolution (which it nevertheless remains). We are accustomed to thinking of evolution in terms of complication—going from the simple to the complex. In one sense—particularly if we examine the technological development of human kind—such a position is a true one. But there is another sense which allows us to see that the constant complications are possible only concomitantly with vast simplification. It is easier to live with fire than without it. The increasing complexity brought about by cultural evolution is material and usually superficial; underneath the complexity lies a growing simplicity.

We have noted above that man seems to have made the first of his simplifying discoveries (if indeed we can say it was actually the first, merely because it is the oldest to have been preserved) when he began to chip stone tools. Cultures have declined, but new ones have risen—and man has never looked back. It would seem that the discovery of fire took place in East Asia perhaps two hundred thousand years ago, and Oliver and Fage in their *Short History of Africa* guess that its use by human beings was introduced into Africa only about fifty thousand years ago. They would surely admit, however, that the data are extremely thin.

We are on surer ground with the two simplifying discoveries to be discussed in this chapter—two more recent discoveries that lie behind African history as well as behind the history of the rest of the world. They are first the discovery of agriculture and animal husbandry, which made vast new amounts of energy available to men, and second the discovery of metallurgy, which made energy more efficiently usable.

THE AGRICULTURAL REVOLUTION

So far as present-day archaeologists are aware, fixed agriculture and urban living developed together in the Jordan Valley about 6000 B.C., on the base of a Mesolithic hunting culture known as "Natufian." In most parts of the world, societies which depend on hunting and gathering for their subsistence are necessarily limited to a few hundred people and must necessarily range over a wide enough area that fixed villages or other dwellings are impractical. Almost the only exception to this generalization is to be found in fishing communities: quite large villages of fishermen may grow up and be permanent over long periods of time. We shall see that fishing industries probably had as great an effect in Africa as they have had elsewhere on the history of the expansion and spread of culture.

The oldest example yet discovered of what is unquestionably a fixed settlement, with agriculture and the beginnings of animal husbandry, is the site of Jericho. Cultivation may have been practiced before total settlement, as it is by some bands of nomads today—catch crops that need little care. Extensive cultivation, however, demands close attention and ultimately settled existence. It both demands and allows much larger populations, and it is safe to say that the world's first major "population explosion" occurred during these millennia.

Both the idea of horticulture and the crops to be grown spread slowly from this base in Asia Minor (which, as we have seen, might as sensibly be called "Africa Minor"). Cultivation brought new securities—and new problems; the increasing population further increased the rate of speed at which new techniques and new cultigens were discovered and adopted.

Nevertheless, it was some two thousand years from the time that agriculture was established in the Jordan Valley to the time that civilization began to develop in the Nile Valley. The crops and animals—wheat and barley, sheep and goats—were the same in the two places. What happened in Egypt is that a strong Asian influence was stamped upon a basically African culture, giving rise to Egyptian civilization. A warning must be issued: "African culture" has nothing to do with the race of the people who practiced it. It has rather to do with forms of social organization, economy, polity, religion, and the like. As we learn more and more about the cultures and civilizations of Africa, we realize that by these criteria Egypt lay culturally as well as geographically between Africa and Asia. Egyptian religion can be best understood only by reference to African religion; many other aspects of Egyptian history and polity are illuminated by African ethnography. It has been stylish in the past to assume that all these social and cultural forms were invented in Egypt and spread to other parts of Africa. Today we know that such was an oversimplification: Egypt was basically an African culture, with intrusions of Asian culture.

In order to see the picture most clearly, it is necessary to go back several millennia. It seems reasonable to believe that some twelve thousand years ago the Sahara was habitable, but dry—not so dry as today, but drier than a wet phase that came later. It seems to have been inhabited by people who were probably of a stock resembling modern Bushmanoid peoples, although the point has not been finally determined. These people also hunted across the territory that was later to become Egypt.

The Sahara subsequently went through a wet phase, in which people encroached upon it from both north and south. We do not know for sure who they were, but it seems unwise merely to assume that they were like modern Europeans or modern Negroes.

In the wet phase of the Sahara, the hunting and gathering subsistence economies seemed to include considerable fishing which, as we have seen, allows of comparatively large populations. It would also seem that the situation of this time allowed of a very considerable gene flow through large areas and diverse populations.

Then, some six or seven thousand years ago, the desiccation of the Sahara began again, which was eventually to bring it to the state that we know it today. With progressive drought, people withdrew from the desert in both directions. With progressive withdrawal, the gene pools, as well as the "culture pools" (if the analogy be permitted) became smaller.

It seems likely that the peoples who left the Sahara and went north were swallowed up into the greater populations of the Mediterranean. Those who went south encountered a far different fate: to say that the Negro race "developed" at this period would almost surely be a misstatement, yet in the new situation the physical traits that today are considered to be characteristically Negroid were undoubtedly intensified in a relatively small, in-breeding population in the sudanic areas south of the growing Sahara.

Not only genes, but culture as well, spread to both the north and the south of the Sahara. Only by some such theory can the genetic similarity of Europeans to Negroes as well as their manifest differences be accounted for.

It is difficult for modern man, that most numerous of beasts, to accustom himself to the idea that a few thousand years ago men were rare animals. The gene pools were undoubtedly small—small enough that a race could be consolidated in comparatively few generations and then, through social practices and limitations, spread throughout a continent, multiplying rapidly.

The story can be summed up this way: As men withdrew from the Sahara to the south, and continued to live in fishing communities, they brought with them the genes of the Sahara population, and consolidated them into a racial "type." They also brought the cultural background that underlies both Europe and Africa and is at the basis of what has been called the "Old World Culture Area." The story is given verisimilitude by the fact that Negroes are, relatively, such a scarce people. Even if the United Nations figure of 250,000,000 Africans is not too high (which it almost surely is), and if we were able to say which Africans are "Negroes" and which are not (a dubious point), it can be seen that there is a very small number of Negroes in the world compared with either Caucasoids or Mongoloids, and it is possible that, under favorable conditions, that number could have been reached in only a few thousand years from an extremely small original population.

The Negroes spread in Africa presumably as fishermen. The agricultural revolution reached them in two waves, both depending on the finding of satisfactory crops for the areas in which they lived. Near Eastern grain crops do not thrive in the sudanic areas of Africa, and will not grow at all in the forested regions. The first phase of the agricultural revolution in Africa south of the Sahara came with ennoblement and spread of the millets and sorghums in the grasslands and sudan. The second came with the introduction of root crops from Southeast Asia and ultimately from America that would thrive in the forests.

There is currently a dispute among prehistorians of Africa about whether the agricultural revolution among the Negro populations in Africa south of the Sahara occurred independently in the western sudan or whether it occurred as a result of what anthropologists call "stimulus diffusion" and the discovery of new crops suitable to the sudanic area that could be ennobled. There is, in fact, still some dispute about the precise area in which the millets were ennobled: the actual data are very difficult to unearth from under a huge overload of claims and counterclaims, charges and countercharges.

Yet, at only a slightly more abstract level, a general picture can be drawn. We know for certain that metallurgy went from east to west. We do not know whether the idea of horticulture was invented once and went from east to west, or whether it was invented twice (the second time in the western sudan with the ennoblement of the millets) and went from west to east, meeting the east–west movement in the upper Nile. Further scientific work and archaeology will undoubtedly provide us ultimately with an answer. Within the whole picture, the point is of little importance. What is obvious is that the fishing and hunting communities in prehistoric sub-Saharan Africa could, when they got agriculture, be very greatly enlarged. And that undoubtedly did occur. Peoples of predominantly Negro type filled the sudanic areas. Yet, this same type of people were in the forests, still living primarily by fishing techniques. It was not until some time later—maybe as late as the Christian era—that they acquired the yams and cocoyams from Southeast Asia, across the Indian Ocean, with which they were to conquer the forests.

EGYPT IN THE HISTORY OF AFRICA

The discoveries of agriculture made in the Jordan Valley reached their highest early achievement in that of the Nile. The position of Egypt in European history has always been somewhat equivocal. Its position in African history is central and perfectly clear, for all that details are yet to be reconstructed from archaeology and from documents as yet unread or even unreadable.

The peculiar situation in the valley of the Nile made it possible for the dynastic period in Egypt to be reached only a millennium or so after the introduction of agriculture. Although there were hunting peoples in the Nile Valley before that time, there was very little vested interest on the part of the hunting peoples and hunting cultures when compared to those who brought about the vast improvement in agriculture.

The agricultural revolution began in Africa in the fifth millennium B.C. and continued into the fourth. South of the Sahara, the time period probably was from about the beginning of the third millennium, but gained momentum only during the latter part of the second and during the first millennium B.C. The spread of agriculture into the forests accompanying the root crops took place in the early centuries of the Christian era.

The earliest Egyptian cultivators of which we have any record did not live along the Nile but rather along the tributaries in what was then dry steppe country. The dates have been confirmed by radiocarbon dating as the second half of the fifth millennium B.C. Fishing equipment, storage granaries, Neolithic stone tools, undecorated pottery, and linen were all present.

During this period, the Sahara was drying up, and the

Nile Valley was shrinking. Oliver and Fage gauge that twenty thousand people is a top estimate for the number that could be supported in the Nile Valley at the time of the beginning of the agricultural revolution, and they note that the population of the Old Kingdom two millennia later has been estimated at from three to six millions. Population explosions are nothing new.

There are good samples of skeletal material from this time; the people were fairly tall and lightly built and probably resembled the modern Somali. We also know from their writing that their language was a branch of what we now call the Semitic family of languages.

Wheat and barley were the most important crops; they were always accompanied by goats, sheep, pigs, and cattle. These culture traits, plus the Egyptian Neolithic stone tools, spread across the north of Africa into Cyrenaica. The parcel of traits did not proceed into the area of present-day Algeria, Tunisia, and Morocco, which instead seems to have developed out of the indigenous north African Capsian tradition.

Egyptian influence moved up the Nile rather than along the Mediterranean. It reached Khartoum by the second half of the fourth millennium. At about the same time, the cultural bridge was probably created between the Nile and the easternmost tributaries of the Niger. It seems sensible to think that the idea of agriculture was diffused along this line and that new crops were sought in the sudanic areas to the west. Any unequivocal archaeological data indicating that agriculture might have been discovered independently in the western sudan comes from a very much later era.

By the middle of the fourth millennium B.C. there were large villages in middle Egypt, and an extensive trade was carried on from the delta, both with the Aegean Islands and with the east. With a growing population there came a spurt in the growth of religious and political ideas in the Nile Valley. Kingship and the priesthood developed together, and as the same institution. Today, it seems surely to be the case that Egyptian ideas of kingship developed in Egypt itself, instead of further east as was once thought, and developed on an African cultural base. The ideas about the nature of the dead that were expressed in the pyramids (which ideas developed with an amazing rapidity once they started) and the forms of the state that emerged are significantly different from similar ideas and practices to be found in Asia Minor. Divine kingship seems to have been an African invention, for the African form differs radically from any other. Millennia later, it could be found in Uganda, in the Benue Valley, along the Guinea coast, and down into Rhodesia. How much was Egyptian influence, and how much was feedback of an Egyptian adaptation of a basically African idea will never be known—mainly because of the fact that the settled population, agriculture, and the scale on which such society became possible were never duplicated in early Africa.

From the earliest dynastic periods, Egypt was in contact with the south, both by land and by sea. Ivory, hardwood, and slaves came from the south. So did incense, boomerangs, and pygmies. In exchange for such items, Egyptian musical instruments, Egyptian cloth, Egyptian basketry, and many other things and ideas went south if their earlier forms had not come from there. By the end of the second millennium B.C., Egypt had influenced all of the area of the Nile in the region of the third and fourth cataracts, where an indigenous society, Cush, had developed an Egyptian-type culture. Cush, which became more powerful during the first centuries of the first millennium B.C., remained a power until about the fourth century A.D. It was at this time that Egypt was in full decline. The Assyrians and the Hittites from Asia Minor had overrun lower Egypt and ultimately in the eighth century B.C. Cush itself was strong enough to conquer Egypt, whereupon the type of culture that we think of as ancient

Egyptian moved south, although mass migrations of people probably did not occur.

About the sixth century B.C., Cush began to extend itself southward, and ultimately the capital of Meroë was founded. We know from the archaeological skeletal evidence that the peoples in the area of Meroë were Negroes. We also know that the incoming Cushites had learned the art of ironmaking from their enemies of Asia Minor. Egypt had no iron ore and no fuel. The region of Meroë has both, and Meroë turned itself into one of the largest iron-producing areas of the ancient world.

Meroë, like Egypt, traded with the rest of Africa. Ivory, slaves, and ostrich feathers were exchanged for iron and the other products of the then civilized world. A new script was invented which to this day has not been adequately transcribed nor read. The subsequent decline of Meroitic civilization in the third and fourth centuries of our era gave rise to an empire in the Ethiopian highlands, which was within the next few centuries to be Christianized and become the basis for modern Ethiopian civilization. Iron had spread from Meroë into Ethiopia. It had also spread to the west. With it went a type of political organization and military power which was to become typical of the medieval African kingdoms and empires. Iron and kings were spread into all parts of Africa.

IRON AND KINGSHIP

The discovery and spread of metallurgy marks the separation of the metal ages from the Neolithic age, just as agriculture is the major determinant for separating the Neolithic from the earlier stone ages. As in all such revolutions, much changed beyond the precipitating cause: in the metal ages, the trend toward urbanism was vastly increased, and another population expansion began which even yet has not been checked.

Ironworking entered Africa at about the same time that

it entered the Greek islands—around 600 B.C. The first Cushitic grave to contain iron objects dates from about 350 B.C. Just as Egypt and the Aegean civilization, in intense contact and trade, spread northward into Greece, so it spread from Egypt southward into Africa.

Meroë has been investigated by a great many pot hunters and by two or three proper archaeologists. Although it is the biggest single site of Cushitic culture—there are over eight square miles of ruins—it is only a small portion of the available remains. When properly trained archaeologists and sufficient money are found, a major job of research remains to be done on the culture of the Cushites.

Ironworking in Meroë was probably closely associated with the priesthood as a source of power—the priesthood and the kingship in Egypt had scarcely been separated. The processes were probably secret, at least for a long period. Even today in West Africa, smithing is associated with social groups that are dissociated from the rest of the clans and tribes, and in many of them there is a correlation between high rank and ironworking—and in a few, between low rank and ironworking.

Meroitic civilization went into decline in the third century A.D. However, many cultures which showed major influence by it flourished for centuries after Meroë itself had fallen into ruins. By 1100 A.D., the iron-based cultures had crossed the forests and had provided the beginnings on which the Ashanti, Dahomean, and Yoruba states were to be based centuries later. It also provided the base for the states of Kongo and Bushong. All of these states developed with the spread of ironworking, as well as many other items of the cultures of Egypt, Meroë, the sudanic empires, and Monomotapa.

Until after World War II, Meroë was considered by even the best historical opinion to be no more than an outpost of Egyptian civilization. Nobody questioned the stereotype "Africans" sufficiently to credit them with one of the high cultures. This fact plus another—that archae-

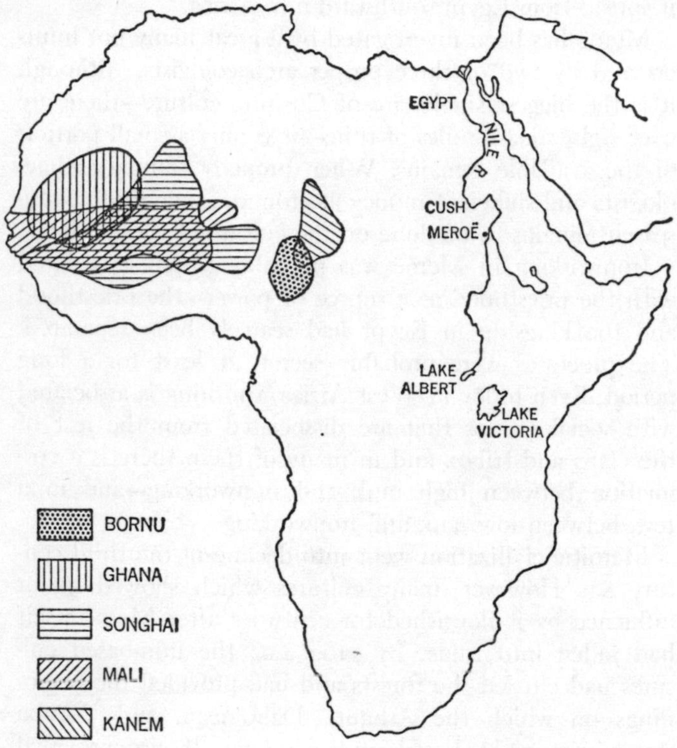

FIG. 4. Some of the old African empires.

ologists have an amazing tendency to account by migrations for changes that might well have come about by diffusion—have led to much pseudo-history, the main theme of which is that the Cushites from Meroë did not merely disappear into a peasant population, but actually fled to the south and to the west before invading Asians. Nobody is sure what happened; nobody knows whether the Cushites went south *or* west, or whether they went any place.

What is very probable, however, is that Meroitic civilization had a vast influence on the sudanic kingdoms to the west, and that there was considerable, but a different type, of influence to the south. In Tanganyika, and farther south, there are several peoples of whom the best known are probably the Iraqw, who speak languages that seem to be unrelated to the other African languages surrounding them, and who are said to "look different." Scattered throughout this area are also to be found large numbers of megaliths, that look like, and probably were, degenerate outliers of the old Egyptian pyramids. Further south, and much later, there are ruins of stone temples and towns of which Zimbabwe is probably the best known.

From just such evidence, and from East Africa myths which tell of a superior people who came in from the north, and after a few generations went on to the south leaving behind them kingdoms and ironworking, Diedrich Westermann, G. P. Murdock, and many other scholars have postulated that the Cushites fled to the south to escape invading Asians. Murdock goes so far as to say that it was these fleeing Cushites who ultimately took up the Pacific yams and sweet potatoes in the Mozambique area and were responsible for diffusing them back into the forest regions, thereby allowing fixed agricultural civilizations to come to the rain forests.

The archaeology of the civilizations of the bend of the Niger, and in the sudan has only just begun. Reading of the Arabic writers who from the eighth to the eighteenth centuries kept careful records has also just begun. Yet, for all that, the outline seems clear. The metallurgical revolution which spread from Meroë by east–west trade routes and perhaps by movements of whole peoples as well, led to the organization of the great state of Ghana, from which the modern state of Ghana has taken its name.[3]

In about 100 B.C. to A.D. 200 or 300, and probably for some time before that, the sudanic area of West Africa was pretty well covered by a culture known from its pottery and terra-cotta figurines as the Nok culture (the name comes from the small village in northern Nigeria where these terra-cotta sculptures were first discovered). It is generally but not universally conceded that ironworking, the Egyptian-Meroitic-type divine king, and the political institutions which accompanied him, were grafted on to the Nok-type cultures to produce Ghana and the subsequent empires. Iron, being secret and kept to the ruling groups, was the fundamental source of weapons, and hence of power. It gave its possessors the kind of superiority that enabled them to shape the African divine state on the foundations of African tribalism.

The state of Ghana was in existence until about the tenth century, when it was overrun by the Moslems. Arabic writings record several things about it—its capital was said to have been two cities six miles apart, in one of which the king lived, surrounded by a walled fortress, and in the second of which there were mosques, and a market, and a merchant city.

Ghana's main advantage came from the fact that it lay between the salt of the north and the gold of the south. Prosperity came from trading in the two. Ghanaians obvi-

[3] Some scholars are of the opinion that the "Cushite theory" is no more than a restatement of the "Hamitic theory"—that Africans imported rather than invented much of their culture—and that Ghana arose independently. *Only* archaeological research will answer such questions.

ously extracted tribute from surrounding peoples, had a complex tax system, and a customs organization. After being overrun by the Moslems, however, their whole state and the cities (which survived into the thirteenth century) fell badly in decay.

Well to the east of Ghana, and overlapping with it in time was the kingdom of Kanem, to the northeast of Lake Chad. Records about it are more spotty, but it seems to be of a very similar type to Ghana. Its rise and fall were based on the same phenomena.

Between Kanem and Ghana, but at a later date, there arose the empire of Mali, whose main cities were Timbuktu and Djenne. To the east of them came the Songhai empires. During the thirteenth and fourteenth centuries there was considerable warfare between Mali and Songhai. There was also considerable influence on Mali from northern Africa. To the south were the Mossi raiders who sometimes overran and sacked Timbuktu, which nevertheless withstood them until well into the sixteenth century, when the Mali and Songhai empires had fallen apart. A little earlier than this, the forerunners of the Bornu empire in what is now northeastern Nigeria were also beginning to be developed, probably out of the remains of Kanem.

The rise and fall of iron-based empires dominated by divine kings lasted up until the time of the Fulani *jihad*, or holy wars, which ended only late in the nineteenth century with the period of colonization.

The whole history of the sudanic kingdoms and of the Saharan trade might, in an oversimplification, be said to be written politically in iron and religion and economically in salt and gold. Empires rose and fell on their ability to dominate trade by the power that came from dominating the art of metallurgy. Perhaps the arch problem of all, however, was that the kings of the sudanic kingdoms never solved the problem of political succession. The Egyptians, and to some degree their successors, had deified the king in an involved series of myths. They created ritual through which divinity could be captured after its escape from the dead king, encapsulated in an image, and then again by ritual means reintroduced into the new king at the coronation.

Even in Egypt, and certainly in the other areas, most new kings had to fight their way to the coronation. Where the fighting was not real, it was very often, nevertheless, re-enacted in ritual. Where polygyny was extensive there were many more contenders. Egyptians and some of their followers solved this problem, insofar as it can be solved, by allowing the kings to marry only their sisters—their concubines' children were not considered to be adequate successors although there were some who nevertheless contested the succession.

The divine king throughout the sudanic area, as in Egypt, was more than a political figure. He was the religious symbol of the political organization, and of the society. He lived a constricted life surrounded by taboos and ritual, at the same time that he enjoyed tremendous power over individuals. Like all persons in positions of power, however, he was himself bound by its constraints. Divine kings are said never to have been allowed to die natural deaths, for that would have meant the downfall of the kingdom. They were strangled by their wives, or other attendants, and their deaths kept secret until the succession had been at least to some degree confirmed.

All of these devices, however, did not prove adequate to the solution of what is a recurrent problem in mankind's political life: handing on of power from one generation to the next. Many solutions were attempted. The Nupe, for example, even in the colonial period, recognized three lineages as royal, and the king was "supposed" to be taken from each in turn. In addition to the dynastic wars that racked the sudanic empires, they were constantly subject to revolts and palace revolutions, and family wars.

All of the sudanic kingdoms were based on ironworking, agriculture, and herding—a hierarchic state organization with a ruling clan and caste which dominated and controlled the iron; a large sedentary farming population; and a large herding population constantly on the move and trading with the settled peoples. In most, organized markets appeared early. All were marked by thriving cities, huge armies including mounted cavalry, chain-mail armor and spears, iron shields, broadswords, and helmets. For fifteen centuries such kingdoms rose and fell, until the process was stopped by the incoming Europeans and the era of colonization.

There was considerable Arab influence in the sudan after about A.D. 700. There was extensive pre-Islamic Arab influence. Then after the tenth century, sudanic West Africa was vastly changed again by Islamized Arabs. It is with Islam that conquering the kingdom was turned into the *jihad*, or holy war.

THE SPREAD OF IRON AND FEUDALISM TO THE SOUTH

The influence of Meroë seems to have spread south at about the same time it was spreading west, with different results because the indigenous societies to the south were of a different sort from those encountered in the sudan. Indian trade, Arabia, and Persia had given a flavor to them. The land of Zinj, the Arabic name for East Africa, was populated by dark peoples, from the eastern horn of Africa to about the present-day Mozambique. Arab sailors and adventurers did not sail much south of Mozambique, because the winds changed in the Mozambique Channel.

The written records of the Arabic contact go back well beyond the tenth century A.D., and the much older archaeological records are beginning to emerge. From these we find that the main coastal trade was in the hands of the Arabs who came to the east coast of Africa early, and were well established by 200–300 B.C., when there are Greek records, including a periplus, or seafarers' atlas, that includes the coast down to about modern-day Mombasa. By the ninth or tenth century A.D. the Arabic geographers had the coast pretty well mapped, but like seafarers everywhere, were ignorant of anything ten miles inland. The inland trade was totally in the hands of the Africans.

Peoples in this area traded ivory, gold, slaves and, later, iron. Shipments of iron ore went from the east coast to the southern part of India, where it was made into steel, which was itself reshipped to Persia and Asia Minor, and worked into the so-called Damascus blades. African ore was smelted and made into steel in India for swords made in Damascus. Obviously there was an extensive trade in the Indian Ocean.

There are several Arab writers, from the seventh to tenth centuries A.D. (translated into French in the nineteenth century), who gave us good records of the African areas at this time. But it was not until our own era that we began to know the extent of the trade, and of the contact with India and China. Sir Mortimer Wheeler, the British archaeologist, has said that the history of Tanganyika can be written in Chinese porcelain. There are places, especially along the Swahili Coast, where he and Gervase Mathew have discovered sites in which one can shovel up the potsherds of Chinese porcelain. Undoubtedly Chinese and Indian cloth were also brought in extensively in this period, though cloth does not of course leave remains over long eras of time. The Chinese, by the fourteenth century A.D., had four- to seven-mast sailing ships of at least two thousand tons that plied from Java across to eastern Africa. Some of the Arabic records earlier than this indicated that Javanese ships could carry as many as two hundred people, and there is one recorded occasion when as many as twenty-seven thousand Chinese landed in East Africa.

There was, in short, a very considerable east coast trade.

The archaeology of it has not yet been done—and the reluctance of scholars to learn Arabic and search the Arabic record is as nothing compared with their reluctance to learn Chinese so that they can search the Chinese record. We do know, however, that in one of the most interesting changes of policy in history, the Chinese, in about 1500, decided to scrap all their ships, close their shipyards, and give up being a maritime power. Even before the arrival of the Portuguese, the Chinese had ceased to be a power in the Indian Ocean. The Arab trade continued, but never with the naval efficiency of the Chinese.

Another factor in the Indian Ocean and along its African coasts was the presence of the Malays, who eventually settled in Madagascar. Some Malagasy languages are Malayan in type, and many of the main crops of the area have their origins in Indonesia. The root crops of Africa—taro, sweet potatoes and Indonesian yams—undoubtedly came into the continent from the east coast. And undoubtedly we do not know the full story of their travels: just who picked them up on the east coast is unknown. Murdock says it was the Megalithic Cushites; Oliver and Fage opt for fishing communities of Bantu. Whatever the route—and the matter has still to be argued with a shovel—it was not merely Indonesian crops but many other traits of Indonesian culture that found their way into all of the forested parts of Africa.

Africa has, in short, been almost at the hub of the meeting of cultures from the Near East, from Europe, from India, and from Indonesia. All have been implanted on African cultures. The myth of African isolation is disappearing before our eyes, and yet it is still necessary to explain why the explorers of the eighteenth and nineteenth centuries and the missionaries and administrators in the early twentieth nevertheless still subscribed to the view that Africa was the "dark continent."

Chapter 7

Darkest Africa

It was about six thousand years ago that the Sahara became dry enough to offer a major barrier to human movement. From that time until the middle of the fifteenth century, Africa and Europe moved continually farther apart. There were major paths of communication down the Nile Valley and across the caravan routes of the Sahara. We know that goods and people never ceased to move across it. Nevertheless, European civilization, particularly in the Middle Ages, got farther and farther away from Africa. Africa, the last major continent to be mapped and explored by Europeans, was the "Dark Continent."

THE GREAT TRADITION AND THE LITTLE TRADITION

The disparity between Europe and Africa lies not so much in the community cultures of each as in the civilizations of each. Although this distinction can be traced back to Sir Henry Maine and beyond, it can best be understood in the terms given it by Robert Redfield, the American anthropologist. He claimed that there was, in all the "old" civilizations of the world—that is, civilizations grafted on earlier cultures and peoples rather than founded anew as Anglo-American and Australian civilizations were—a disparity between a "great tradition" and a "little tradition." Redfield was led to this formulation by his interest in peasant cultures; unlike "primitive" societies and unlike civilizations, the social groups that exhibit peasant cultures all depend to some degree on the existence of the "manor"—the city or the church or some other carrier of a "great tradition." The peasants—the carriers of the little tradition—do not themselves participate fully in the great tradition, although in most cases at least some of their members may move into the social groups that represent the great tradition.

Africa and Europe shared a little tradition that diverged on amazingly few points. But both areas also developed great traditions, and there it was that they most tellingly grew apart. Onto a more or less common village community structure came to be grafted widely divergent institutions. In Europe the institutions of the great tradition were feudalism, the Church and its various political manifestations, the heresies and the Protestant movements, and finally the Industrial Revolution and all the changes that it wrought.

In Africa, the great tradition lay in the ideas of divine kingship, associated as it was with the major technological developments of metallurgy and ultimately of everything that follows from it.

With the expansion of Arab culture across North Africa and down the east coast, the situation developed in which all of North Africa and the Eastern Horn became associated with the Near East. Arab occupation of Europe was stopped (with a few exceptions) at the Bosporus and in the mountains of the Iberian peninsula. Marc Bloch, the eminent French historian, has pointed out that one of the reasons that medieval Europe could develop as it did is that there was no invader to destroy European culture as it developed. We are used to thinking of the Teutonic tribes destroying Rome; we are not accustomed to realizing that from the eleventh century on, there were no major invaders of Europe. The medieval civilizations—the great traditions—of Europe and those in the sudan were in some regards alike. But the Arabs destroyed the civilizations that were developing in Africa. Had the Arabs got past the Spanish or the Turks, the medieval and modern history of Europe might well resemble that of Africa much more than it in fact does.

Moreover, Arab intrusion into Africa offered an easy path for Islamic influence once the Arabs themselves were Islamized. Islamic influence was never felt extensively in Europe except as an external factor—what Toynbee has called a "challenge." Africa did not and does not combat Islam. Christendom, through missionaries and other forces, is still combating it.

Thus, the shutting out of Africa from the European consciousness began with the desiccation of the Sahara. It was reinforced when certain aspects of Egyptian civilization came to be important influencing factors of Aegean and Greek culture, while differing aspects of the same Egyptian civilization went south to Cush and the kingdoms south of the Sahara. Then throughout the era that is known in Europe as the Middle Ages, both Europe and Africa turned inward to their own affairs, but in Africa those affairs were vastly changed by the Arab influx.

Yet through all the medieval period, there was trade—sometimes extensive trade—across the Sahara via the great kingdoms of the sudanic areas and the peoples of the northern littoral of the African continent. We know, for example, that Africa was, in the thirteenth and fourteenth centuries, flooded with cowrie shells which were brought by the Venetians from the Maldive Islands, and which crossed the desert. Cowries during this period became a type of currency in many parts of Africa, and ultimately became so plentiful that their value underwent serious deflation; in the most important centers they all but lost their value. We know also that the flow of Negro slaves across the Sahara never totally ceased. Comparatively few got as far as Europe, but some did. During the period that European civilizations were largely cut off from the civilizations of Asia Minor and India, the commerce and other interrelationships between eastern Africa and Asia were at their height. It begins to look as if Europe were the Dark Continent.

When Europe began to rediscover Africa, along with her rediscovery of the rest of the world, a series of occurrences took place that made smooth and amicable relationships between the peoples of the two continents almost impossible. If we follow tradition and take the exploration voyages sponsored by Prince Henry the Navigator of Portugal as our starting point, we discover that the exploration of Africa can be thought of as a continuation of the movements that began when the Iberians organized to force the Arabs out of the peninsula. In the years after 1407, when Prince Henry of Portugal took part in the sacking of Ceuta, opposite Gibraltar, he formed an academy and was instrumental in letting out on contract the task of exploring the west coast of Africa. His explorers received certain rights and rewards in exchange for claiming these areas in the name of Portugal, and more specifically for bringing back items that could be used in national (not to say royal) trade. Among the earliest imports into Portugal were Moorish slaves. Negro slaves were not far behind.

In the next two or three centuries the exploration of the African coastlines was tied irretrievably with the slave trade. As we shall see, slavery is an African institution which has peculiar forms that are totally unlike the institutions of servility that were found in medieval Europe. For this reason, there was an effective misunderstanding between Africans and Europeans about just what slavery consisted in, and yet Africans were able, because they had a tradition of slavery, to exist and even to prosper in a slave situation. This fact led Europeans to state that they considered Africans to be "natural" slaves and "born" hewers of wood and drawers of water. As we have seen in our investigation of the development of racial attitudes, this idea very quickly implanted itself and led to disdain on the part of Europeans for Africans and African culture.

The abolition of the slave trade added fuel to the fire. For all that it was a humane movement and one which the modern world of that time had to undergo in order to develop industrialism to the point that it desired, the way in which it was carried out was ultimately most uncomplimentary to Africans and destructive to the relationships existing between Africans and Europeans. As we have seen, minimal claims were made for Africans—they were, after all, "fellow creatures" and the implication was left that they might not be much more.

The situation was certainly not improved by the explorers of the late eighteenth and nineteenth centuries. These men, who were driven out of the European cultures which culminated in the strictures of the Victorian era, were, for the most part, either malcontents or men of overweening ambition searching for position and power. Such men were in no position to understand or even to perceive the intricacies of African civilization or the basic similarity between the "little traditions"—the peasants—of Africa and those of Europe, although some of them—Mungo Park and David Livingstone—did see the similarities. Men like Cruickshank and Winterbottom also could see what they were dealing with and reported fully and correctly. The same could be said, however, for very few.

It was in this era that the idea of the Dark Continent—the phrase was Stanley's—came to the fore. With the exploration and with the expansion of the West which accompanied industrialization and the vast social and cultural changes then going on, Africa was a prime target for colonial expansion. In order for colonial expansion to take place, it became necessary to consolidate the view of African cultures as savage and barbarian in order to justify one's activities.

Europe and Africa, which had once been culturally close together, grew successively farther and farther apart. Africa, at the time the colonial empires emerged in the late nineteenth century, was thoroughly the "Dark Continent," subject to almost all the stereotypes that remained in effect until after 1945. If one begins with Carthage, and has one's thinking dominated by events in a Europe cut off from the spread of Islam, and then by the modern colonial situation, the justification of the view becomes clear: Africa south of the Sahara is one world, and the Mediterranean is another. But the picture must be expanded at both its ends.

PRINCE HENRY AND THE BEGINNINGS OF "DISCOVERY"

After the Arabs, the next great influence on African development came from Europe. Europe had, as we have seen, long been involved in its own troubles. It had had its period of feudalism, which of its own weight was beginning to break down. The very reasons for the breakdown were associated with outward pulsations from Europe on almost all fronts. The Italian city-states were expanding their commerce into Asia in search of exotic goods to fill their market places; improvements in seafaring equipment and other technology were keeping pace; Marco Polo and other voyagers made their reports. The Crusades had led generations of Europeans "against the Saracens"; now the Arabs were driven back out of Spain, and an impulse was begun that could not be stopped. Backed by a rapidly developing technology, trade and empire were the aims of all those political entities that were fast becoming recognizable "nations."

Intelligence—that is, the knowledge of the doings of others—is always necessary to turn a profit or to win a military victory. One of the Rothschilds is said to have trebled his fortune because he had—long before the telegraph—a carrier pigeon service to bring him the latest information about the outcomes of battles and of "deals." Knowledge is intelligence, and in the search for wealth and for domain that characterized an "awakening" Europe, princes and merchants turned their forces to acquiring better intelligence.

Geographical research was in those days intelligence—even in our own day, long-range weather reports can be "classified information." By the late Middle Ages, various kings and princes in Portugal, Majorca, Italy, and Sicily were subsidizing academies of geography. The same developments had taken place a little earlier in Arab lands. In Europe in the fourteenth and fifteenth centuries, geographical intelligence was the basis of developing mercantile empires.

By 1444, there was a thriving market in African slaves in Portugal. By the time of the discovery of the New World, there were provinces in Portugal that had more Negro slaves than Caucasians. Obviously, a rapid change that bordered on revolution had occurred in Portugal. From a few slaves, the number became legion.

The Portuguese expeditions of Vasco da Gama got around the southern tip of Africa and up the east coast in 1498. What they found was an extremely prosperous coastal culture that had been built up with the assistance of Arab and Chinese trade. They destroyed whatever they could of it in their search for gold and spices and the mythical Christian kingdom of "Prester John"—a figure who held the same sort of fascination for Prince Henry's era as the abominable snowman has for our own. It was at this time that Portugal captured Goa and settled down to occupy various ports all around the coastlines of the Indian Ocean. Soon, however, Portugal gave up her position in Africa.

Her African claims turned out to be poor in the commodities she wanted—spices and gold—when compared to the New World and the East Indies, so Portugal lost interest in Africa. Her associations with it languished. The Portuguese left Africa for the simple reason that there were greater profits to be made elsewhere.

Portugal today claims that her African occupation goes

back to the fifteenth century. Although she was there at that time, she actually established her African empire no earlier than 1870; she then "projected backwards," quietly —even unconsciously—a postulate of continuous occupation. The entire Indian Ocean operations of Portugal were run from Goa, not from any port in Africa.

However, the Portuguese had started the slave trade; other European countries had begun settlement of the New World and an economy and society based on slavery were growing there. Portugal pulled out—but the rest of Europe rushed in to fill the vacuum.

SLAVERY AND THE SLAVE TRADE

The nature of slavery is not always understood by modern Westerners. Both the Europeans and the Africans at the time the trade developed had a tradition of slavery, but the two traditions were of very different sorts. African slavery (usually called benign, domestic, or household slavery) was a domestic institution—there were only a few exceptions on the continent. Domestic slaves are interesting because their economic value was not the most important thing about them (although they may, like housewives, be of economic value). It was rather their value as political followers and as indicators of prestige that was dominant.

It is necessary to do *something* with war captives, with criminals, and with the generally bad lots that are found in small numbers in all societies. The African answer was to turn them into slaves, which meant giving them a special (and humble) status in which they—either rejected by or removed from kinsmen—could be carefully watched at the same time that they were given security and position. The word "slave" in this sense refers to people who are attached to domestic groups by non-kinship links of a sort that contain elements of servility. Many slaves could occupy high positions within households—such was also the case with some slaves in classical societies—and to this day, an African will take up arms, joining his slave, if the slave is "insulted" in public by being addressed as such.

A slave was, thus, a kind of kinsman—with different rights from other kinsmen, different positions in the family and household from other kinsmen, but nevertheless a kind of kinsman. Slaves had either to be captured or they had to be acquired from their kinsmen who were "selling them into slavery." This means that, as a form of banishment, some groups took their criminal or generally unsatisfactory kinsmen and performed a ritual which "broke the kinship" and then sold him. The people who bought such men brought them into their own domestic groups and attached them by non-kinship, but kin-like, links to various "huts" within the household. Such slaves did work —often the hardest work—but they married, brought their families into the social group, and formed a thoroughgoing part of the extended household.

Indigenous African slavery was benign in another sense —there were not very many people involved in it. The wars that Africans fought, until they met Europeans or until the Zulu and Ngoni began their progress through South Africa in the eighteenth century, did not produce very many captives. And very few people are totally unsatisfactory to their kinsmen.

Throughout Africa, slaves were no more than otherwise kinless persons who were attached by non-kinship links into households. The few exceptions are those in which they were attached to kings and courts, and in one or two places such as Dahomey, where there were plantation slaves working for the king (probably a feedback from New World institutions).

One of the most important distinguishing characteristics of the American Negro slaves is that they too were kinless people. We who live in such a loose kinship system as that of middle-class America forget the tremendous importance of kin. But even in works of Harriet Beecher

Stowe, one finds the classical distinction between the good master and the bad master: the bad master "broke up families." Every slaveowner in the New World had the right, obviously, to break up families. To this day, in lower-class Negro families, the matricentric family, consisting of a woman and her children with the link to the husband-father weak and ephemeral, is commonly found. When Negroes move into middle- or upper-class culture, this trait disappears. However, in the lower-class culture and through much of the Caribbean area, such is the standard family pattern, left over from the days of slavery. Slaves, even in our own society in the nineteenth century, were kinless people. In the African situation, this is about all that slavery amounted to.

In Europe slavery was a very different institution. It arose on a different basis, had a different history, and led to totally different conditions. European slavery was, from the beginning, primarily economic—perhaps it would be better to say that domestic slavery was the exception, for all that it existed side by side with economic slavery both in the classical world and in the American South. Even in Aristotle's time there were economic slaves being worked to death in salt mines—that expression has been with us for a long time.

Particularly in the medieval world, the form of subservience or servility was scarcely "slavery" in the African sense at all, because it consisted of the institution that European history knows as the "bond servant." Bond service was of an almost purely economic character. For reasons of debt, or some other, it was possible for me to bond myself, or a member of my family, to work until the debt was paid. The whole notion of bond service developed out of a feudal ethic and carried over into the subsequent period.

What happened in the slave trade is that the economically dominated feudal version of servility from the European area met the basically benign, family-dominated slavery from Africa. Like many other aspects of culture, they met first in the market place. Africans saw nothing wrong in selling slaves. Europeans found nothing wrong in buying them—indeed, many of the Negroes in the earliest importations were treated as bond slaves, their bondage limited by contract to a period of years. But the idea that each had about the role of the slave in the world's work was totally different from that of the other. Supply of slaves became expensive, and the "bond" became permanent. From the meeting of the two and the establishment of new nations and new economies, a new institution—New World slavery—emerged.

Given this particular impetus in the form of a labor force, Portugal got a tremendous shot in the arm. Spain was not far behind. And as Portugal went down the coast of Africa, with sea captains under contract to the princes, working on a commission basis, they found themselves by 1460–70 in the Bight of Benin. They built fortresses along the coast at a slightly later date.

The Dutch were not far behind the Portuguese. The Brandenburgers, the Danes, the English by 1540—all got into the trade.

When the Portuguese came down the coast, they found large African kingdoms on the Guinea coast and at the mouth of the Congo. The sources of slaves extend from Cape Verde down the coast deep into Angola. Slaves going into Latin America and Brazil tended, after the first few years, to come from the coast south of the Cameroons; those into the West Indies and North America from the Guinea coast. Portuguese slavers eventually even exported slaves from the east coast, particularly from what is today Mozambique, into Brazil.

The slave trade that the Portuguese found in full tilt along the east coast was of a different sort. It seems to have been somewhat smaller in volume (the records of the west coast trade are good; those on the east coast trade, carried on by Arab dhows, are either poor or unexplored or both), but the whole of eastern Africa was involved in a slave trade, carried out by Swahili contractors for Arab traders who shipped Negroes to Arabia, Persia, and India. The conditions under which they were shipped make the justly infamous middle passage from West Africa to the New World seem benign. The Arabs organized the Swahili traders along the coast. The Swahili organized the immediately inland tribes, who raided farther and farther toward the center of the continent. The captives then had to carry ivory and other goods to the coast; during the trip they were inadequately fed and housed. Livingstone in the nineteenth century made some startling estimates about the vast number of slaves who died on this trip. The slave markets in Dar es Salaam, Zanzibar, and Malindi, and particularly those on Pemba Island, are well described in the eighteenth century and even earlier by Arab travelers. The slaves were packed, like cordwood, into dhows, with sometimes as little as eighteen inches between the decks. Not surprisingly, after the exhausting trip to the coast, many more died at sea.

By the beginning of the nineteenth century, the African continent was more or less in chaos, produced from the slaving operations carried out from both its coasts. The goods that were traded for slaves included large proportions of firearms, and the power structure of African societies underwent vast change. African chiefships and kingships fell to those who controlled the most force, could thereby raid most effectively, and ultimately get the richest. It was with this new power situation, based on the ancient African tradition of kingship, and the wealth produced by the slave trade, that the new empires of the Ashanti, Yoruba, Dahomey, and of the Kongo were enlarged, and on which their new export economy was being erected. The records for Dahomey and Abeokuta and others show that every year the armies of the kings scoured neighboring tribes in slave raids.

Africans did not, of course, take to enslavement kindly.

But they did not perish under it as some other peoples have done. They had slavery institutions that they knew; to a degree, they knew how to behave as slaves. Certainly they knew how to survive as slaves. They were neither puzzled nor terrified by the institution itself. The Spanish had done their best to enslave the American Indians of the West Indies; the West Indians had a freedom-or-nothing attitude and seem to have lacked a cultural tradition of slavery. So many of them died that Las Casas (who lived to regret it bitterly) and many other leaders of New Spain sought the royal permission that ultimately led to wholesale importation of African slaves. The African slaves fought it, and many escaped from it into the hills of Surinam (to form the present-day tribes of "Bush Negroes") and into Middle America. But die out they did not.

ABOLITION OF THE SLAVE TRADE

The slave trade was accepted in all of Europe until late in the eighteenth century—even by those who disapproved of it on moral grounds. There were individuals and small associations who talked and moved against it. But it was not until the first decade of the nineteenth century that the forces in favor of abolition of slavery, and certainly abolition of the slave trade, had won out. The ethics—and the growing industrialism—of Europeans ultimately would not allow them to carry on with slaving. The Church had been against slavery from early times, but in many periods had done nothing about it. Priests in Spain, for example, put the responsibility for the welfare of the West Indians squarely on Queen Isabella's soul—it was not her fault, poor mortal, that she had absolutely no control over what was going on in the New World. The voices of men like William Wilberforce, the archetype of the anti-slavery reformers, became louder and louder. The demands of machine industrialization that made a mockery of the by-now traditional types of slavery (other degrading types of servility were perhaps yet to be invented) found more and more spokesmen. Ultimately all of these forces working together brought about the abolition of the slave trade from the western coast of Africa. The East Africa trade went on somewhat longer—probably well into the twentieth century.

Slavery—still of the benign, domestic sort—lingered in Africa itself. The status "slave" became illegal in Nigeria only in the 1930s, although the slave *trade* had been quite effectively stopped internally by about 1908 and had been illegal from the time Nigeria was founded in 1900. There are, however, even today constantly to be heard on the lips of Africans, rumors that so-and-so is a slave and charges that there are still people who steal children to sell into slavery. It has become, in all probability, a bogeyman. But it is a bogeyman with a long history.

THE EXPLORERS

In a situation of slave raiding, it is not possible to maintain a stable government or to create security for a population. In Africa, the slave trade had so worked up the whole continent that by the middle of the nineteenth century, nobody trusted anybody. Kingdoms rose and fell at an ever-increasing rate. In many areas, social chaos reigned. It was just such chaos, added to the stereotype of Africans that already existed in Europe because of the slave trade and the fact that Europe had otherwise turned away from Africa to the supposed greater riches of America and the East, that reinforced the stereotype.

A century or so after the Portuguese had crawled southward along the edges of Africa, other European nations followed them. The Dutch, who had recently ridded themselves of colonial status in Spain's European empire, had by 1595 outfitted a navy and were exploring the western coast of Africa, carrying their dislike for Iberians with them. By the middle of the sixteenth century the dubious distinction of major carrier in the Atlantic slave trade had passed from the Portuguese to the English. Sir John Hawkins is probably the man most often derided in this context—he was the "first" great slaver, and he had on his coat of arms a "moor in chains."

The English also formed a series of chartered companies to exploit Africa as they exploited India, the Americas, and the other parts of the world into which they were expanding. The first Africa company was formed by Elizabeth in 1588. It was not successful, another was formed in 1618 by James I, and still another in 1631 by Charles I, which had as its impossible goal reaching Timbuktu by going up the Gambia. In the twentieth century, when Britain was computing the length of time she had been in Africa, the date 1631 was taken as base line because, at that time, they established a "permanent" base on the Gambia.

The Danes were in Africa by 1670. Danish power down the coast of Africa continued until about 1810, when their claims were sold to Great Britain for £10,000. At that time they had three castles on the coast and probably a few treaties with the local chiefs. Brandenburg (long before the unification of Germany in 1871) had navies along the coast and claimed castles and "allies" among treaty-bound chieftains.

The castles along the western coast of Africa were fortresses built by the European powers, primarily as home stations for trading vessels and traders' representatives. They were as often fortresses against hostile European powers as against hostile Africans.

The Dutch formed their first settlements at the Cape about the middle of the seventeenth century, and have been in South Africa ever since. There are, in fact, several Afrikaans myths that need exploding: perhaps the most virulent one is that there was no one at the Cape on their arrival. It is quite true that the Bantu peoples were coming south and had not reached the Cape when the Dutch arrived, although they seem to have been farther south than the Boers today claim. But to say that the place was empty was to overlook a lot of Bushmen and a very great many Hottentots. Apologists for Afrikaaner policy sometimes lambaste the United States' Indian policies and compare their Bantu policies favorably with them. Without in the least trying to whitewash or justify the American record in regard to the Indians, it is still fair to point out that the real comparison lies not with the Bantu but with the Bushmen and Hottentots. Between being systematically exterminated and interbreeding with the Dutch to form the present-day "colored" population of South Africa, the Hottentots have all but disappeared and the Bushmen are fast disappearing. The Dutch were a pioneer people, of the same sort and at the same time as the pioneering peoples of the American West. They met the Bantu coming south and fought some bloody wars with them. The resulting problems, however, are far different from any that American society faced or faces. To insist on superficial similarities in "race problems" is only to becloud the issue.

Before 1815, major efforts to tame America and a constant, almost domestic, set of wars in Europe took so much of the energies of Europeans that there was little time left for Africa. Trading stations existed, but no Europeans went more than a few miles inland—the slave trade inland was carried on by Africans—except the Dutch in South Africa. The only exception is the French in Senegal, which was a department of France early in the nineteenth century.

The rest of the nineteenth century was taken up with the cessation of the slave trade and its replacement, at least in some degree, by trade in other goods such as palm products, and ultimately coffee, cocoa, tea, and hemp. Most important, this was the age of African exploration.

Throughout most of this period, there was little tendency beyond the intrepid explorers with their various motives (escape, trade, and missionizing) to penetrate Africa and colonize it. Exploration of the interior of Africa began in the late eighteenth century with the founding in Europe of several societies for exploration; exploration was in many cases also underwritten by governments or by combinations of merchants. There were a number of cogent mysteries: the source of the Nile; the source of the Niger and the location of its course and its mouth. Most of the interior of Africa was a blank space on the map in an era in which, more than ever before, blank spaces represented challenges.

Late in the eighteenth century Mungo Park set out to solve the problem of the Niger; Bruce had investigated the upper reaches of the Nile, and even Napoleon had outfitted expeditions to "solve" the Nile problem. Early in the nineteenth century, expeditions crossed the Sahara and discovered Lake Chad. Clapperton and the Landers had discovered the course and mouth of the Niger. Caillé had visited Timbuktu in 1828. Baker, Speke, and Burton finally discovered the sources of the Nile.

By the middle of the nineteenth century, the great German geographer, Heinrich Barth (who, of all explorers has left the most useful ethnographic record) had done his travel in the interior of the sudanic countries of Africa, while the great lakes in the east were being discovered by Burton and Speke.

The greatest explorer of all—at least, he has become so to people of the modern West—was David Livingstone, who crossed and recrossed the continent, and whose fabulous moral and physical strength, and whose missionary zeal and works tend to overshadow the fact that he was a fugitive from the rigors of social life in his native Scotland.

In the last third of the century, the era of picturesque exploration gave way to large numbers of local and more thorough explorations on the one hand, and to great and

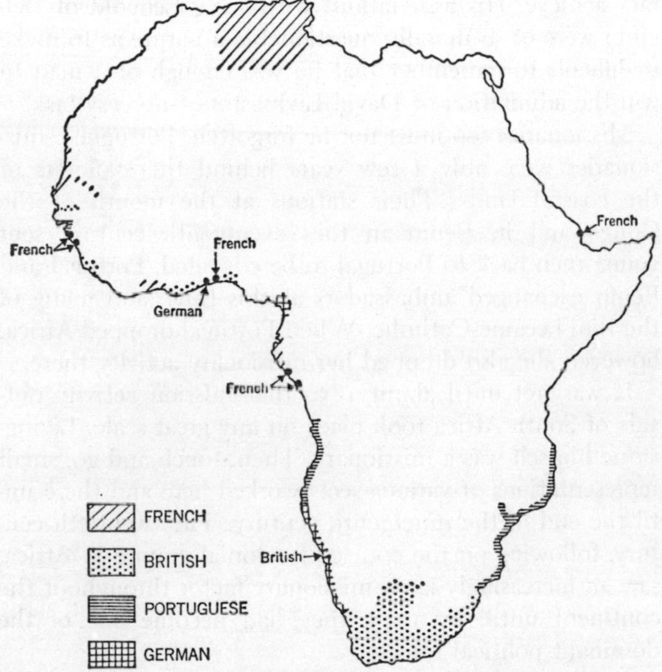

Fig. 5. European toeholds in Africa, 1884. This map shows the spheres of influence of the various European powers prior to the Berlin Conference. The dots indicate the footholds or trading stations. With the exception of two French trading stations in Senegal, European influence was entirely restricted to the coastal areas. (Adapted from L. Dudley Stamp, *Africa, A Study in Tropical Development.*)

even vulgar showmen like Henry Morton Stanley on the other. Stanley himself was such an unpleasant person that it is difficult to be honest enough to give him credit for the vast explorations along the Congo that he did in fact achieve. His associations with King Leopold of Belgium were of so morally questionable a nature as to make it difficult to remember that he was enough of a man to win the admiration of David Livingstone—no easy task.

Missionaries too must not be forgotten. Portuguese missionaries were only a few years behind the explorers of the coastal lands. Their stations at the mouth of the Congo and in Benin in the seventeenth century sent young men back to Portugal to be educated. Portugal and Benin exchanged ambassadors at this time, and many of the Bini became Catholic. When Portugal dropped Africa, however, she also dropped her missionary activity there.

It was not until about 1850 that mission activity outside of South Africa took place on any great scale. Livingstone himself was a missionary. Then, touch and go, small representations of various sects worked here and there until the end of the nineteenth century. The twentieth century, following on the course of colonial empire in Africa, saw an increasingly large missionary factor throughout the continent until, by 1945, they had become one of the dominant political forces.

THE SCRAMBLE FOR AFRICA

In 1884 there were little more than a few trading stations along the coasts of Africa, missionaries spreading out from them, and explorers seeking to fill in maps. The main European peoples interested in Africa during this period—to the extent that they were interested—were the French, the British, the Portuguese, and the Germans. Soon after German unification, a tremendous colonial drive formed in that country. Had it not been that German explorers were so intrepid and kept killing them-

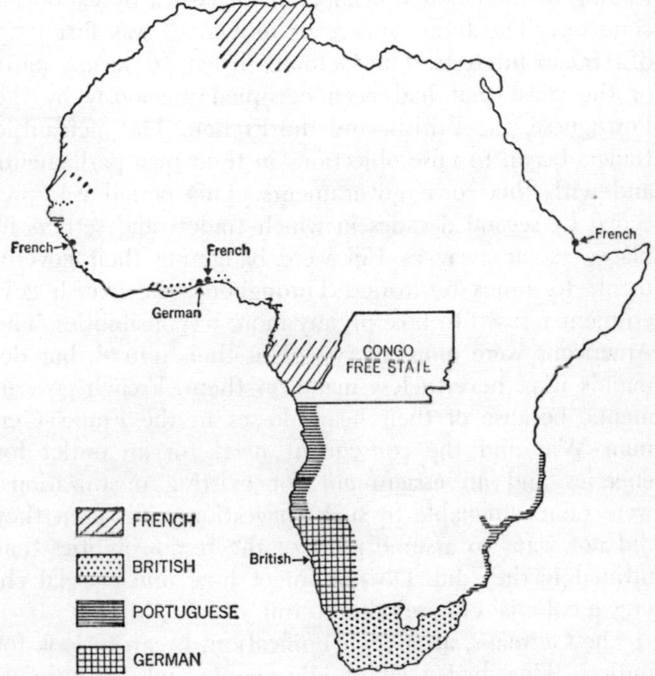

Fig. 6. Europeans in Africa after the Berlin Conference, 1885. (Adapted from L. Dudley Stamp, *Africa, A Study in Tropical Development.*)

selves off, Germany might have had a larger stake in Africa earlier than she in fact had.

It was the intensification of German activity and the entry of Belgium into Africa which created the catalyst leading to the colonial occupation of Africa by European countries. The term "sphere of influence" was first used of African interests. The Germans began to occupy parts of the coast that had been occupied previously by the Portuguese, the British, and the French. The mercantile traders began to raise objections in their own parliaments and with their own governments. This period was preceded by several decades in which traders and settlers in places as far away as Fiji were badgering their governments to annex territories. Throughout, the British government refused to take on any more responsibilities. The Americans were more successful in their refusal, but demands were nevertheless made on them. French governments, because of their heavy losses in the Franco-German War and the consequent need for an outlet for energies and an assignment for existing organizations, were more amenable to such suggestions. Yet even they did not want to assume most of the responsibilities that ultimately they did. Do not forget how *much* social energy a colonial empire takes to run.

The Germans, after their unification, began to look for outlets. They had a lot of idle people and an organization that needed something to do. After Waterloo, the same factors began to affect the British, but not with the same force. It was at the same time—the middle nineteenth century—that Europe became a market-dominated society. It is difficult for us to realize today that it was not until the first third of the nineteenth century that England became unequivocally a market-type society: the need for all persons, in order to live, to sell one of the factors of production in the market. Always before that, people could stand outside the market or enter it only peripherally. It was with the Corn Laws and the Poor

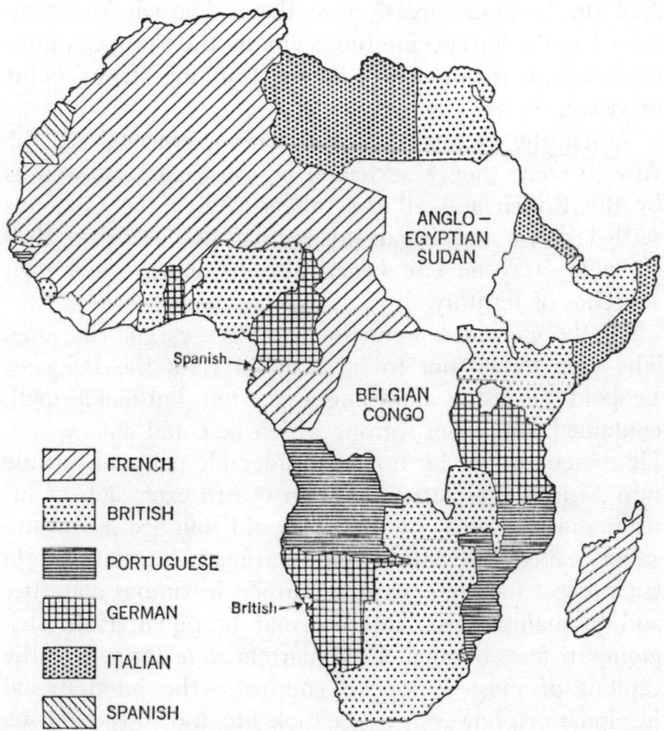

Fig. 7. Africa in 1914. The colonialization of Africa was complete—the four South African colonies had united to form the Union; the Congo Free State had been annexed to the Belgian Crown; the Anglo-Egyptian Sudan was well established as a condominium; the French had established themselves in Morocco, the Italians in Libya, and the British protectorate of Egypt was declared. Subsequent changes, until 1957 with Ghana's independence, were in boundaries or in occupying power.

Laws and the Speenhamland Act of 1832 in England—later on the continent—that people were pushed into the market.

Something had to give. The organization was there. And the "colonial areas" were there. The whole got involved in the internecine fusses among the European principalities (as it might best be put from an African point of view).

When the Germans, a new nation, emerged on the African scene they were feared by the French, as well as by the British and all the others. When the Germans settled down and began to occupy the countries they claimed, everyone else began also to occupy their own stretches of territory.

All the chessmen were now in place except the king. The king turned out to be Leopold II of the Belgians. Leopold was just as ambitious as the rest, but had a small, contained country in Europe which he could not expand. He thereupon put his not inconsiderable personal fortune into African exploration with an eye to expansion of his realms in that area. In 1876 Leopold founded an organization called the African International Association. He tried to get national chapters formed in various countries and to maintain the international headquarters in Belgium. In fact, national headquarters were formed in the capitals of most European countries; the international headquarters, however, never took fire and to the end remained no more than the Belgian chapter. Americans sent representatives to the meetings of the various societies although they never formed a society themselves.

With the Germans occupying the position they did, and with Leopold wanting an outlet for his energies, his people, and his capital, a conference in Berlin was called by Kaiser Wilhelm I in 1884–85. The Berlin Conference did several things: it regulated trade on the Congo and internationalized it. It regulated trade on the Niger-Benue. Perhaps most important of all for subsequent events, it laid down the rule that if a country was going to make a claim to territory, that territory had to be actually occupied. The result of this conference was that the occupation of Africa—the so-called "scramble for Africa"—began.

There followed a series of bilateral treaties among various European countries dividing up the coast, and stretching inland. Leopold got the others to agree that he could establish a free state in the Congo Basin. He was the king of both Belgium and the free state. The Congo Free State did not belong to Belgium—it belonged to Leopold. All of the money that went into it was his. So was all that came out. Stanley, in the hire of Leopold, proceeded up the south bank of the Congo signing treaties with the chiefs; he was all but paralleled by de Brazza on the north side of the Congo signing similar treaties for the French.

The British action in the scramble took place almost entirely in terms of trading companies: The South Africa Company, the Central Africa Company, the Royal Niger Company, and others. These companies manned colonial governments and maintained private armies long before the British government became involved directly.

The French government was much more directly behind the activities of Frenchmen. From their position on the Ogowe they pushed north, and from their position in Senegal they pressed eastward, the two forces meeting in the vicinity of Lake Chad.

Out of the scramble the Germans got Togo, Cameroun, South-West Africa, and Tanganyika-Ruanda-Urundi. The Portuguese reasserted their rights to Portuguese Guinea, Angola, and Mozambique. The British, the Portuguese, and the Germans were all fussing about Angola—the decision in favor of Portugal (but perhaps with the connivance of some of the British factions who wished to avoid the responsibilities of empire) was made by President Grant.

The Congo Free State was left, in Leopold's will, to

Belgium. So did it become the Belgian Congo. Cecil Rhodes dreamed of a railroad and British domination from the Cape to Cairo. The accompanying maps show the positions of European nations in 1884, 1885, and 1914. The face of the African map was changed overnight. The face of Africa was, however, to take longer.

Important actions in World War I were fought in Africa, when Germany lost her hold. Then Africa settled down to being forgotten again—until after World War II. The quietude of colonialism was upon her.

Although Africa had felt the impact of Europe for centuries, it was not until after World War I that so-called "competent" administration was established over all of the areas of Africa. Northern Nigeria's middle belt did not have a stable administration until about 1918—Africans before that time had been widely influenced by Europe, but in most areas that influence was material and superficial until the 1920s. At the same time, there were to be found along the coast and in South Africa situations in which third, fourth, and even fifth generations of Christianized, educated Africans were to be found. The tremendous range is still there.

With the scramble for Africa, the African populations became what might be called "frozen." Migratory movements did not cease, but did slow to a crawl. And all Africa was gripped in the vise of false stability which is the earmark of every successful colony. Boundaries were established, chiefs were appointed, and "responsible" leadership was ensconced in foreign-dominated political systems.

And for the next decades, it looked to Europeans as if "traditional" Africa was slow, unchanging, eternal and, indeed, sleeping. Africa had been effectively darkened.

Part III
TRIBAL AFRICA

Chapter 8

Tribal Africa

When the colonial regimes slowed down the movement of peoples in Africa (for all that individual mobility eventually increased), an illusion of fixedness and stability was created. Colonial administrations—at least the early ones—were under the illusion that African societies tended to be mutually exclusive, when in fact many of them ran together and intermixed. The gesture of interdigitation is the one Africans use to discuss this intermixture of culturally differentiated peoples. Moreover, early scholars as well as early travelers made the assumption, more or less overtly, that boundaries between peoples either existed or could be created and that the various peoples of Africa put on a map that resembled a map of the nations of Europe. The result has been a long series of tribal maps of all or of parts of Africa. Murdock, in his book *Africans and their Culture History*, is the latest and by far the best. Yet all such maps suffer from the fact that they require the cartographer to draw lines on paper which do not necessarily correspond to natural or social divisions in terrestrial space. This is not to say that tribal maps have no value, but only that their limitations are too often misunderstood or overlooked.

In order fully to understand the nature of the problem, it is necessary to look into the kind of unit that can be put on a tribal map of Africa. In short, what is a tribe?

The word tribe, when applied to African peoples, certainly refers to something far different than does the same word when it is applied to North American Indians of the seventeenth century or to the Australian aborigines of the nineteenth century. Some African tribes are what have been described as village states; others are empires of several million people spread over hundreds of thousands of square miles. Some African tribes are language groups; some others are congeries of indefinite or indiscriminate groups that have been classified together under a term, usually pejorative, by their neighbors. Probably the classic case is to be found in the Northern Territories of Ghana, where some of the so-called tribal names that were meticulously recorded by early administrators and students turn out to be no more than derisive terms for culture traits that have come from one direction or the other, while the peoples of the area refer to themselves by names that take their referents from local places and who, in fact, have scarcely any organized groups larger than the ordinary homesite or compound.

Tribal maps are of very great use if we do not take their boundaries too seriously. Yet the pressures on administrators and indeed on anthropologists to get the Africans "straightened out" and "classified" are tremendous. Colonial administrators treat a colony as if it were a cupboard. It is to be kept neat. Then things can be found, justice can be achieved, and one's own life proceeds smoothly. The cupboard assumption has often led, as it did in the Belgian Congo and South Africa, to a system of passes in which Africans have to get written permission if they are to move outside their restricted tribal areas. They must carry papers to be presented on demand. Colonies are neatest if everybody can be found in the right place.

The anthropologists wanted the Africans straightened out for their own reasons. For better or for worse, they, being dedicated to the useful proposition that cultures are to be considered as "wholes," carried their concern a step farther than it should have gone. Many of them—by no means all—figured that whole cultures took up space from which other groups were excluded. They explained and then disregarded the interdigitation; they disregarded foreign fishing villages set into the midst of farming communities. They disregarded nomads who crossed and recrossed the territories of settled peoples. All were reduced to maps and, on most maps, all were given exclusive territories.

The problem then was to get everybody in, and to get him into approximately the right place—either to govern him or to study him.

Anthropologists have gone farther. They have created not merely tribal maps, but "culture areas" and maps of them. In the United States, in the nineteenth and twentieth centuries, American museums were organizing the loads of American Indian material in their storehouses. They discovered as a principle what they had already used as a working device: that museum material—costumes, tools, and art—was different from one geographical area to the next. They were able to create a number of more or less discrete areas in which such material culture exhibited more similarities than differences. The Great Plains area, the Eastern woodlands, the Northwest Coast area, and so on. North America was divided into "culture areas" earlier than any other continent. It provided the model. And, largely because the Indian cultures of North America were, by the twentieth century, what anthropologists call "memory cultures"—they are not practiced in any significant degree—the spread of the culture area concept to non-material matters went unchallenged. The exigencies were those of museum exhibits: all other "culture traits" were assumed to follow.

Amazingly enough, it was not until the 1930s that Africa came into the ken of a few American anthropologists. Among the first—and certainly the earliest to publish a systematic review of the culture areas of Africa which can still be used—was Melville J. Herskovits. He performed the tremendous task of combing the reports of missionaries, traders, and a few anthropologists such as the Seligmans and Labouret who had visited Africa. His task was to coordinate the culture traits and divide the continent into culture areas of the sort that were stylish at the time. Herskovits' culture areas of Africa probably did the job as well as it can be done; certainly it was superior to earlier ones which he meticulously cites. A German ethnologist, Hermann Baumann, has suggested another set of "culture provinces" of Africa which are rather more numerous, and which do have some contradictions to the Herskovits system—and which are probably about as good. The point is not that one scholar is right and another wrong; it is rather that the uses to which a culture area approach can be put are extremely limited.

Some aspects of culture undeniably go by area. Some culture traits are diffused from a center and are found only in limited areas. Others are rejected in all but limited areas. The environment does influence—and sometimes limit stringently—the way people do things.

There are, however, just as many or even more aspects of life that do not go by area—or, if they do, the areas of different traits are not congruent. It may be that they are not affected by the environment so directly, or at least that they are not affected by the same aspects of the environment. It is, for example, possible to have almost any kind of political organization or any kind of religious dogma in almost any geographical location. It is true that some of the symbolic references in the religion or in the polity will be drawn from the local area. Such is, however, very different from a form of agriculture that is affected by limitations in rainfall.

The combination of climate, area, and technology may limit the size of the domestic group. Yet it is usually true that a large number of types can occur within a single area, and that the same types may be found in all areas. Kinship systems, myths—both may diffuse and therefore both may be representative of an area. On the other hand, some mythical themes are of worldwide distribution, and kinship systems are notorious for the change they undergo at diffusion.

The weakness of culture area schemes is that except for material culture such as house types or fish trap forms, for art styles, and for ways of getting a living, the same entries occur as descriptive of most or even all the culture areas. Few of the areas of Africa in any scheme fail to exhibit both centralized and stateless societies; few areas do not exhibit kinship systems and religions similar to those of most of the other areas.

The question must be asked, then: What *can* be mapped? How many maps is it desirable to have? The corollary of such a question is: Except for museums, are culture areas or cultural provinces really sensible? The answer is almost certainly, no.

In this chapter, two maps will be presented: one for language and one for ecological adjustment. Both will be explained in some detail. Although art styles will be discussed at some length in the next chapter, no map will be attempted for the simple reason that authorities disagree with vehemence about which aspects of art style are to be definitive in drawing the boundary lines. Therefore, no two of them look much alike. It would be possible either to opt for one of the existing ones or to create a new one. Neither course would face the issue, which is that every culture trait or every stylistic element in Africa can be mapped. And when it is done, the meaning may not be very significant.

THE LANGUAGES OF AFRICA

African languages have sometimes, in the past, been said to be so simple that they contain vocabularies of only a few hundred words or so difficult as to be unlearnable by ordinary Europeans or Americans. Obviously, both statements are false. African languages are highly developed and fine instruments; they are as expressive and as expandable as their speakers care to make them. It is true that some African languages contain consonantal sounds not elsewhere found: the four clicks of the Bushman languages, that have been taken over by some of the surrounding Bantu, are probably the most famous. The double consonants of the west coast languages—*gb*, pronounced by releasing *g* and *b* at the same time is a case in point—are also to be noted. African vowel systems tend to be simple compared to those of Indo-European languages such as French and English.

Many African languages are tonal—a fact that scares off many potential European speakers who are preconvinced that tone is difficult and who hence refuse to sing. Such people may be assured that they can, if they lose their *amour-propre* and try, learn to speak African languages. Speakers of Indo-European languages can learn most African languages with somewhat greater ease than they can learn a language like Arabic or Chinese, or even one like Hungarian. On the other hand, they are not to confuse a knowledge of kitchen Swahili or trader Hausa with knowing an African language.

There are many languages in Africa. Eight hundred is the classic number, but Joseph Greenberg, who is the foremost American authority on these matters, considers that the actual number is probably considerably greater. The problem should be familiar to us: in the same way that we had problems in differentiating men from premen, and the races of men from one another, so it is difficult to distinguish one language from another. The divisions in nature are not always precise—there must be man-made criteria added to make sensible classifications. By a trick of definition, it would be possible to make the number of African languages come out to almost any number that is required. This situation may be made quite precise within the next few years, as linguists study interintelligibility of languages. To date, however, such studies are in their infancy—and in Africa they have scarcely been begun.

The vicissitudes of the classification of African lan-

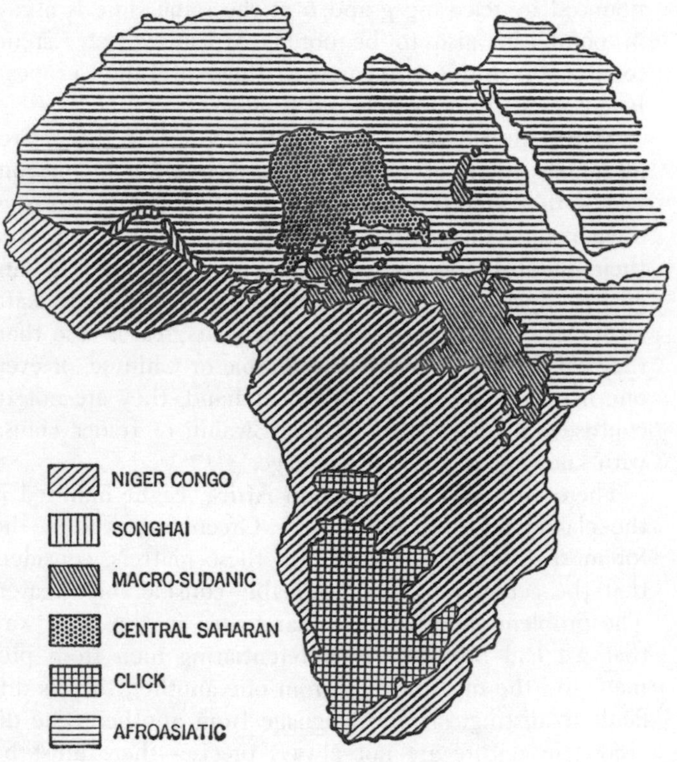

FIG. 8. Language areas of Africa. (After J. H. Greenberg.)

guages can be traced back to 1810. Every few years a basic change has had to be made in the classification, following upon better information. Such is still the case. Greenberg in America and A. N. Tucker in Britain find it constantly necessary to revise their classifications as more and more information becomes available to them. Greenberg's latest classification—and the information is now becoming good enough that the changes become less dire with each renewal—contains four major language groups, shown in the accompanying map. Far and away the largest of the language groups, covering by far the largest geographical area of the continent, is the group that Greenberg calls the Niger-Congo family and divides into seven subfamilies. One of these subfamilies is the well-known Bantu. Bantu languages cover most of central and southern Africa—but all are closely related to one another, reflecting the fact that it has been only in recent centuries that the Bantu peoples have spread into the forest regions and down the eastern and southern highlands.

The second large family is called Sudanic. It includes the languages spoken by the Nilotes, as well as many spoken in the western sudan and the area of the middle Niger River.

The Afro-Asian group of languages is related to the Semitic group—indeed, Greenberg considers Semitic a subfamily or branch of the Afro-Asian. This group includes ancient Egyptian, Berber, Cushitic, and the various languages spoken today in the Horn of Africa, and some of the languages spoken around Lake Chad, of which the most significant is Hausa.

Finally, there are those languages spoken by Bushmen and Hottentots, and by a few remnant peoples in Tanganyika, which Greenberg classifies by their most obvious identifying characteristic as "click languages."

Dialects of English are the native languages of populations in Liberia and Sierra Leone on the west coast, and dialects of Dutch—indeed, a new language called

Afrikaans, which developed out of a systematic simplification of Dutch—developed in South Africa. As any English speaker who tries to make sense of Krio (from the word Creole) in Sierra Leone, or any Dutch speaker who tries to cope with Afrikaans can vouch, there are today indigenous forms of Indo-European languages in Africa.

There is another map of African languages that it would be desirable to draw, but for which information is simply not available. This is a usable map of the *linguae francae* of Africa. In the first place, there are two important European languages that are used among Africans who cannot otherwise communicate and which are, as a matter of fact, the official languages of most African countries: English and French. There are in addition large areas centering on Tanganyika, Zanzibar, and Kenya, but overlapping into Uganda, the Congo, and even into Mozambique, in which Swahili or a pidgin form of it is a commonly used *lingua franca.* Hausa, or simplified forms of it, is used throughout northern Nigeria, up the Niger, and into Ghana, as well as overlapping into most of the adjoining areas. Bemba in Central Africa, Lingala and Kongo in the Republic of the Congo, and many others of less extensive distribution are to be found.

The problem of the *lingua franca* can best be seen if we take the case of Swahili. Swahili is a Bantu language of the Niger-Congo family whose vocabulary has been significantly affected by Arabic. There are three main dialects of it, spoken in Zanzibar and along the eastern coast of Tanganyika. It has been taken over in simplified form by all of the peoples of East Africa. Those who speak Bantu languages tend to speak fairly decent Swahili, even as far away as Uganda. On the other hand, those who speak Sudanic, Afro-Asian, or Indo-European languages limit their vocabularies and certainly butcher the grammar of Swahili into an almost unrecognizable form. European settlers in Kenya, for example, may (a few of them) speak excellent Swahili; many more speak what is locally called "kitchen Swahili." So far as I can find, no study has even been made of the degree to which communication can in fact be carried on in African *linguae francae*.

The future of most African languages is in doubt. Swahili, Hausa, Lingala, Bemba, Yoruba, Twi, and many others will undoubtedly be preserved. Literatures are growing in them. But the languages of many of the smaller groups will just as surely disappear—just as certainly as the various dialects of the Germanic and Celtic languages have disappeared, and for the same reasons.

SUBSISTENCE AREAS OF AFRICA[4]

Africa can also be divided, on criteria of geography and dominant subsistence practices, into a number of overlapping zones or belts. Distinctions between herding and farming, and among types of animals herded or among types of staple crops grown correlate rather more widely with other cultural activities than perhaps any other single aspect of culture. Subsistence activity shows a close correspondence with the working habits of both sexes; with the size and composition of work groups; with trade; with diet patterns; indeed, even with musculature. It is also true that subsistence patterns are those least changed by the colonial experience.

The staple products, and therefore diets, of Africa can be classified meaningfully by the source of food. There are a few remnant groups who still subsist on a foraging economy: the Pygmies are primarily hunters and gatherers (although trade with neighboring tribes brings them vegetable food); so are the Bushmen. The most important group of foragers are the fishermen on the coasts and rivers. Fishermen are among the few Africans who do not show some dietary deficiencies; they usually trade a part of

[4] Another version of this section has appeared in my article "Africa: Peoples and Cultures" in the Encyclopedia Americana.

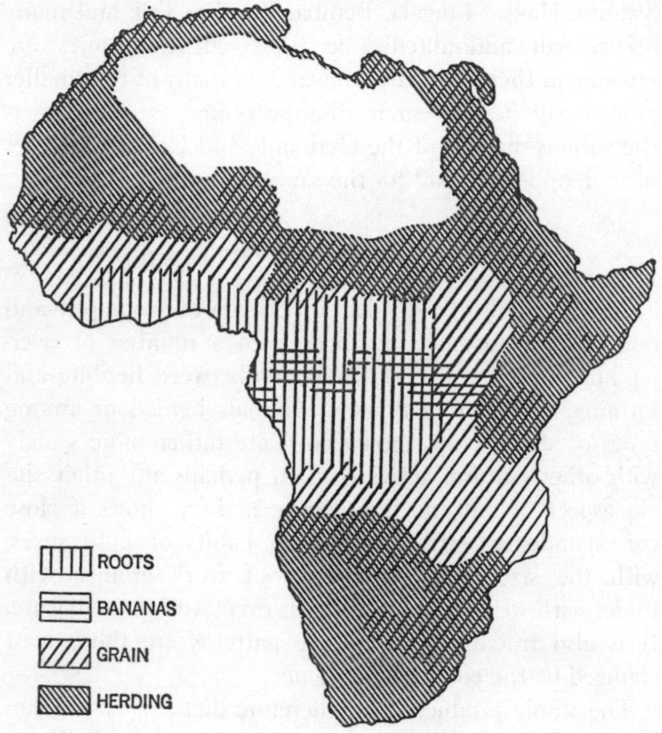

FIG. 9. Subsistence areas of Africa.

their catch for one of the starchy staples, or else the women of the group grow some grain or tubers.

African herders are primarily cattle herders, although the Sahara shelters a few peoples who keep camels, and the Serengeti plain and other areas in East Africa are the home of peoples who keep large flocks of goats (that animal being all but ubiquitous on the continent, however). Herdsmen's diets are either a milk staple or (in a few parts of East Africa) a diet in which the major protein is a mixture of blood and sour milk. Almost all herding peoples add starchy staples to their diets, either by harvesting their own catch crops or, more commonly, through well-integrated methods of trade with settled agricultural peoples.

By far the greatest number of Africans are farmers. They can be sensibly divided into three groups: those in which grain crops are the major staple, those who grow root crops, and those who grow tree crops. Bananas are the basis of the diet in a belt stretching westward from the vicinity of Lake Victoria to the Atlantic. The grain changes from one area to another of the "grain belt" and there is a variety of root crops, but these distinctions are of somewhat minor importance when it is realized that Liberian rice farmers and Rhodesian maize farmers use very similar methods of cultivation, and the yam cultivators of Nigeria and the manioc farmers of the Congo would quickly be at home in one anothers' work habits even though manioc takes much less work.

Camel herders are found throughout the inhabited Sahara and on the Saharan fringe, both north and south, as well as in the eastern Horn. The "cattle belt" of Africa runs from the Atlantic in Senegal, along the corridor between the forests and the desert with only a few breaks; it turns south along the Nile and from Lake Victoria proceeds both eastward and southward, and eventually swings back to the Atlantic in Angola, between the forests of the Congo and the Kalahari. In much of the area where cattle are of the greatest concern of East and South Africa, cattle nevertheless do not actually form the subsistence base, or provide the staple part of the diet, and these areas must be included in the "grain belt," the staple being maize or sorghum. Cattle do, however, form the basis of the morality and prestige activities of the men of the tribes of that area, and many pastoralists get grain in exchange for dairy products.

There is a great deal written about the East African herding peoples, for example, who tap blood from the neck veins of their cattle, mix it with sour milk, and eat the mixture. Actual studies by food economists, dieticians, and geographers, however, have recently indicated that blood accounts for at most a few hundreds of calories a week. Milk and butter are much more important, but some starchy staple enters the diet of almost all African herdsmen. They seldom kill animals for meat, but do of course eat those they sacrifice.

The grain belt of Africa forms a crescent, inside of and overlapping with the herding crescent. There is another, smaller grain belt along the Mediterranean coast, in which the staple grains are barley and wheat—European grains. South of the Sahara, however, the grains are of a different sort. Farmers from Senegal south through Liberia and into the Ivory Coast grow an indigenous African variety of rice as their staple food. They grow it either as upland rice or sow it into patches which they have cleared out of the forest. Although rice has remained a staple in this area, much of the acreage has been put into Asian rice, which is considered even by Africans themselves to be superior.

As one proceeds westward from Senegal, the grain changes to sorghum and millet. Still further east, in the southern sudan and Ethiopia, the primary grains are eleusine, teff, and fonio. As one turns south, east of Lake Victoria, maize and sorghum are the staples; there is some pearl millet in the southern Congo area, and in a few others, but aside from that, maize and sorghum form the staples all the way to the southern end of the continent.

Throughout the grain-producing areas of Africa, the mode of agriculture and the nature of the diet are similar. The chief agricultural implements are the hoe—short-handled in most places but long-handled in parts of Rhodesia and the Congo—and the long knife called a matchet in western Africa and a *panga* in Swahili-speaking areas. In some places the digging stick, with or without a metal tip, is still to be found. The plow, pulled by oxen, is found today in parts of eastern Africa. In most places —but there are, as usual, exceptions—the heavy work of clearing the land is done by men, who also prepare the fields for planting and may even do the planting. The women then take over—if they have not indeed been doing the work already—and take care of weeding and harvesting. It is also the women who carry the grain back to the homestead or to the drying platforms. It is stored in granaries which are made, in most areas, something like the houses but smaller and usually set up off the ground to give some protection from termites, rats, and other pests. These granaries—and the food in them—are often the property of the household head, but the food is just as often considered the property of the woman, who is obliged to feed her children from it as well as her husband who provided her with land and cleared it for her.

Except for rice, which is cooked whole, grain in Africa is ground—traditionally by hand, on stone, today often by hand-operated mills or even by power mills at the village center—and cooked into porridge. A thick, malleable porridge is Africa's bread. It provides most of the calories of most African diets. It is eaten dipped into a sauce prepared of meat or vegetables or both. Oils and fats are plentiful—the particular one varies with the part of the country from shea butter to palm oil to peanut oil to sesame oil and many others. They are part of the sauce, not of the porridge.

A woman's day is taken up with farming, grinding the meal, cooking the porridge and the sauce. Yet most African women find time to attend markets, visit relatives, and even sometimes to rest.

Men's work is more strenuous, more varied, and—like farmers' work everywhere—seasonal. During the time of clearing land, African grain farmers may put out almost unbelievable amounts of work in a day. They have, moreover, to carry out the political and judicial affairs of the country, which in most African societies takes a lot of time on the part of many of the men.

The subsistence area based on root crops forms a core in the Congo, with a long strip along the Guinea coast. Crops are yams, manioc, taro, sweet potatoes, and a few other minor root crops. None of these roots, it would appear, is indigenous to Africa. The yam is Malaysian, and manioc is South American. Root crops, as food, are generally considered by Western dieticians to be inferior to grains, because they are short of some of the essential vitamins and minerals. Their culture puts a little more work on the men of the community, who must, in this shallow soil, make two-foot mounds in which to grow yams, or smaller ones in which to grow manioc or sweet potatoes.

Roots are either cooked green or else dried and made into a flour, then mashed or stewed into porridge and eaten with sauces.

There is also a relatively large area in the Sahara where dates form a staple, and there is a large stretch across equatorial Africa and a few spots on the west coast in which bananas are the staple. These bananas are not the sweet bananas that Americans and Europeans eat for breakfast or dessert, but are plantains—scarcely sweet, much starchier, and of a less oily consistency. Plantains are cooked and, like the grain and the roots, made into porridge.

It is important to note that not only food, but drink,

follows these general areas. Again to oversimplify, herders drink honey beer—except those who are Muslims. Some make beer from traded grain. In the grain belt, arguments rage about the virtues and faults of beer made with maize, sorghum, and millet. In the banana country, bananas are mashed and made into beer. The root crop country is approximately the same as the oil palm country, where the staple beverage is palm wine.

It is important for Westerners to realize that Africans are well fed. Although protein shortages exist in some areas and vitamin shortages in most areas, there is little gnawing hunger: bellies are adequately full. Today, when one travels in Africa one nowhere finds the beggars or hangers-on that commonly surround travelers in the Near East. What few beggars there are seem to have resulted from urbanization and the impact of Western ways. Famines in Africa have, in the past, been severe. But they have also been local, and with modern transportation, they can be ameliorated if not averted.

Yet Westerners who are thoroughly familiar with the market economy and with the particular tensions and insecurities it brings, would do well to remember that subsistence economy also brings its own tensions: one is totally dependent for one's food during the next year on one's own labors, and on the fruits of one's fields, more or less ameliorated by dependence on kinsmen. Droughts and floods, locusts and birds are personal enemies. Religious myth and ritual, like insecurity, centers around food production. Many Africans are, today, entering market economy and adjusting to new types of insecurities. But with most of them, subsistence is a major psychic as well as practical problem, and in creating it one must work and must cooperate with kinsmen and with the forces of the gods.

Chapter 9

African Arts

All art can be said to have two sweeping characteristics: it embodies a message within an idiom of communication, and it arouses a sense of mystery—a feeling that it is more than it appears to the intellect to be. "Good" art is that which, no matter what its cultural origins or uses, can arouse this sense of mystery in many persons, from many cultures (although all are probably blind to the arts of some cultures and some ages).

In that sense, Africa has an extensive "good" art. Its ineffable quality can be widely perceived, and it has taken its place in museums and in the collections of many art lovers.

Yet art also bears a "message" from artist to viewer. The message must be carried out within an idiom that, like language, can be broken down into a sort of grammar —the parts of sculpture or the parts of music, analogous to (but probably more complex than) the parts of speech. In fact, it is impossible for an artist *not* to convey a message, whether his metier be measured realism and calls up the calm of a forest twilight or it be abstract, perhaps (but probably not) calling up associations as widely divergent as Rorschach tests.

Art then may be valued either as a message-bearing comment or as mystery. It may in fact be valued for both of these things at once. Usually, however, it is not. Too often art appreciators—those who prize the mystery for itself—object to the people who intellectualize and put into words the messages that are conveyed. On the other hand, anthropologists and others who use art to get at the temper of a culture (much as critics use it to get at the temper of an age or of a creative mind) usually denigrate the mere appreciator. Fullest comprehension implies both.

The mystery of good art comes across cultural barriers. The message probably does not. In order to appreciate the art fully, something of the cultural background must be known to make the message clear.

ARTISTIC COMMENT

Art is of the essence in analyzing culture because it supplies the media in which some of the most perceptive and original thinkers in any society communicate their experience. Therefore it is to the arts and sciences that we must first turn to know what the people of another culture—indeed, of our own culture—may be thinking. It is, ultimately, not art that holds the mirror up to nature—it is social and natural science. In art, everything is simplified, stripped to its essentials; the mirror of art is a burning glass.

Art then includes communication, comment, and criticism. The message may be trite or propagandistic. The message may be extremely distasteful; it may also be obscure. Yet artists are thinking people—which does not necessarily mean that they are intellectualizing people. So are consumers and critics of art. They are the people on the receiving end of communication. The critics translate for us, who may have less perceptive vision, what it is that the artist is saying—the postulates that lie behind his message. Artists may hate critics. If they do, it may be because the critic was obtuse, but it may be because the critic was extraordinarily perceptive and the artist is unable to bear the bold statement of his message in an idiom and in a symbolism different from that which he himself gave it.

African art can be understood on three levels. It can be studied as form and technique. In the second place, the purpose and the meaning—the aesthetics, indeed—of the art must be garnered not merely from the artists but from the critics in the society. Finally, African art can be evaluated for its impact on Western (or some other) art—an impact that was, earliest and strongest, that of the mystery rather than that of the message.

THE FORMS AND TECHNIQUES OF AFRICAN ART

The main forms of African art that have become widely known outside of Africa are limited to sculpture and music. African music is coming into its own as one of the world's great musics that has several specific contributions to make. Undoubtedly the most dramatic of the special attributes is its polyrhythmic structure. Polyrhythms are complex combinations of fairly simple but different rhythms, all played concurrently. Western music has the "classic" situation of "two against three"—the triplet played against two "full-value" notes during the same time span. Rarely, in Western music, a third rhythm may be added. In African music, on the other hand, five such rhythms are common, and as many as a dozen at a time have been recorded.

Although African dancing has been for a long time one of the two favorite sights of tourists in Africa, few outsiders have been able to realize its full quality and artistic achievement. The point of African dancing in many parts of the continent, at least, is for various parts of the body each to accompany one of the rhythms in the orchestra so that the polyrhythms in the orchestra are reproduced by the dancer's body. The head moves in one rhythm, the shoulders in another; the arms in still a third, the trunk in another, and the feet in still another. Once the viewer has learned to see and feel the polyrhythms in the dance as it reflects the music, he can appreciate that African dancing both demands great precision and allows great freedom of expression to the dancers. African dancing is still a folk art; there have been a few attempts to produce it for the stage—notably the Ballets Africaines of Guinea—but too often the European and American audiences have not been sufficiently sophisticated and the individual dances cut too short to give the dancers sufficient play for their imagination and the variations that each dance requires if the rhythms are to be fully explored.

In African literature the great form is the dramatic tale. African tales have affected the literatures of many lands, particularly of the southern United States and the Caribbean area, where the so-called Brer Rabbit stories have become standard. Collections of African folk tales are also quite common, even though they are usually studied only by specialists. In all of these manifestations, however, the true quality of the original has been left behind in Africa. The mere tale on a page will produce little more than would the retelling of the plot of *As You Like It* in two paragraphs, with a moral tacked on at the end, fable-fashion. These dramatic tales in Africa have a theatrical quality. They are told and acted out before audiences who participate in musical choruses and in spoken responses. The individual tale-tellers may be assisted by a dozen or more people who are costumed and "cast" as in any other theater art. The tale-teller also makes up songs, centering around the situation of the tale; he teaches the choruses of the songs to the audience and assures himself audience response whenever he needs it. The stories of the tales are well known. The achievement of the individual artist is to be found in the music and in the version of the tale and the way he manipulates the dramatic elements in it to enlarge or point his moral. The result is living theater. It cannot be overemphasized that African folk-tales, written on half a sheet of paper in a Western language, lose all but the so-called "plot" of the original. The art is gone. Again, it should be noted that the dramatic tale demands of its performers compliance with a certain set of activities, and then encourages individualization and free expression.

Nevertheless, the best known of the African arts, outside of Africa, is sculpture. It is to sculpture that most attention is to be given here. With a few notable exceptions, such as the soapstone carvings of Sierra Leone, the iron sculpture to be found in a few isolated places, and the ivories of Benin and the Congo, African sculptors work either in green wood or in various alloys of copper, tin, and zinc that hover around bronze and brass.

African carvers work almost exclusively in green wood. The carver must know a great deal about the qualities of different woods, so that they will not crack too much when dry, although cracks appear in most pieces of African art—even in Africa, let alone when they are subjected to the high and dry temperatures of American and European homes and museums.

Woodworking is done with an adze and is finished with a double-edged knife. In some parts of the continent, some sculptors use rough leaves as sandpaper. The carvings may be painted with all sorts of mineral and vegetable colors (and today with imported colors), the most common being lampblack set by the sap of any of several trees.

Indigenous African sculpture falls into three sorts: one is the figurine, which may vary from small and simple figures only a few inches high, to elaborate carved house posts, stools, or other functional forms. The figurines are fundamentally adaptations from the tree trunk, with the heaviest weight at the bottom, proceeding in columnar form. The next form is the mask. African masks are among the best known in the world and artistically are among the most satisfying. They come in three main shapes: those that are worn over the face, those worn on top of the head, and the "helmet"-type masks which fit down over the head. The third form is decoration of various useful objects, ranging from doors to spoons to bobbins.

African bronzes are all cast by the lost-wax method. Each piece is therefore unique. In this method, the technique is fundamentally additive, rather than subtractive as it is in carving. Over a core of some sort—usually dried mud in the traditional forms—the sculptor models in wax whatever he wants to reproduce in metal. When the core is thoroughly dry and the waxen model completely set, it is covered by several coats of the finest pottery slip clay available. The whole is then covered with coarser pottery clay, leaving spaces or passageways for the wax to run out. The trick in casting, then, comes from pouring the molten metal into the cast in such a way that the wax is melted and runs out, to be replaced by the metal in the desired form, avoiding air bubbles.

It is commonly believed that African painting was not highly developed before contact with the West, in spite of the fact that rock paintings several millennia old and some decoration on buildings has been reported from the earliest times. Modern African art, as we shall see, has a large element of painting, and although much of that art is of traditional import, it is commonly said that the techniques are almost wholly those of the West.

THE HISTORY OF AFRICAN ART

Except for Egypt the earliest sculpture that we know to be unequivocally African comes from the Nok culture, around 200 B.C., in the sub-Saharan sudan area. The distribution of Nok sculpture runs from northern Nigeria (where it was first discovered in the course of tin-mining operations) to the east of Lake Chad and west to the great bend of the Niger and beyond. Nok art, as we know it, is almost entirely a pottery or terra-cotta art. Working in terra-cotta, as in casting brass by the lost-wax method, the artist is working in an additive technique of sculpture in which he starts with a core and builds out. Nok art is done in fine pottery, excellently fired: hollow figures, three-quarter life size, in some cases. Such an art is technically very demanding. Nok culture is now represented by several score of examples—heads, limbs, and some furniture; there is not as yet a good record of it published in any one place.

Among the finest pieces of measuredly naturalistic sculpture ever produced are the bronze heads of Ife in Nigeria, which date from about the twelfth century A.D. Because they are in a measured and classical naturalistic style, it was assumed when they were found, in the early twentieth century by Frobenius, the German ethnologist, folklorist, and adventurer, that Africans could not have made them. Therefore, "obviously" it was the Portuguese who did them. The fact that there was no technique of this sort known to the Portuguese or any other Europeans at this time was not allowed to intrude against the stereotype. Once carbon-14 dates made the age fairly precise, it became necessary to admit that they could *only* have been done by Africans.

Frobenius turned up a good many of these Ife heads in terra-cotta and one in brass. The brass piece that he discovered he "bought" (in a manner of speaking) from the Oni, or king, of Ife. The British administrative officers on the spot refused him permission to export it. After considerable contretemps, Frobenius returned the bronze, and some of the terra-cotta. In the 1940s, however, Leon Underwood, a well-known British sculptor, discovered that the head Frobenius had originally discovered was a sand casting, whereas all the other Ife heads were lost-wax castings. No African artists had ever done sand casting. The assumption is unavoidable either that Frobenius had not returned the original or else that he was not the true discoverer, and discovered only the copy. The complete set, including the copy returned by Frobenius, is now in the possession of the Oni of Ife and housed in his small but magnificent museum.

Another ancient art that deserves attention is that of

Benin, some eighty miles east of Ife. Benin art flooded Great Britain, and indeed the Western European museums, at the very end of the nineteenth century. At that time, 1897, the consolidation of European power in Africa was being carried on most furiously, with the colonial powers, in accordance with the Berlin Conference, busily occupying the territories they had claimed. The Ashanti in the Gold Coast fought and held out for some years. The people of Benin—who call themselves Bini—also fought. The Bini had a form of religion in which a royally sponsored art, made by highly organized craft guilds, was a major component. The content of the religion embraced safety, salvation, fertility or increase; sacrifice at altars played a major part. The art was based on altarpiece heads of cast bronze, each of which had a place in the cap of the skull into which a carved elephant tusk could be inserted. The tusk swept back and up from the head. An altar might have more than a dozen such pieces, magnificently wrought and carefully preserved. The other major component of Benin art was the bronze plaques which were set into mud walls and pillars of the house. There are a large number of such plaques known. Some are of historical importance: since they show Portuguese in medieval European armor with arquebuses and crossbows that we know from other sources, we can reasonably assume that they show as accurately those aspects of African culture to which we have no other direct contemporary evidence.

Benin is well known for the fact that during its last years human sacrifices were performed in the most gross exaggerations. There were sacrifices made just before the capture of the city by the British—almost frenetically performed sacrifices aimed at staving off the encroaching enemy. The first major work on the area and the art is called "Benin, City of Blood."[5] Only in later years was the pre-

[5] Bacon, R. H. *Benin, City of Blood.* London: Edward Arnold, 1897.

cise symbolism of these sacrifices determined; the word "Benin" was, in parts of Europe, synonymous with depravity at the turn of the century. Today, when these matters have been forgotten, there is a new, derivative, but hopeful art being made in Benin. The organization of guilds is still more or less intact, and it would seem that royal or governmental patronage may lead to an efflorescence of art, in a new set of styles containing some traditional elements.

The African art that is best known in the West and best represented in African museums stems from the nineteenth century—from the era just before the culture and ethnogeography of Africa were frozen in place by the colonial era. The art from that period has been divided by William Fagg of the British Museum into three major areas: the sudan, the Guinea coast, and the Congo. Most other books on the subject have selected a larger number of areas: like race, it is easiest left to the three major stereotypes, thus avoiding the contradictions of experts. Trying to put the elements of style from the three areas into words inevitably erects a screen between the viewer and the artist. Thus, the student of African art, or any other, must learn at the same time that he makes the classifications for scholarly purposes to supersede them for purposes of direct communication. The sudanic art is a quiet, inward, smooth-surface, rather intense sort of art. The Congo provides a more flamboyant, decorated, exaggerated, extroverted (it has been called) kind of art. The Guinea coast lies stylistically as well as geographically between them.

THE PLACE OF ART IN AFRICAN SOCIETY

Westerners have often, in the past, confused the examination of the place of art in society with the historical development of art. They have been wont to seek for the "origins" of art rather than to perceive its uses. Origins and histories of individual art styles and forms can, of course, be usefully made; but "the origin of art" is too amorphous a question. Sometimes religion is the assigned "cause," sometimes something else. Art can no more have a cause or a single origin than can language. Just as apes did not suddenly one morning awake to find themselves men, so art did not, one day, suddenly spring into being from the fertile mind of some prehistoric genius. Art is a form of communication, and therefore it grows with culture and develops with the beast—and it has always been so.

The forms in African art are by and large associated with religion. So is much of Western art and every other art. This fact has led some art critics and some anthropologists to exaggerate the claims of religion for art. It is quite true that many pieces of art have religious associations. Of course African art has a religious connotation—but the very same claim can be made for its having a political connotation or an economic one or a domestic one.

African masks are one of the most common art forms and are worn as part of a costume. In the court or the ritual, the symbolized forces of politics and religion can be made carnate, so that the drama of justice or of myth can be re-enacted. The myth is not assumed in most societies, as it is in our own, to be pseudo-historical and about the past. The myth is rather used to explain—indeed, to communicate—the here and now. Much African masked drama is a reincarnation of the basic myths of creation, the power structure of the society, the myths of history and religion, and even the myths of settlement patterns. One of the best ways to assure the efficacy of the myth is to sanctify the objects which Westerners call art. Then it is possible for the priests, or the kings, or simply the public to loan their human vitality to the mythical principles that are symbolized.

Figurines are not "worshiped." They may be used as symbols of forces, ideas, historical events, myths, which are very real in society and held sacred. That is a grave difference. The "heathen" do not "bow down to wood and stone." Neither are saints' symbols in our own society worshiped. Rather they stand for something important and holy. Figurines can be consecrated in that same sense, and for the same purpose.

Giving living reality to the myth through drama and art is the most vivid way of making people recognize their dependence upon the myth and upon the society whose members live more or less by it.

Sometimes, too, African art is for fun. I would even say that some "art" may be no more than playful decoration added to the basic ideas for producing something that is "needed." Art supplies a "need" that is felt or expressed. It is art, in one sense, if it is decorated and goes beyond the mere need. Omitting taste (criticism within a culture cannot omit taste but comprehension across cultures probably must), art is decorated, needed objects. The communication in it is greater if it is great art; so is the mystery. But art for fun both supplies needs and is decorated. As with the Jefferson Memorial, the image draws attention to the principle.

Art permeates African culture, which in turn permeates African art. Art is not set aside from "real life"—it cannot be among a people who do not make such distinctions.

THE AESTHETICS OF AFRICAN ART

It is critics rather than artists who create aesthetics. Only in a hopelessly intellectualizing culture such as that of the modern West does the artist have to become his own aesthetician. Therefore, for social sciences it is from the critics that the greatest knowledge is to be gained. It is the critics and the consumers of art who relate art to the rest of culture and therefore create data for social scientists.

The screen that comes between the viewer and the artist is the thing that has been intellectualized and nurtured among Westerners. We should be made aware of it. I first experienced the existence of the screen at an exposition of Portuguese art in London. The earliest piece in the show was a fourteenth-century crucifix about eighteen feet high, done in wood, magnificently displayed so that as one came in the door he was hit by it. It was immediately evident that the sculptor had had absolutely no set of principles between him and the wood. There it was—indeed, there he was, immersed in the idea. The communication was immediate.

Around the corner in Cavendish Square, Epstein's madonna was perched high on a convent wall. The Epstein intensity was, I now saw, of a completely different nature from the intensity achieved by the unknown Portuguese artist of the fourteenth century. Sir Jacob Epstein had to settle down and create an intellectual aesthetic. In our era, it is necessary for at least some people to intellectualize the aesthetic: to verbalize all communications first, even when the ultimate medium is not verbal. For the Portuguese artist, such intellectualization or verbalization was not necessary. What he was saying about his belief and his convictions and his vision was a direct representation—almost a union between him and the wood. Epstein may have achieved something greater, but he had not achieved that union. Their achievements may, indeed, be all but incomparable, joined only by the word "art."

It is such direct union that can be discerned, felt, in the greatest pieces of African art: there is no intellectualized aesthetic or verbalized purpose between artist and art.

There *is*, however, a screen of "aesthetic" between a piece of art and the viewer, probably in all situations. There is certainly such a "screen" between African art and the European—indeed, for most modern African—viewers. Whatever disadvantage may be felt here can be turned to advantage if one completes the process—creates a full intellectualization so that the screen is known and hence can be systematically disregarded. Directness—or a reasonable substitute—can thus be achieved by the viewer as well as by the artist.

In order to appreciate the African aesthetic, then, we must first recognize a few points in our own. Probably the most important one to note is that even in the mid-twentieth century, Americans have an unshakable conviction that "art" is something special—a little off to the left of life. Art is, we are taught, a separate world; it is done only by special kinds of people who are not very "practical." Such an opinion cannot be held by a people who have no word for "art" and none for "society" or "reality."

The aesthetics behind African art are seldom verbalized. Any European critic or scientist who does so must realize the extent to which communication in European language warps the original perception.

There is, for example, a great deal of discussion among students of African art about whether African sculpture is "portraiture," but only comparatively little sensible discussion of what defines "portraiture." It is a phony question. The use of small figurines in the Ivory Coast, for example, is as a place or site into which the spirits of departed ancestors can settle. In Western portraiture the point is to capture the personality—we are told by our severest critics that we overvalue the cult of the personality. Likeness, even the caricature of individuality, is prized. If you doubt that caricature is prized in twentieth-century Western art, examine Graham Sutherland's painting of Maugham or Epstein's bust of the ninth duke of Marlborough, or almost any of the Sargent portraits. It is the very individuality that our religion, our culture—and, of course, our art—make us seek to recapture. The Ivory Coasters are seeking something quite different when they make the figurines for shrines to contain the spirits of ancestors. They are after a principle that lies behind both the religion and the kinship system. Strip the personality—and the principles of humanity, of ancestorhood, remain. With us, it is the personality that must be kept, not the principle or the relationship.

Getting at these ideas is difficult precisely because, among other reasons, the people we study do not look at such problems intellectually. We must find out what we require of art before it is possible to discover what somebody else requires of it. A background in traditional aesthetics doesn't help much in that process. Honest examination of exotic art is only just beginning.

One reason that some educated Africans do not like African art is not merely that it is associated with tribalism and therefore "backward" and injurious to their amour propre; rather it is that they have actually lost the culture which allows them to see immediately the relevance of much of this art, to cathect it, at the same time that, for whatever reasons, they have not been interested in developing a capacity to "appreciate" it through intellectualization as some Europeans can. They have the same problems as the Europeans have in looking at it, without the motivation or the techniques for understanding it that have been drilled into educated Europeans.

There have been very few attempts systematically to get at the aesthetics of African art. The most notable one is documented in a slim volume by Hans Himmelheber called *Negerkünstler*, about the Atutu peoples of the Ivory Coast. Himmelheber went into the area armed with first-rate interpreters, and with questionnaires. He found nineteen artists with whom he spent several months. He watched them work and he filled in his questionnaires. In the book, written in German, one of the questions he reports that he asked was "when you are working, *fühlen Sie noch Schöpfungsfreude?*" ("do you feel any joy in creation?"). The question was asked in French, interpreted into and answered in Atutu, recorded again in French, and reported in German—yet Himmelheber is aware of the difficulty and says specifically that he thinks that his interpretations came through the buzz of language pretty well. The reaction he got was: "Good heavens, no—not that!" Artistic joy is something that all Atutu denied.

Himmelheber could not help being put off when Atutu artists claimed that they worked mainly for money. Himmelheber was a little sentimental here: artists in our society do not expect to make a lot of money (neither do the Atutu), but they like to make a living at their art. They *all* do it for money, in one sense: yet we have a sneaking suspicion—left over from the nineteenth century and the Great Depression—that doing something for money is a sign of the prostitution of talent.

African taste in art, like taste in art everywhere else, is created ultimately by the consumers. The second most important function in any art tradition is that of the critic. We in America have assumed that only the people who create have a God-given right to criticize. Americans dislike the notion of criticism—criticism is tantamount to carping. We have a special term, "constructive criticism," under which we are allowed minimal expression of our critical capacities.

Everywhere there is an exchange of views between the artist and the critic-consumer. Realization of this point makes us see that most of the comment about "preserving" African art is the grossest sentimentality. Unless the art conforms to the cultural patterns and values—the views of the society and the ideas behind the expressed views—it is meaningless. Thus, art is "cheapened" by African workmen for Europeans. The reason is simple: the only "feedback" is that of the market place. There is a widespread and mistaken belief that only the bad taste of Europeans has spoiled African art: that African art has gone to pot *because* of European curio trade, etc. The real reason it has "gone to pot" is that the demands of the consumers have changed. African art, obviously then, has no glorious future—if that future is measured solely by the nineteenth-century tradition. But then neither do copies of the French impressionists. There is a tremendous body of modern African art being produced. Much of it is plastic art, as the tradition of great African art would lead us to predict. Such sculptors as Gregory Mukoba, such painters as Selby Mvusi, are doing interesting, arresting work. Their subject matter is drawn from the world in which they live: and that world is modern Africa, not nineteenth-century Africa. Their society has fallen heir to European as well as African tools; to European as well as African ideas. They do not sculpt like traditional Africans any more than Pollack painted like Whistler—and for the same reasons. Like other Africans of talent, no matter what their field, these artists are pushed all out of proportion by demands made by both Africans and Europeans—indeed, by two streams of evaluation and criticism.

For African artists to do "authentic" African art would be equivalent to the most distressingly precious folkloring. Folk song in our own society can be made viable only when it is modified and recast into the mid-twentieth-century idiom of performance: Joan Baez is not "authentic" in any sense save that she uses material that is traditional, but uses it—and well—as a highly sophisticated performer. Her relationship is with an audience, not with a "folk."

If there were no African artists we might decry the "death of African art." But the continent is full of them, as it is of writers and musicians. As everywhere else, artists in Africa are "oddballs." Everywhere they are specialists, given a different set of moral demands by the public. Artists are special people—that is as true in African as in Western society. African artists are trained today and they always have been. The training may take a formal form as it does among the Ivory Coast tribes in which an apprenticeship may last up to five years; during that time the apprentice is made to copy the master's work and live in the master's household. In such a way, style is handed on: yet individual styles are immediately distinguishable to the trained and aware eye. Today they are trained in universities and art schools as well as by traditional means. So are artists everywhere.

AFRICAN ART IN THE WESTERN WORLD

African art broke upon the Western world in the early twentieth century, when it was discovered by a few English army officers and a few French painters. General Pitt-Rivers, Torday, Picasso, and Les Fauves were all involved in their various ways. It was a sort of general discovery in France, however; and to this day some of the finest collections are in France, and it is easier to buy good African art in France than elsewhere (although the price may be higher). No one should jump to the idea that Picasso's women who look two ways at once, or anything else about his work, is a copy of something he discovered in African art. There was little direct, stylistic influence, although some can be discovered by latter-day critics. Rather, what happened was that with the discovery of African and other exotic art, the way was discovered for breaking out of the confines that had been put on European art by tradition—perspective, measured naturalism, and anti-intellectual sentimentality. African figurines could give the "modern" artist courage to foreshorten, to emphasize by changes of scale, to adjust scale to message. Looking at African art made such artists see what some of the earlier great painters had already known—El Greco stretches his human figures—that one sees passionately quite differently from the way one sees mensuristically. To get inside the vision, it was necessary to get outside the inherited canons of art. And African and other so-called "primitive" art was one means of taking such a journey.

Yet, African art had been present in Europe for many years. It had never really been looked at by artists before the late nineteenth and early twentieth centuries. It is, of course, a very old art.

For modern Westerners coming to African art, it should be stressed that American museums are full of good collections, but that looking at plastic art is no substitute for handling it—and unfortunately, museums cannot allow their specimens to be handled. Tactile sensations are as important in learning about African sculptures as are visual sensations. It is easiest to learn if one can get it into his hands. The memory of it, like the sensation of it, comes through the muscles and the sense of touch as well as through the eyes. Dahomean brass sculpture is tactilely sinewy and tough and not at all delicate as it appears to the visual sense: actually, of course, the combination tells one a great deal about Dahomean culture. Some African wood carving is in heavy, earthbound wood; other is in wood so porous and so light as to seem almost spiritual. To make such remarks is *not* so much to interpret African art (which they do not) as to prepare one for the fact that there is more in it than the artists put there and that the something more is derivative of the cultural image of the human condition. The more we know of the human condition, and the specific picture of it which lies undelineated behind the pieces in question, the more the art can be made to mean.

African art, like any other, must mean something to the artist and something else to the viewer or the critic. The anthropologist tries his best to make the African artist's view as palpable as possible to the European viewer, and such is a worthy intention. He is not, however, within his province if he claims that any other interpretation of it is wrong. Art is embodied vision. African art speaks both for the culture and for itself. Like all art, speaking for one human culture allows it, in some degree, to speak for all.

Chapter 10

African Families

In the ordinary course of reading the newspaper, it is possible to pick out every few weeks an article that displays the vast European and American ignorance about African families. And, interestingly enough, these articles all say the same thing; their content seldom varies, although the language and degree of detail varies with the audience of the papers. An article in *The National Observer* (whose audience is presumably educated, conservative, and fairly well-to-do) in July of 1962, serves as well as—but no better than—any other to make the point. One of its headlines reads:

> *"Lobola" is Still Paid*
>
> "ONE MAN? ONE WIFE?" CRY WOMEN OF RHODESIA AS A NEW ERA DAWNS

Americans seem to have an inexhaustible interest in polygyny and in bridewealth—enough that the vast reaches of similarity between their own family lives and those of Africans tend to be almost forgotten. In order to understand either that interest or the facts—and especially to untangle the two—it is necessary to follow the same procedure as that in the last chapter: we must examine some of the ideas and practices to which Americans are accustomed, and then something about extrafamilial kinship groups about which modern Americans know next to nothing from firsthand experience, while looking at the family institutions of Africa and the values and ideas that underlie them.

FAMILY LIFE

Family life is a universal; it takes care of completely universal human requirements. Indeed, it is the only economical and workable way of controlling and satisfying the most fundamental needs of the human animal: the need for secure and predictable social companionship, for food, for sexual expression and regulation, for reproduction, for teaching and training the young. Therefore, attitudes toward the human condition are found very close to the surface in the family philosophy, for although it is universal it is also subject to an amazingly wide variation.

A family is based on the mammalian animal quality of human beings. A great deal of effort, energy, attention, imagery, and imagination must go into the perpetuation of the species, the control of sexuality in order to avoid social chaos, and the bringing up of children to be "human," however that may be culturally defined. These processes take, in all societies, a tremendous amount of time.

It has often and correctly been said that the family image is at the foundation of the images of all social relationships. Whether we make the statements from a psychic or a social, a historical or an evolutionary point of view, it is incontrovertible.

Kinship is, actually, a simple business. It springs out of the fact that a man marries a woman and they beget and bear children. These are "the facts of life." On such facts, all sorts of changes can be rung; and only a few of the possible changes are not found institutionalized and valued somewhere. Therefore, it behooves us to look at African kinship practices in order to understand Africa and better understand ourselves.

There are two kinds of kinship. One is a relationship of descent; the other is a relationship of sexuality. Each may occur in two modes: the direct mode and the shared mode.

"Male" assumes the existence of female. "Child" assumes the existence of parent. Such are the direct mode relationships. But co-wives assume a common and shared husband, with no direct "organic" relationship. Just so, siblings assume a common shared parent (perhaps more than one), with no direct "organic" relationship no matter how many genes they may have in common. These are indirect modes of kinship.

Out of these differences, and the relationships which exhibit them, all kinship groups have to be built. The only building blocks there are are those of sexuality and descent, which English-speaking Westerners see as the relationships of husband-wife, mother-son, mother-daughter, father-son, father-daughter, brother-brother, sister-sister, brother-sister, and co-spouse relationships. The blocks can be compounded into great edifices; nevertheless, the blocks themselves are of a very precise nature and number.

American families contain all the relationships except those of shared sexuality. African families, being polygynous, contain all the relationships familiar to Americans, plus that of co-wife to co-wife, and the ramified relationships of half-siblings and of "father's wife-husband's child."

In all cultures, such kinship relationships must be given a more or less restricted content. It is necessary to know what husbands are supposed to do, as husbands; and what wives are supposed to do, as wives; what fathers are supposed to do, and what daughters are supposed to do. Then, on the basis of these understandings, human beings can act more or less comfortably as they make their compromises between reality and the ideal.

The content of the mother-child relationship bears greater similarity from one society to the next than does the father-child relationship. The brother-brother relationship can go all the way from the minimal content which Americans give it today, to the maximal content that some African patrilineal societies give it, where it is fundamental. The husband-wife relationship, and the kind of content that it involves, can vary just as widely: from the maximal content that Americans give it to the minimal content that some African societies give to it.

What, then, is polygyny? A married man marries a second or third woman, and they produce children. The content of each husband-wife relationship will be altered; the relationships of the co-wives and half-siblings have been added. The difference between monogamy and polygyny is contained in this: it is possible, even if it is not usual, to create a deeply intense relationship between husband and wife that probably most men cannot enter into with two women at once. If the intense and unique quality in that relationship is what is most highly valued, then polygyny must be opposed. But if something else—say security of position and the road to children—is most highly valued, polygyny is not a contradiction. Indeed, the added relationship among co-wives may provide some of the very cultural content and psychic satisfaction among adults which modern Americans try to cram solely into the husband-wife relationship. And it is no more fair to say that a rewarding husband-wife relationship cannot develop in polygyny than it is to say that intense community of interest among women cannot develop alongside monogamy.

The birth rate in a polygynous situation is never higher than the birth rate in a monogamous situation. It is usually lower. A man may beget many more children in polygyny than in monogamy. A woman does not bear any more. We can cease to worry about the birth rate in polygyny, because the moment that enforced monogamy comes into the African situation, the birth rate always soars (although monogamy is not the only factor—enforced monogamy is always accompanied by many other factors which change the way people live). African women do not, in their indigenous cultures, bear more than one child every two and a half or three years. They achieve this spacing by the only sure means—continence during the time they are nursing a child. When the situation changes so as to favor monogamy, their inclination and opportunity to shun their husbands for such a long period of time is usually reduced. In the indigenous culture, polygyny gives security to both husbands and wives during the time when a mother withdraws from cohabitation with her husband during a nursing period. The number of men in any society who can undergo such a long period of celibacy is small. If you are a wife in a polygynous society, would you rather have your husband at home with your co-wife or galavanting around the countryside?

Americans think that the impossible thing to share is the husband. If American women would really look into their souls, they know that it is really the kitchen that they would refuse to share. And the wives of African polygynists do not try. There are separate houses for each wife or for each group of wives; there is also usually a separate sphere for the husband.

Obviously, to make polygyny work it is necessary constantly to re-create a situation in which the rewards and obligations among co-wives are as neatly and precisely stated as are the obligations and rules among parents and children, husbands and wives. There are some things that a co-wife must do to be a good co-wife. There are others that she must *not* do if she is to be a good co-wife. If she does the one cheerfully and well and refrains from the other, she is by definition a good co-wife, whatever her husband's other wives may do.

If one examines divorces in Africa, he will find that some women leave their husbands not because they do not like their husbands but because they do not like their co-wives. Living in an impossible situation, whether that impossibility is created by husband or co-wife, leads in some societies and under some conditions to divorce. There are African women who divorce their husbands because they can't stand their co-wives; there are others who stay with impossible husbands because the co-wives are congenial. A good senior wife or mother-in-law may be as important in providing security, pleasant surroundings, and a rewarding place for a woman to bring up her children as is her husband.

If they have separate quarters and a pronounced code of behavior known to everybody, it is possible for co-wives not only to live next door, but to share their husband and even to become quite fond of one another. They have a great deal in common. The ideals of polygyny always are such that harmony among co-wives is possible. At the same time, in many African languages, the word for co-wife springs from the same root as the word for jealousy. The situation is fraught with difficulty—but are not all family relationships fraught with difficulty: the husband-wife relationship in monogamy? The parent-child relationship everywhere? The polygynous family is more complex than the monogamous family, and there are certain difficulties built into it. But the rewards involved may be great: it is possible, in a polygynous family, to spread your regard, your love, and your dependence over a wider range of people. You don't put all your emotional eggs in one basket. For this reason alone it can be seen to have great rewards. A large group of people has the welfare of each member at heart. And in the worst of all possible situations, the very number may dilute the hate pointed at each one.

Women in polygyny have grave trouble only when the interests of their children are involved and when real or supposed slights from the father toward one set of children or the other affect the smooth running of the whole. A woman, as a co-wife, can learn to accept all sorts of real or fancied slights. The same woman, as a mother, will have difficulty in accepting either real or fancied slights to her children. Here is the source of the difficulty: tension between my mother and the mothers of my half-siblings.

Polygyny has nothing to do with the position of women

in society. African women, by and large, have a high social position: legal rights, religious and political responsibility, economic independence. Where there are kings in sub-Saharan Africa, there are queen-mothers. At the basis of every secret cult of men, there are women: the innermost secret of every religious club barred to women is the male's ultimate dependence on women. Women are often excluded from rituals, but there are two things that initiation into religion and society involve: initiation into society is a ritualized teaching to the novitiates that they embody, in themselves personally and in their relationships collectively, the moral force of society—they are themselves the gods (not God) and the sanctions. Initiation is also a ritualized teaching to the initiates that women must stand behind and support men. In the Ivory Coast, for example, initiation has two denouements: one when the boys find that the masked dancers who have represented the gods and the social forces suddenly take the masks off and put them on the boys themselves; the other when the innermost hidden secret of the men's religious societies is exposed to them—and turns out to be a woman.

Women in Africa are not, in short, a deprived group as they were in the nineteenth-century Western world. African men ritualize rather than deny their basic dependence on women.

The next myth that must be banished is that polygyny has anything to do with the concupiscence of the male. Polygyny is a state into which most African men enter with a certain trepidation. If you think that one wife can henpeck a husband, you should see what three in league can do. If co-wives live up to the ideals of the roles, even just barely, no man exists but is under greater strain and control than he would be if there were only one woman involved. The man who has a strong senior wife is a fortunate individual, because she will run the household and will straighten out the fusses among the co-wives. He will not have to bother. If he does not have such a wife, two-thirds of his energy goes into administration.

Men must treat their wives in accordance with the station of the wives—not necessarily with absolute equality, unless the society dictates that their stations are those of absolute equals. The greater number of societies lay down quite precise obligations on the part of the husband, but others insist that the obligation is to make the personal adjustments necessary to keep all the parties contented.

It is all but inevitable, in all probability, that polygynists have favorite wives. It should never, however, show up in the way the husband carries out his obligations: clothing them, feeding them, giving them children. Occasionally romantic love enters into this situation. I have seen an old Tiv chief with seventeen wives who loved them all, but loved one of them in the sense given that term by the troubadours and adapted by latter-day American marriage counselors. The senior ones had given him families and had comforted his years. But unfortunately —and even he considered it unfortunate—he "fell in love" with one of the younger ones. It kept him from being a good family man; it kept him from being a good chief. I judge that romantic love occurs in an African familial situation about as commonly as it does in a European or American one. The difference is that Westerners have a series of myths which make them simulate romantic love to see them over the time between initial attraction and the regard that sensitive and sensible living together, breeding, and growing together can foster. The myth makes it possible for Westerners to select their spouses on something besides random choice—indeed, under it they can arrange their own marriages.

Old-fashioned Africans select their spouses by "giving in to their parents' wishes." But in most cases in which the parents' wishes do not correspond with their own, they elope. Seldom do Africans make their children marry someone they do not like.

The other aspect of African family life that is most likely to be misunderstood is the institution of bridewealth. Initially, the European observers who went to Africa said that Africans bought their wives. In a sense, that is true. It is *not* true that wives enter the market place or that they are commercialized or anything of the sort. It is easiest to explain by noting that part of the marriage contract in any society is that the wife gets certain rights in the husband and he gets certain rights in her. The rights of each are the obligations of the other.

Initially the husband has to make a bridewealth payment that is tantamount to posting a bond that he will carry out his obligations, thus guarding his new wife's rights. The analogy can be carried too far, because the nature of the bond and the purpose of the bridewealth changes, and ultimately its nature is in the sphere of legitimizing the children. But, in return for his "bond" and his obligations, the husband gets certain rights.

To sum them up quickly, a man may get in his wife, domestic rights—the right to establish a domestic unit with her and to her domestic work and time and care. He may get rights to her extradomestic economic substance or labor; such was the case in the late nineteenth-century West, but is seldom so in Africa. He gets sexual rights in her and obligations toward her. Finally, he may or may not get the right to filiate that woman's children to his kinship group. In most African societies, traditionally, a man acquired such rights in exchange for cattle or ceremonial currency such as spears or pieces of iron, or else for service of the sort Jacob performed for his two wives, in the Book of Genesis. The difference between matriliny and patriliny can be summed up by determining whether it is common to transfer the rights to filiate the children.

It is these rights that the bridewealth purchases, these

obligations that it symbolizes. If a woman "has cows on her back," as the East African idiom has it, then her children belong to the man and to the social group that paid the cows. This is a matter of legitimization. It is, indeed, a symbol of legitimization.

If the marriage breaks up, the bridewealth must be returned, totally or in part.

Polygyny does not necessarily mean that some men do not have wives, but only that men marry later than women. Polygyny must also be distinguished from concubinage. Concubines are not wives, for all that in some places they have legal rights. In many societies there are, besides concubinage, several "degrees" of marriage, and in some there is allowable sexual and other relationships which may not be granted the status of full marriage. Indeed, in the Roman Republic there were two forms of marriage—heiresses would not marry by the ritual that gave their husbands control of their property, but rather formed a recognized, common-law union in which this economic right was not transferred. There were, thus, two "types" of "marriage": one involved the acquisition by the husband of all the rights; the other of only part of them. Many—probably most—African societies exhibit just such variation in the possible marriage arrangements.

Rights in women are considered, in most African societies, to be heritable. If my father or my older brother dies, leaving a couple of wives, I may inherit his rights in those not my mother. Since all rights involve obligations, it would be more accurate to say that I inherit my father's obligations to his wives. If the widow has several children and her children are members of her late husband's kinship group, she has an important position within that kinship group, even though she is not a member of it. Her position in life, indeed, may depend upon her children —thus underscoring the hard fate of a barren woman. Her natal group has little obligation to her after her initial marriage—ultimately none. As some Africans put it, "your wife of long-standing becomes your sister." A woman's status derives from her being a mother of lineage members. Therefore, it is only sensible for her to remarry into that group. And most widows are women of maturity (which may, of course, begin at twenty); they do not expect from a second marriage what they expect from a first—sometimes the second may be happier for that reason.

The result is the institution of inheritance of rights in widows. In one situation the widow is inherited as a wife; there is another, quite different, situation in which (to use the Old Testament term) the brother of the dead husband raises up seed, which is to say that the widow moves in as his "wife," but that the dead husband remains the legal father of any children that she bears. Such an arrangement is called the true levirate. The new husband acquires domestic and sexual rights in the widow; he does not acquire rights to filiate her children, which are thought to be part of the "spiritual property" of the dead husband.

It is possible, in most African societies, for a widow to decide not to remain with her deceased husband's people. She therefore probably marries someone else and the bridewealth is adjusted.

American and Western European society docs not cope very well with widows. They are an anomaly. They occupy an insecure position, are to be pitied, particularly if they have children; they are not quite to be trusted, although the divorcee has in the twentieth century taken over the role assigned to the widow in the nineteenth. African societies cope well with both divorcees and widows—getting them back into families quickly and simply. Loneliness is not an indigenous African problem.

NONFAMILIAL KINSHIP GROUPS

In addition to families, there are other sorts of kinship groups in Africa based on a more limited range of relationships than are families. Extended families can have only a certain size—after that, the members cannot know all their kinsmen, or respond equally to them all. Since the functions of the family are usually associated largely with households, the household limit—certainly the neighborhood limit—is, in most cases, the effective limit of the family. But certain types of limiting kinship groups can gear their purposes to other ends and still use kinship amity as the sanction for carrying out the cooperation of the group and the achievement of its ends. The descent groups contain fewer relationships, but can control much larger numbers of people.

There are two sorts of descent groups: patrilineal descent groups, which includes the father-son and father-daughter relationships and the three sibling relationships. The matrilineal descent group includes the mother-son and mother-daughter and the three sibling relationships. Each of these, being limited in the way that they are and specifically not being able to take care of the basic functions of bearing and rearing children, can be brilliantly adapted to political and economic ends.

Descent groups may contain several million people and use the sanction of kinship obligations—"blood is thicker than water"—to reward their members and bind them to "right" courses of action. These groups can be called lineages; some types are called "clans." The word "clan" in the anthropological literature is used broadly—it may cover any kinship group that is not a family, and even some extended families (the Chinese *tsu*, usually called a "clan" in English, is in fact a type of extended family).

Unilineal descent groups are very widespread in Africa and were—indeed, still are—the basis for most of the extrafamilial social organization. They form political groups, religious congregations, and even production and land-owning units. They are still strong. They are strong among the educated as well as among the "bush" people. They will continue to be strong.

There is a favorite myth among anthropologists that the African family and the other kinship groups are breaking down. The unilineal descent groups—the uses to which they are put—can be truly undermined by only one thing: that is a police system so effective that contractual obligations can be maintained with as great security and less responsibility than by kinship groups. In the absence of such a police system, there must be *something* else. And the African answer is the efflorescence of the descent group. The economic and legal sanction is to be found in kinship obligations.

There are some societies in Africa in which unilineal descent groups are not found, but such groups are overwhelmingly present in many more. It is loyalty to the descent group, as well as to the family, that is under discussion when Africans talk about their obligations to "their" people.

In addition to the economic and political purposes that such groups can be made to serve, they are often central to religious ritual and belief. They are, moreover, often associated with the history and the view of the cosmography. They are, in short, one way in which the small world of the family can be tied to the greater world and ultimately to the supernatural.

African children grow up in an intense situation of kinship and family. They continue throughout their lives to learn their family obligations and family histories. And, perhaps most importantly, they learn from a very early age to spread their regard, their rewards, and their concern.

Among the Tiv of eastern central Nigeria, for example, a child when he is about six months old is assigned to an older sister or brother, preferably the same sex as the child; the older becomes the nurse of the younger. For the next three or four years—almost until the younger child is ready to become a nurse, they accompany their nurses everywhere. When they cry, the nurses take them to their mothers. When the nurses go out to play, the babies go with them. The bond between a child and his nurse becomes an enduring bond. I have been many times introduced by old men to men just older who had been their nurses. Children learn a great deal about the culture from one another and especially from their nurses. In our society, children more and more learn from adults.

Tiv children, as an example, are allowed to go any place, so long as they keep quiet. They can go into the most solemn court proceedings and sit down and listen. The moment one of them makes a noise, out they all go. Older children of eight or nine often get interested in court cases or political meetings. When their younger charges will not behave, they have to go away; therefore they are very adept in silencing the babies. There is nothing from which children are excluded, unless they misbehave and intrude. As a result, they tend to be well-behaved children, aware from an early age of what goes on in adult culture. The abrupt break such as Westerners know, between children's culture and adult culture, is not to be found.

African children get into their cultures early, and there are no abrupt shifts. After they are twelve or thirteen, and sometimes earlier, boys form groups that range the countryside, hunt, and (where there are cattle and goats) tend the herds. Girls by this time are more closely kept at home and are on the brink of marriage.

At marriage, the vast majority of girls shift homesteads. They leave the households in which they are daughters and join those in which they are wives and in which they will become mothers. Men do not undergo this kind of change, but continue to live imbedded in a group of their own kinsmen.

It is probably impossible for anyone who has never lived in a kinship-dominated society to realize the combination of security and bondedness that it implies. In discussion, Africans always emphasize the positive factors: a group of their own, on which they can depend totally and to which they owe allegiance, a group which transcends them and gives them position in society and in history—importance and status as well as physical necessities or even wealth. Nevertheless, they do, to some extent, chafe under the demands of their kinsmen. Until the present century, there was no "way out" of the kinship situation. There was no place to go if one was exiled. The kinship sanction was sufficient to control all of one's behavior. Modern Westerners would see such a fate in terms of the lack of individuality and freedom. Africans do not. Although today many of them do leave when faced with choices in which they consider that they must give more than they get, few intend to stay away for good.

Africans who felt it necessary to maintain their relationships within their kinship groups have discovered ways and means that have made them all but geniuses in personal relationships—at least it is so at a kinship level. The story is told of a South African chief whose murder was attempted by his brother. The brother got out of prison several years later. The chief met him and welcomed him back to the fold of the kinship group. The balance between individuality and security is solved quite differently in a kinship-dominated society from the way it is solved in a contract-dominated society.

Parenthood is important everywhere. It is trebly so in a society in which rights to the most important parts of all aspects of life are dependent upon kinship, and when most of one's status derives from kinship factors. Only on the birth of a child does a woman become truly a kinsman in her husband's group. Only on the birth of a child is a man assured of the "immortality" of a position in the genealogy of his lineage, or even of security of esteem among the important people of his community. Only on the birth of a grandchild is a man in a position to be truly sure that his name and spirit will live in the history and genealogy of his people. This factor, combined with that other factor that is so true everywhere—that grandparenthood allows a perfect and rewarding position for summing up the meaning of the life cycle—makes grandparenthood enviable, and elderhood the finest estate.

Many Africans express concern lest the kinship groups to which they are bound will wither and perish in the course of industrialization and mechanization of the new Africa. They are determined that, if possible, no such fate will befall them. It will be an interesting experiment. From it we may learn whether or not it is truly modern technology and the development of contract which destroys the ramified kinship system, or whether Western reasons for abandoning it were quite different from those they themselves use to explain their distrust of all kinship groups save the nuclear family.

Chapter 11

African Land and Labor

Polity and economy are of a piece—they can be separated only by the most rigorous "scientific method." The moment that pure economics turns to the realm that it calls "the empirical"—indeed, even before—the actions of governments must be taken into account; political science is impossible without consideration of the means and institutions of production and distribution of our daily bread and annual income.

Put into the very broadest scale, human beings are animals and therefore they take up terrestrial space. Being animal, they must exploit that space for their daily nutritional requirements in some way that is at least minimally predictable. The predictability implies some minimal "political" order. These inseparable attributes of the human animal are the starting place of what, in the old days, was called "political economy." Political economy involves law and international relations; production, distribution, and consumption. Put in another way, it involves the specifically human forms of territoriality and dominance. But, let it be repeated, these factors are never separable in the real world, but only in the world of science.

SPACE AND TERRITORIALITY

The African view of terrestrial space tends (there are half a dozen exceptions) to be one based on the regulation of social relationships. The Western view of the same space is irrevocably based on exploitation. In order to understand the African idea more easily it is well first to etch the dominant outlines of the Western concept—one we scarcely know we hold.

Land (terrestrial space) is a "thing" that modern Westerners cut into pieces that they call parcels which they can then buy and sell on the market. Such an activity is very rare among the societies of the world—it is recent in our own. Neighborhoods are the result, in twentieth-century Western society, of the buying and selling, renting and leasing of homesites. Local communities are, in fact, epiphenomena of the market.[6] Such was never the case in Africa. There a community was and is built fundamentally on relationships within social groups based on some principle other than "economics"; that community is set into space, by other than associations of "ownership" as we recognize it, and exploits the space around it.

Think about the map of the world that Westerners are taught. Maps—and you must file your deed when you buy land—are records of astrally determined points and lines on the surface of the earth. These records are made by representing the grid which we have imagined to cover the earth, according to a known scale, on a flat surface. We discovered that if a surveyor takes a sextant and "shoots the stars," that place can be relocated on the map. We are the only people in the world who use seafaring instruments to determine our position on the ground.

After the position on the earth is astrally determined, measurements are made of the plot by other surveyors' instruments such as transits and plane tables. These measurements are also translated to the paper. And it is whatever corresponds to the representation on the paper that you "own." In this system, a piece of property is deter-

[6] This is not a simplistic argument. I do not mean to imply that there are not non-market reasons for peoples' decisions to make the market choices that lead to communities, for obviously there are. The basic point is, however, true, as status seekers, real estate brokers, and integration leaders know.

mined by its position in relation to the stars, not its location between North Salt Creek and Squaw Butte.

The Western map is, as a matter of fact, a strange kind of map. All the peoples of the world have maps of one sort or another—usually they are not written, but the raw material is there for a "map." A view or image of the terrestrial world. None save modern technical civilization have maps in which precision is so essential. There are a few peoples who divide up the world by natural boundaries such as rivers and hills. Most, however, see it in terms of social relations and the juxtaposition of social groups.

In order to understand the way such peoples are associated with the land and with one another in terms of land, and hence the way the political power system and the economic system of exploitation work, it is first necessary to understand the way they see themselves in relation to the earth.

African societies did not split land up into pieces at all. Here we shall mention two methods by which an area can be made into a socially recognizable "map." One of these is by a series of specific terrestrial points which are given particular recognition and either economic or ritual meaning by the people concerned. The Plateau Tonga of Northern Rhodesia hook their social organization to the earth not by means of anything we would ourselves consider land tenure, but by means of a set of rain shrines, each of which is associated with surrounding villages, and each of which is specifically placed on the earth—possibly but rarely subject to move on ritual authority. Opportunity for individuals to move from one village to another is great, and one's acceptance as a resident in a village automatically carries with it not only fealty to the shrine but a right to make a farm nearby on any land not farmed at the moment nor claimed as fallow by another resident. Tonga farms can be cultivated for five or six years before the soil is exhausted. Tonga can be seen to have short-term "farm tenure," as it were, in the village area near the shrine.

The Bedouin Arabs of Cyrenaica are another well-documented example in which the tribal lands are attached to points—in this case to saints' graves and wells. Many pastoral societies and most of those that practice shifting cultivation see the land in this sort of association with society. The pastoral Fulani, with their long, sweeping cycles of movement, and the slash-and-burn peoples of the Congo forests, with their relatively short moves, can all be included in this classification.

In the other mode of connecting society to space, the social organization is conceived in terms of pure space, and is only incidentally linked with the physical environment by vicissitudes of farming or other land uses for very short periods of time. The Tiv of central Nigeria are an example of a farming people who are characteristic of this type. They see geography in the same image as they see social organization. The idiom of descent and genealogy provides not only the basis for lineage grouping, but also of territorial grouping. Every "minimal lineage" is associated with a territory. This minimal lineage (two or three hundred males derived from a single ancestor, whose wives and daughters live with them) is located spatially beside another lineage of precisely the same sort—that is, from the brother of the ancestor of the first group. In reference to the father of the two apical ancestors of the two minimal lineages, they form an inclusive lineage, and their territories form a single spatial unit. This process continues backward genealogically for several generations, until all Tiv are included; it continues spatially until the entirety of Tivland—some two hundred miles in diameter—is seen as a lineage area, segmenting into increasingly smaller lineage areas.

This "genealogical map" of Tivland moves about the surface of the earth in sensitive response to the demands of individual farmers as those demands change from year to year. The "map" in terms of which Tiv see their land is a genealogical map, and its association with specific pieces of ground is of only very brief duration—a man or woman has precise rights to a farm during the time it is in cultivation, but once the farm returns to fallow, the rights lapse. However, a man always has rights in the "genealogical map" of his agnatic lineage, wherever that lineage may happen to be in space. These rights, which are part of his birthright, can never lapse. A mathematician friend has suggested to me that whereas the Western map, based on surveys, resembles geometry, the Tiv notions resemble topology, which has been described as "geometry on a rubber sheet." The Western map is necessarily rigid and precise if the principle of contract is to work; the Tiv map is constantly changing both in reference to itself and in its correlation with the earth, thus allowing the principle of kinship grouping to work. For the Tiv, the position of a man's farm varies from one crop rotation to the next, but neither his juxtaposition with his agnatic kinsmen nor his rights change in the least. Tiv, like Tonga, might be said to have "farm tenure" but they do not have "land tenure."

Thus, instead of seeing their maps primarily in terms of "property," Africans see something like a map in terms of social relationships in space. They emphasize the spatial aspect of their social groups and provide themselves with a social map, so that they are left free to question the ways in which they attach either social groups or individuals to exploitational rights in the earth. In the past they were usually imprecise, because group membership was the valued quality. Westerners, on the other hand, think about their map in terms of property and values, and see the social system which results as fundamentally a series of contracts and hence open to question. As a result, in any situation of change, Westerners question the social system that lies behind land usage, while Africans question the property ideas associated with the systems of land usage.

This relative inability on the part of Westerners to question whether or not a land system is in fact a property system—that is, the assumption that it always is, even if land does not enter the market—has led to the continued life of a silly concept called "communal ownership." Now, in a technologically developed, contractually oriented society like Europe and America, communal ownership can and does exist. That is to say, the commune, whatever its nature, can be viewed as a jural person. As a "corporation aggregate," it is capable of owning property under the law. The difficulty arises because this fiction has so often been used by Westerners to make sense out of African land systems. A more farcical situation is difficult to imagine.

Sir Henry Maine pointed out long ago that in a community based on kinship, the land is an aspect of the group, but not the basis of grouping. Notions of "communal ownership," manipulated by people who assume property and market as the basis of society, have made the land the basis of grouping in a system in which spatial extension and concomitant rights to exploit the environment are mere aspects of the social group. The indigenous basis of grouping is kinship in some parts of Africa, while in others it is a village community similar to those Maine studied in India and Europe. In no place in Africa did the basis of grouping depend indigenously on contract.

Property, in the Western sense, and its resultant contractual relationships, are the fundamental basis of grouping in the Western type of national state. In a developed market economy, a land market emerges—with whatever agony to the people who must see it to fruition. Therefore, as African societies become Western-type national states, as they come to have more fully evolved market economies, the problem before them is how to preserve certain of their valued kinship groups. Their answer is the same as the one found by some of the more prosperous of American Indian tribes such as the Osage. They are turning their kinship groups into corporations aggregate before the law. This means that they can maintain at least some of the valued qualities of the kinship group at the same time that they are making themselves into corporations—sole or aggregate—which are the units of "modern societies," based on contract and on the market.

The Osage, when they struck oil, turned their tribe into a limited corporation under the laws of the State of Oklahoma. The Yoruba people in the western region of Nigeria turned their extended-family compounds into landholding units before the law, under the "Communal Land Rights (Vesting in Trustees) Law" of 1958.

This law, in brief, makes a matter of legal record the change in the nature of the Yoruba lineage group called the *ebi,* though it does so in legal language which eschews mention of the *ebi.* The *ebi* in traditional terms was an agnatic descent group which shared a common residence. Every quarter of every Yoruba town had several *ebi,* and on some occasions an *ebi* could split into two or more *ebi.* This body of agnatic kinsmen, with their wives, also had an estate—a more or less precisely determinable area within which they traditionally farmed, and which they protected from encroachment by others. Within the *ebi,* the members farmed not in specific places which they considered their own, but the group moved its farms about within the area so that they could remain as a unit to take advantage of the best soils and to control the system of fallowing. Nobody "owned" anything, but every member had a right to a farm sufficient to support his immediate dependents. These rights to a farm were inalienable. The *ebi* had a head and a council which ran the agricultural affairs of the *ebi* in a kind of committee.

This mode of spatial distribution and concomitant exploitation of the environment left several things to be desired in the new society which has developed under colonialism. In the first place, it granted a man land rights *only* insofar as he was a part of a lineage. The moment he ceased to be an effective member of his lineage, his land rights were forgone until he again became an effective member. Under modern conditions, Yoruba often want to remain members of their lineages, but also want to have land rights of a different sort. Sale of land was impossible in the old system because land was the spatial dimension of the *ebi* rather than a commodity which could be considered "property" and sold in the market, but sale of land became desirable when the economic system changed in such a way as to make such sales feasible. Immediately, a sort of pull or pressure was set up between the *ebi* land unit and the individual. Either a man had to cease being an individual in the new system, or the *ebi* land unit, as an institution, had to go.

"The Communal Land Rights (Vesting in Trustees) Law" is, then, a legal mechanism by means of which this particular difficulty has been solved. European analysis of Yoruba land tenure has, from the beginning, classed the *ebi's* spatial dimension as "land owned in communal tenure." The *ebi* is certainly a community of sorts, and since it was associated with land, the European notion of "tenure" was automatically applied without question as to whether it fit or not. Such an assumption had the result of turning the *ebi*, in European eyes, into a corporation aggregate before the law. With this European analysis in terms of legal corporations, a subtle change was introduced. The Europeans, in the legal system they fostered, gave the *ebi* a legal reality which it formerly had not possessed. From being only a social group, it now became a legal entity. Yoruba were late in recognizing what had happened. But having recognized it, they and their legislators have seen in it a means of preserving the *ebi* as a social group fulfilling some of the basic needs of what we would call social insurance and community center at the same time that they have strengthened the institution of private property.

Thus, in the indigenous system, the *ebi* did not "own" land communally or any other way. In the modern system, the *ebi* of the Yoruba has been turned into a legal entity, before the laws of Nigeria, and can therefore "own" land. "Communal land ownership" assumes that the commune is, before the law, the same sort of unit as the individual. That idea has penetrated Yoruba cultural values and, indeed, communal land ownership under the law is actually taking place.

With changes in the economic use of land—that is, with "economic development"—the dimensions of society are necessarily affected. Land as a factor of production assumes a greater role than it formerly had, compared with land as the dimension of society.

LABOR

If land provides the fundamental dimensions of society, work provides its gyroscope. If one's work is changed, the balance of one's life is changed in the process.

Until the development of the "economics of development," economists viewed labor merely as one of the primary factors of production. And so it is, but it is more. People at work create not merely products; they also create a web of social relationships. They fraternize with one another in terms of quite specific sets of rules; each takes home to his family at least some residue of these relationships with his pay envelope. Indeed, all of life is involved with one's work habits. In addition to some of the most dominating of one's social relationships, even such fundamental aspects of life as how and when one sleeps, and what and when one eats are influenced by one's work. The concept of the "labor supply" is only one way of looking at the social structure—a way limited by and to certain economic and political problems.

During the Industrial Revolution in Europe and America, work with all its social ramifications underwent a profound change—it entered the market place. The dictum "He who does not work does not eat" became "He who does not sell his labor or his brains on the market does not acquire the means to buy the wherewithal to support himself and his family."

Like the Europeans in the days before the eighteenth century, Africans before the middle twentieth century did their work in groups, and by arrangements that were not fundamentally geared to the market. Traditional forms of labor in Africa took place within the sphere of the family, the local government, the age-set, and other such organizations. They specifically did not take place in the form of any organization set up to buy labor and the other factors of production on the market, in order to turn out goods to be sold on the same market in which the labor was hired and the other factors acquired.

Before the revolution of the mid-twentieth century, the major part of the work done in Africa was done in carrying out one's obligations within the fundamental family and kinship groups. The domestic economy was not severed from "the economy" in the way that has been the practice of our own society in our own age. People helped one another in their work for an approximate return in kind. The men of a local community, however it may have been defined, got together to perform community work such as road and path construction and bridge building, clearing the market place, or putting up a new shrine. The economy was thus no more differentiated from the local government than it was differentiated from the family. Part of one's duties as a citizen, to put it into modern terms, consisted in carrying out one's portion of the work of the community. One of the favorite ways of getting sizable working groups together—and there are some jobs that must be done, in all societies, that take sizable working groups—was for members of an age-set to work together.

The age-set of a community in most African societies could furnish from twenty to one hundred men. The organization within the set was already established so that few or no new lines of authority based primarily on the job at hand and the purpose in mind had to be established.

It is customary—and correct—to think that the African "production unit" is the family or kinship group. It is necessary, however, to recognize the more basic situation: that kinship groups are less specialized in traditional Africa than are kinship groups in modern America. Production was and is done in family groups because subsistence production does not require any others.

There have been, from so-called time immemorial, a few people in Africa who sold their labor on the market. To overlook this point would be to report falsely and—more serious—to deprive one's self of the most sensible explanation of why the Africans took to market labor with such alacrity when the opportunity came for them to do so. Traders have existed throughout many parts of Africa for centuries. Although they often depended on slave labor, more often they were able to hire labor. If they depended on sharing with their kinsmen rather than hiring strangers, their reasoning can be seen because there were no courts to adjudicate their rights.

Thus, most Africans "always" knew that it was possible to hire themselves out, and to sell their labor at a going market rate. However, only an infinitesimal proportion of them ever did so. By and large, their work, like their land and like the other factors of production, and indeed like the mode of distribution, was organized along non-market principles and not for purposes of increasing production or creating "economic growth."

In the West, and in the technologically advanced parts of modern Africa, one still works for the sake of one's family, for the sake of one's citizenship, as well as for the sake of one's sanity. But in the West, and in the new Africa, one works in a different social context: that of the "firm." The firm is a type of social organization put together on the basis of the principle of contract—a principle that was very little developed in most parts of Africa, even by the colonial governments who imposed it on their African colonies. It has often been said, correctly enough, that Africa, for all the fact that she was the home of great legal systems, never developed a reliable system of contract law. The reason is that she never needed it. Law always follows social development, and contract-oriented forms and rights and obligations had not yet taken a dominant enough place in society to make the law follow in spite of itself. In a firm, those aspects of a contractual relationship which lawyers call the "consideration" are of the essence. In short, through firms, people sell their labor. With the establishment of this new type of organization, new types of obligations and rights came into being in African society much as they had come into being in European societies several centuries earlier. Obviously, they are not as painful to African society as they were to European society during the Industrial Revolution because there is a model to go on—it would be a sad comment on us all if some lesson had not been learned from the European experience.

Perhaps the most important point to be garnered from our discussion is that whereas Africans had always worked, like everybody else—and they worked extremely hard, and still do—they have, as a result of the introduction of firms and of the spread of the market to include the factors of production, become "labor." The word labor in English means not merely work, it also means that sector of the population which sells its work. *Some* Africans became and are becoming labor, in this new sense, and with it they have taken on new identities and new obligations.

In the nineteenth and early twentieth centuries, those Europeans who brought capital and entrepreneurial experience to Africa in order to create a new economic milieu and make their marks in the expanding societies in which they lived came with another and related idea. Africa, they reckoned, was a pool of "cheap labor." If they supplied their factors of production—capital and entrepreneurship—then the Africans would profit by providing those others, land and labor. They were so sure that their social system was superior to anything else in the world at the time, that even had they recognized that they were working unfathomable change (and some Europeans since the time of Robert Owen had recognized it), they would have considered the game worth the candle.

The more amazing thing is that Africans considered it worth the candle too. Although they did not see the "game" in these terms, what they did see was a new and admittedly technologically superior culture. No matter how repelled they may have been by some non-material aspects of the culture, their attraction to its material advantages overcame what repulsions they may have felt.

What resulted was the institution of so-called "labor migration." It became part of the life experience of most young men on the continent to leave home at the age of eighteen or so and to spend several years in the cities, or industrial complexes, or on the farms of the European settlers. The greater the density of European settlement or development the higher the rate of African labor migration. What occurred was thus a classical dual society. Africans did not participate fully in modern society lived by the Europeans; the Europeans did not participate fully in the society in which the Africans lived. This was no mere difference in class and culture. The society was a closed one for both groups. The two sectors met in the market place: the market place into which the factors of production had inserted themselves along with the products.

Much has been written, and many special pleas made, on the subject of labor migration. Among them are the obvious facts that living conditions in barracks and among groups composed solely of men were depressing or unhealthy or both; that the quality and standard of the agricultural work in the African villages and farms deteriorated badly; that morals were undermined. Perhaps the most serious charge of all—and it is a true one—is that governments were enabled to hide unemployment problems and welfare problems by turfing workers back into what had become an outworn tribal system. In some cases, the tribal groups themselves overhauled their organizations to cope, in some degree, with this new situation. But these so-called "transitional forms" were not really satisfactory to anybody. Africans began to realize that life and labor could be made more pleasant than those they currently knew, and European firms began to realize that cheap labor was not cheap.

The problem for both Africans and Europeans came to be: how can Africans be committed to a market system? To Europeans, the Africans appeared to be "target workers." The stereotype appeared of the man who would come, work until he had achieved the sum necessary to buy a bicycle (it was always a bicycle), and then would return home, until he wanted something else. To Africans, the stereotype was a very different one: a man could not give up his loyalties to his tribal groups until he had the welfare that it provided him assured in some way—his kinship group was his insurance society, his old-age pension, his community.

These problems still exist. They were inherited by new governments from colonial governments. It will be illuminating to see what sort of compromise Africans are willing to make between the economy they are seeking to achieve and the social groups in which they get many of their major rewards. What form of government can best make the compromise? How, in fact, can society and economy be most happily wedded?

Chapter 12

African Politics and Courts

Just as land and labor lie behind all of production, so territorial distribution of people and the nature of the power relationships are the givens on which the solutions to political problems are based.

Africa did not learn politics only in the twentieth century any more than Africans learned to make a good living only in the twentieth century. African political sophistication at the local level is such that even mayors of major American cities could take lessons both in chicanery and in effective welfare. Learning something of the African idea of politics in the period of the "deep freeze" of colonialism, and before it, is necessary in order fully to appreciate African political problems in her postwar states.

Politics as a practical art deals with two vast subjects and organizations, and it deals with them in two ways. On the one hand it has to do with internal problems: law, and the comfort, protection, and welfare of citizens. On the other hand it has to do with international relationships—between those inside and those outside. In either of these spheres, the activities can be of two sorts—they can be violent or they can be nonviolent. It would seem that one of the major problems of civilization has been to get more and more political problems solved by nonviolent means rather than by violent ones. It would also seem that there has been more success in achieving these aims internally or domestically than there has been in the international arena where the problems of power, equality, and indeed the very perception of the good society may be at odds.

African politics, like any other, must deal with these

problems and it must do so in terms of geographical space, however that may be conceived. First, how did Africans maintain law and welfare among their peoples? Then, how did they maintain cultural integrity and keep other societies and peoples from overrunning them? Again, in order to discover traditional African answers to these problems, we must at the same time expose our own traditional ideas so that we can recognize those answers when we find them.

There were two basic types of indigenous political systems in Africa. One is familiar to Europeans and Americans because they too now utilize it and have done so for long enough that many of them seem to believe that it is synonymous with order and civilization. That is the political form called the "state." A state is a bureaucracy organized specifically to carry out political activities. The bureaucracy may or may not be based on some other kind of social group such as the family—that is to say, the criteria for achieving entrance into the bureaucracy may be almost any that a society chooses. In a state there is an interlocked system of offices or positions that must be filled by officials. Authority is then made inherent in these interlocking positions, which both reinforce and act as a check on one another. In well-run states, the power system is the same thing as the authority system. In states in which such is not the case, the result is likely to be tyranny or chaos or both.

The special bureaucracy called the state is not, however, the only organization capable of carrying out the political requirements of a society. Africa has had its share of glorious and effective states. It has also had its share of stateless societies.

A stateless society would seem almost a contradiction in terms to modern Westerners. In spite of the fact that through the Middle Ages there were many such represented in Europe, it was these very stateless societies that the officials of European colonialism were unable to understand and therefore very seriously misjudged when they discovered them in Africa in the nineteenth and early twentieth centuries. "States" are conceptually simple, but organizationally complex. Non-states are the opposite and are hence difficult to conceive for those who understand only the concept of the state.

Colonial powers confused the state, which is one form of political organization, with political organization itself. Occurrences of this sort almost always happen when a people has found a vast simplifying mechanism (in this case the statelike bureaucracy) to take care of a vast number of the problems of life. No matter how complex states may be, they make life simpler for the people who live in them. Organizationally complex as it may be, civilization is nevertheless parsimonious in its use of social principles, and therefore the people who are used to the simplicity of civilization cannot immediately comprehend the complexity of smaller-scale societies. They failed to realize that there were ways other than the state to achieve political aims.

STATES

Egyptian and Meroitic civilizations and the sudanese kingdoms that were influenced by them were effective forms of the state based on a royalty which had deep religious duties as well as commanding position in the hierarchies of authority and power. But although some of these states—some are even called "empires"—lasted for several centuries, the problems that have been solved in various parts of the world by process of election, unencumbered royal succession and the like, as a way of passing authority from one generation to the next, remained fundamentally unsolved.

States of nineteenth-century West Africa, such as Ashanti, Dahomey, the Yoruba kingdoms, Benin, and states of the Congo Basin such as the kingdoms of Kongo and Bushong, are well known and easy to understand, once the facts are revealed. The only serious barrier to direct understanding by modern Westerners is that religion played a vital role in the political process, and the fact that political tasks as we have defined them above were not carried out wholly or solely by the state, but that some of them were assigned to other organizations, based on other organizational principles, particularly to families, village communities, age-sets and religious congregations.

Jan Vansina, a Belgian anthropologist and historian now teaching in America, has made an enlightening comparison of the qualities of African kingdoms—and all the indigenous states of Africa were kingdoms of one sort or another. He accepts the recognized criteria of centralized authority, administrative machinery, and judicial institutions, which assumes that territorial sovereignty, a specialized bureaucracy, and the monopoly on the legal use of force are aspects of the African state.

Vansina's most signal contribution is in making us realize that the idea of centralized authority means no more than that the state must have a recognized head from whom the authority, and presumably also the power, derives. Beyond that requirement, singularities are common. Most of the political organizations which have this kind of king, however, surround him with councils and with courts. Almost all have institutionalized means to keep him from abusing his power. Authority is usually delegated from the king through the so-called administrative machinery, or bureaucracy, to the heads of smaller territorial units, which are provinces or principalities. The association between the heads of the provinces and the king may be of many sorts; in some parts of Africa they are kinsmen, in others there is an almost feudal type of arrangement, and in still others there is an arrangement that would seem to amount to contract.

African kings are divine kings. This term was given a special meaning by the early anthropologist J. G. Frazer and his followers. Although in some African cases, the classical type of the "Divine King" has been considerably attenuated, in general the person of the king is sacred or else sacredness resides in the insignias which are his so long as he is king. The king is the physical symbol of the kingdom, and therefore must be physically strong and sound. The killing of old or ill kings when they were no longer suitable symbols for the vigorous wholeness of the nation has been found in many instances (whether their execution was actually carried out or not is another problem), and the kingship was usually surrounded by taboos and restrictions, which sometimes seem bizarre until their meanings are understood.

The king usually had his hands full merely being the symbol of the kingdom, and its religious center. Delegation of authority usually amounted to delegation of almost all authority save religious—and on a few occasions, even religious authority was delegated. Kings, because of their special positions in the religious system, had certain fundamental rights which we would tend to think of in terms of sanctuary, ultimate judicial appeal, and the like. It was, however, up to their henchmen to carry out the trappings of justice, even when the king was the ultimate symbol of justice. The heads of the provinces made laws, and sometimes even waged war on their own.

The ways in which authority might be divided up for delegation and redelegation varied vastly. The lines of the delegated authority were also used in reverse order for the payment of tribute.

In African kingdoms, chiefs held whatever authority they held by reason of its delegation from the king. This delegation was admitted by the chiefs, no matter how powerful—power and authority may not always go hand in hand—and their association with the king was primarily in terms of a religious idiom. In their provinces, they were the chief sources of justice and law. They were also the chief raisers of tribute for their kings.

Vansina has found from two to five levels of delegation of authority within African kingdoms. At every level, the chief was the delegate of the king to the people, and representative of the people to the kings—typically the chief must be acceptable to both. In the central and southern Bantu kingdoms, people could move about from one chiefship to another almost at will, and the chiefs and headmen were in considerable competition for subjects. Movement, while not impossible, was much more restricted in the kingdoms of the Guinea coast, mainly because local communities were organized on a more consistent kinship principle.

Tribute passed from the lower man to the higher man in this ladder of delegation, and in fact its presentation and acceptance symbolized the delegation. A king would not accept a tribute from a man who was not, in his view, a legitimate chief. A chief would not give it to one who was not a recognized king. Tribute was generally of small economic value, and sometimes was purely symbolic in that it had no economic value whatever.

All African kingdoms that Vansina investigated utilized some form of "taxation" in the form of tribute, labor, and calls upon the subsistence of subjects for purposes of sacrifices, feasts, or celebrations within the kingdom. Tribute collected at one level of the system of authority is handed up, in part, to the next higher level so that ultimately a part of it from everywhere reaches the top.

As Vansina has noted, all the strata of authority of subchiefs, chiefs, paramount chiefs, and king received wealth from the system of tribute so that they could perform their obligations. This did not mean, however, that in the indigenous system kings or chiefs were notably more wealthy or had more than their subjects. For the tribute was dissipated again as fast as it was collected.

The hierarchy of delegation also acted as a hierarchy of appeal courts. In some cases, the chiefs and kings had oracles as well as courts, and a hierarchy of oracles was established for settling those disputes that could not be settled through human judicial activity.

Astoundingly little is known about the military organizations of these states—mainly because of two facts: that the studies were made during a time of enforced colonial peace, and that the sociology of war in a comparative framework is astonishingly poorly developed by social scientists.

The lines of communication between chiefs and king may vary, although the most common means is for the chiefs to form councils, or to send representatives as intermediaries on the councils of the king. The membership of the councils which are the primary deterrent to tyranny of kings changes vastly from one of these kingdoms to the next. The "constitution," so to speak, varies, while the form is more or less constant.

The state was one of the most notable features of preconquest Africa. However, scattered among the states and within the states were other, stateless societies, which too have added much to the political character of the continent.

STATELESS SOCIETIES

It was with the stateless societies in Africa that one of the major difficulties lay for colonial governments. It is with them that one of the major difficulties lies for their independent successors. Whereas most members of stateless societies can understand the notion of the state—indeed, their attitude may be that they understand it only too well—most members of states (even African states) confuse stateless societies with chaos.

"State" is, to repeat, a very simple idea, even though its manifestations may be terribly complex. As with most simplifying ideas, it allows (but obviously does not require) suspension of more complex alternatives. Modern Westerners use the institution of the state to avoid tyranny (the while knowing from experience that a bad state may impose tyranny); they see the absence of the state as chaos. Africans who live in stateless societies tend to see the state as unavoidable tyranny; they seek and find order in other institutions.

There are two known organizations that Africans have used as alternatives to state political organizations. One of these is the maintenance of justice and of cultural and territorial integrity through the extended family organizations and the invocation of kinship behavior not only in domestic but in wider spheres. The other answer is a system of checks and balances in which a principle very like that in international law—two power centers instead of one—can be applied at all levels of the community. Such an arrangement assures that no single bureaucracy of the sort that characterizes the state can arise. The first of these two forms is characteristic of the hunting peoples such as the Bushmen and the Pygmies and probably of a few of the most primitive of the farmers in the "Middle Belt"—that stretch of the sudan between the forests and deserts of West Africa. The second is found widely distributed throughout the continent.[7]

Both of these types of nonstates use, for the most part, kinship idioms and the norms of kinship behavior in their system of sanctions. They must not on that account, however, be confused with one another. Their uses and limitations are easily distinguishable. The familial solution to political problems has never worked well face to face either with efficient modes of production or with larger groups of technologically more advanced peoples. The second solution (what one might call the international law solution) works better because it can accommodate sev-

[7] Extended discussion and examples will be found in: Meyer Fortes and E. E. Evans-Pritchard, editors, *African Political Systems* (London: Oxford University Press, 1940); and in John Middleton and David Tait, editors, *Tribes without Rulers* (London: Routledge & Kegan Paul, 1958).

eral million people and can frustrate—indeed, baffle—technologically advanced groups. The family solution is easy for foreigners to understand, and easy for them to demolish. The second is neither.

The "international law solution" to political problems at the local level depends on an arrangement of power reminiscent of what used to be called the "balance" of power. It is most often (but certainly by no means necessarily) expressed in terms of kinship with brothers and their groups of descendants balanced against one another —and, at a more distant ancestral remove, large groups of descendants of brothers or other "equivalent" ancestors balanced against one another.

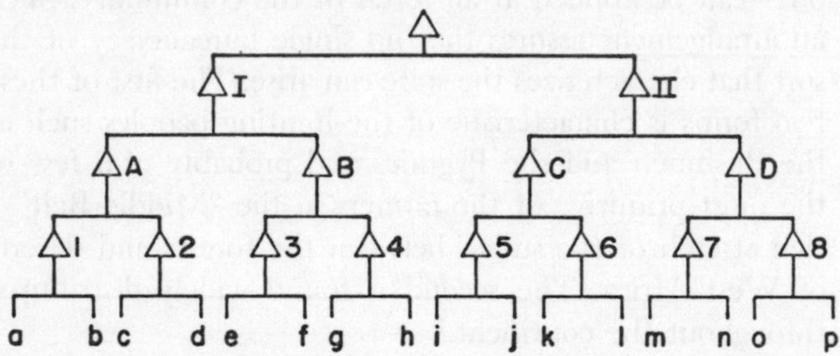

It is a postulate of most of the societies of the world that brothers fight with one another, but that when somebody steps in to stop their fighting, they are likely to join together to turn upon him. Furthermore, though brothers may fight, they must because of their very brotherhood ultimately reach a *modus vivendi.* If we examine the diagram, it becomes quite obvious that if Brother *h* fights with Brother *g*, then anybody who steps in will be regarded as an interloper. If, on the other hand, *h* fights with *f*, *g* will come to the aid of *h*, and *e* will come to the aid of *f*. If the dispute lies between *h* and *d*, then everybody who is a descendant of *B* will come to the aid of *h*, and everybody who is a descendant of A will come to the assistance of *d*. In the same way, I and II are equivalent segments in such a unit.

When we discover that each of the units may contain several hundred men with their wives and children—all the sons and the unmarried daughters—it becomes obvious that a certain narrow band of kinship norms can be used to control warfare and to carry out the legal proceedings. Warfare is in fact stopped automatically by the nature of the system—at very least it is contained. Outsiders, instead of joining in, are usually peacemakers, because they are kinsmen to both warring parties.

Laws are maintained in this situation not through a system of chiefs, but through opposed sets or councils of elders. If there is a dispute between the members of Lineage 3 and those of Lineage 4, the elders of each group will meet, often on the borderland or marches, often in neutral territory, and they will hammer out a solution to the problem because, after all, they are "brothers."

This kind of system has no bureaucracy which is vested with authority. Rather, all disputes, all solutions, all agreements are hammered out between segments whose power is "equivalent" and who are balanced against one another, with the rest of the outside world having no basis for taking sides one way or the other. In one sense, every court case, every legal dispute which is decided amounts to a treaty rather than to a court decision.

Formerly, the Tiv of central Nigeria organized almost a million people with this system. The Nuer of the southern Sudan organized well over a quarter of a million. The Bedouin Arabs throughout North Africa, and over into the Arabian Peninsula are all organized in this way—indeed, there are remnants of such a system to be seen in the royal houses of the various Arab states. There are in such systems no officeholders, there are only representatives of groups. The moment that the representatives of Group A finish dealing with Group B, and turn back into their own organization, they are members either of Group 1 or Group 2, and therefore their "authority" is automatically limited. In the same way, within Group 2, they must belong either to *c* or *d*. In just such a way, authority within groups is checked at the same time that power in intergroup relations is given full force.

Early political officials from European countries sought responsible officeholders in such societies. Obviously, they did not find them. But they did of course find leaders, and when these leaders did not turn out to be "responsible" authorities, the government officials tended to underestimate both their intelligence and their actual power. Throughout the colonial period, the inclination on the part of colonial governments was to give such leaders authority—to force it on them. Wittingly or not, colonial officers tried to create some sort of a state organization and bureaucracy. Almost without exception, their attempts were baffled. Even when such peoples clamored for chiefs—and sometimes they did—these chiefs were treated as the external representatives *par excellence* of the tribal group, or segment of it. Within the tribe, they had little authority and what little they had was considered tyrannous by the people under them.

Stateless societies of the international law type can be seen to be bicentric organizations—or rather organizations in which two equivalent centers are activated at any particular time. They reach compromises rather than make decisions. Judgments must be concurred in by both sides —there are no sanctions from a higher authority. A state is one type of unicentric organization, and because of its single center—no matter how pluralistic that center may appear—its organs may make decisions, their laws can be stated, judgments made, and sanctions brought to bear. The differences between the two ways of seeing "law and order" are so immense that it is sometimes difficult to see that the "other" system does in fact provide them.

LAW IN AFRICAN SOCIETIES

Although many references to warfare among African societies are found in travel books, in historical source materials, and even in ethnographic accounts, there is no study of warfare in Africa that pretends to tie that information together. With law, that other primary political function, the situation is far different. The written material on African law is extensive; although much of it written by Europeans is uncomprehending restatement of substantive norms as legal rules—the pigeonholes of common law filled with exotic fauna—there is nevertheless a substantial body of knowledge about African law.

Indeed, Africa is one of the homes of advanced legal institutions. Perhaps the most famous of these institutions are the courts still found among the Bantu states of the southern third of the continent. Here the local or provincial chief was one of a number of judges on a large and inclusive bench. The bench included representatives of all the important social groups of the community, whether in any particular case they were seen as territorial segments and communities, as kinship units such as clans, or even as age-sets. The judges formed a regular and pronounced hierarchy, and were seated in a row or an arc. The provincial chief sat in the middle; at his immediate right was the second most senior person (however seniority might be computed locally) and at his left the third most senior. To his right, but farther removed, the fourth most senior, and so on, right and left, until the whole court was deployed more or less in a row.

There were, then, certain areas in which the litigants were to stand or, more often, sit on the ground. There were assigned places for witnesses, for the nobility, for the followers and backers of the litigants, and for the community as an audience. These court sessions were often held out of doors, but there might be a building for them

—colonial governments preferred them inside so that regular schedules, based on clock and calendar time, could be maintained even in the face of hostile weather.

There was, in all cases, also a known, and demanded, decorum and order of proceedings. The plaintiff (to use an English term with only a 90 percent fit) made his plea—usually without counsel—and was usually allowed to finish his whole complaint, so long as he spoke well and to the point. The defendant (another translation that does not fit precisely) then made a reply and told his version of the story. Witnesses were called—including what we would call expert witnesses and character witnesses. Then, after the principals had each told his side of the dispute, and after witnesses had been heard, the most junior member of the bench, down at the far end, pronounced sentence. His statements probably included moral lectures, statements of the proper kind of behavior that should have been carried out in the situation, and he may have cited precedent. His judgment would be followed by that of the man at the other end of the line, his immediate senior, who might disagree, and who added new views and new opinions. The third most junior man followed, and so on until they arrived at the middle where the head chief pronounced the final sentence. He had heard everything that the representatives of the community had to say. He had a chance to weigh the evidence, the judgments, and the opinions of his junior judges. His word on the decision became final.

In the southern Bantu states, there were also well-known and highly effective means for carrying out the decisions of the court. The community, having been represented in the audience as well as on the bench, brought both sacred and mundane sanctions to bear. The decisions of such courts were obeyed. Indeed, such communities might be reasonably said to have a "body of law" or *corpus juris* in the lawyer's sense—a body of law and adjudged precedent against which to try each succeeding case.

Law in a stateless society was almost as effective but worked differently. Each case became a treaty-making process. The difference between the two is vital, because in the treaty-making process, the role of precedent is far less commanding and the application of sanction far more diffuse. Indeed, the fact that a solution has been used before may be the very thing about it that a case sets out to overcome.

The difference can best be seen from an examination of our own family law. The norms of family living in modern America are fairly well known and fairly circumscribed. The institutionalization of families is such that these norms are fairly well maintained. A very few of these norms are *restated* for legal purposes: the grounds for divorce, the laws against beating children, and perhaps some others. The large range of family activity is not in any wise made part of a body of *law*, in the narrow sense. The mistake of assuming a body of law in an African stateless society is precisely the same mistake as would be the error of reporting all of the norms for living displayed by the American family as if those norms were part of the law of the land.

In order to comprehend African legal systems fully, then, it becomes necessary to have a new theoretical framework: one which is inclusive of both the law of a state system and that of stateless societies. Such a framework is particularly necessary when we investigate the ways in which the stateless societies are changing on the demand first of the colonial governments and now of the independent governments. These people, who are adapting to state forms on demand, often experience severe difficulty because they see law based on precedent as always and necessarily tyrannous.

There is seldom if ever a special body constituted in order to hear and settle disputes in stateless societies.

Rather these disputes are settled by meetings that can be profitably compared with the old New England town meetings, except that in the case of the African stateless societies, there are always two factions and the actual size of the unit may change from case to case depending on the closeness of the relationship of the principals to the dispute.

There is, in Old English, a precise and accurate word to describe these "town meetings" or settlement of disputes by the important members of the village. This word is "moot." Well into the twelfth and thirteenth centuries Anglo-Saxon communities settled their disputes by meeting outside, under the shade of a tree, in whole communities, in order to discover correct and just solutions to disputes. Such is, in a sense, the origin of the "common law."

Courts, unlike moots, are special organs and require some sort of state organization from which they derive their power. While moots are a mode of the community, courts are special arms of politically organized states.

Moots and courts can, and in Africa often do, exist side by side within the same society. The jurisdiction of the courts may be limited to certain types of cases or to disputes of people of different villages or something of the sort. Vansina has given an extremely cogent example from the Kuba of the Congo. The Kuba state has a very complex court system, the personnel of which changes with the nature of the dispute or offense; at the same time, however, many Kuba cases are settled by moots rather than by courts.

During the colonial era, and undoubtedly down to the present day, such stateless societies as that of the Tiv had a full-blown system of moots which ran side by side with the system of courts that had been introduced by the colonial government. Among these people it was considered to be totally immoral to call one's close kinsman before a government court. However, disputes obviously did occur between close kinsmen. These disputes were always and necessarily settled in moots. In colonial Nigeria charges of witchcraft could not be brought before courts, since "proof" had to be adduced or else the accused could sue the accuser for slander. Since witchcraft is difficult to "prove" in a court, witchcraft disputes had throughout the country to be settled either in moots or in kangaroo courts.

There were devices other than courts and moots by which Africans sometimes settled disputes. Ordeals and recourse to seers and diviners were both fairly widely spread throughout the continent. An ordeal is a means for settling a dispute in the absence of any kind of evidence which can prove or disprove the charge, either because there are no witnesses or because (as in the case of witchcraft) empirical proof is impossible.

Probably no people claims that oracles and ordeals have anything to do with justice. However, they do settle the dispute. Ordeals ran all the way from taking oaths on shrines through the deliberate administration of poisonous substances either to animals or to human beings themselves. These substances were not necessarily lethal, and if the animal or the person did not die, the party was usually considered innocent. Some tribes such as the Azande of the sudan checked and counterchecked their oracular mechanisms by requiring corroboration by a second oracle before they would act on them. Ordeals have all but disappeared from modern Euro-American courts. However, the divine sanctions in which ordeals deal are still a part of such courts because it is still necessary for both witnesses and the principals to take oaths on entering the witness stand.

Africans sometimes resorted to contests to settle disputes. This "game" solution to a dispute is one in which the disputants are either forced to or agree to reduce the field of relevance, and determine a winner; they reopen the field and declare the winner in the game to be the winner of the real-life situation. In the early history of Roman law and others, gladiatorial contests to settle disputes were not unknown.

Perhaps the most important of the sanctions, particularly in the stateless societies, was the institutionalized use of self-help (an example of which is the man who takes a goat from another man who legitimately owes him one). Some degree of self-help is either condoned or required in all legal systems. It becomes even more important in non-state organizations than it is in states because the major sanction, and the power behind it, is to be found in the right and ability of the groups concerned to carry out the decisions made by the elders.

If self-help gets out of hand it becomes, of course, akin to lawlessness—in any sort of society. The boundaries have to be fixed and the use of self-help contained if it is to be an adequate judicial mechanism. In states, such limitations can be defined by legislation or by precedent. In non-states, self-help is controlled, but controlled somewhat differently. In our example of the man taking the goat, his own group will come to his defense if the others try to retaliate. However, if he takes the goat irrationally, and in a way that they believe the moot would not approve of—if he has a "bad case," or if he is a criminal—his kinfolk will not risk their hides and their reputation for him. Limitation is achieved by balance of power and of organizational principles.

African elites in every part of the continent have proved themselves capable of running complex modern governments. The basic ideas behind the political thinking of many of their citizens, however, are still to be found in the type of situation that has been described here.

On the surface, African institutions are changing very rapidly, but the quickening ideas, molded by experience and language, have deep roots in African tradition and history. Because the deep roots of both African and European tradition tap the same prehistoric reserves, and because Africans have passed through most of the cultural revolutions which have, perhaps in other terms, also been the experience of the West, their adaptation has been fast and successful. For all that, however, the distinct idiom in many instances remains. Whatever trouble Africans and Europeans may have in discussing matters with one another in the postcolonial world, much at least is attributable to the fact that they make different political assumptions.

Chapter 13

African Markets

African markets are colorful, noisy, and fun. They provide the place to sell your produce, buy your needs, get the latest news, meet your girl friend, settle your legal disputes, and to pay your respects to (and perhaps influence) your chief or elders. Discussion of the markets had to be left until after both production and the polity had been described, because market places in Africa are almost as important politically and socially as they are economically.

Market places are found indigenously throughout North Africa and the Congo and were especially highly developed in almost all parts of West Africa. They were much less important (though not absent as is sometimes claimed) in East Africa south of Ethiopia, and seem to have been all but unknown in the Rhodesias, Mozambique, and South Africa until they were introduced by European immigrants.

The fact that market places were absent in some parts of Africa does not mean that goods were not bought and sold on the market principle of price, regulated by supply and demand. Nor does the fact that market places are almost overpoweringly present in other parts of Africa mean that the society is dominated by the market principle and its accompanying legal principle of contract, as is the case in the modern West.

To understand the position of the market place in African society, it is necessary first to emphasize the distinction between exchange according to the market principle and the specific place where a group of buyers and a group of sellers can meet. Obviously "the market" extends far outside any market place. In Africa today businesses hire labor, land (particularly in urban areas) may be sold on a real estate market, and today, African grain, palm oil, and diamonds are sold in a "world market."

Conversely, market places are institutions which can be utilized for many purposes besides buying and selling goods. Obviously, therefore, we have two tasks in hand. One is to discover how various processes of exchange and movements of goods help in the provisioning of African societies, and secondly, what goes on in market places. Finally, we want to look at the overlap between the two. We shall find that there are societies without market places, we shall find that there are those in which market places exist but nevertheless very few of the necessities of life pass through them, and finally we shall find in some parts of indigenous Africa and most parts of the modern and emergent Africa, a situation in which the importance of the market place may dwindle but in which the market principle dominates the society much as it does in Europe and America.

A market-dominated economy such as the United States—and the society which goes with it—is one in which not merely products and manufactured items, but the factors of production such as land and labor enter into the same market. These markets may be more or less controlled by political authorities. The difference to be emphasized here is not a difference between free and controlled markets, but a difference that stems from the entry of land and labor into the same market on which yams, corn, cocoa, clothing, and beer are exchanged.

In a society dominated by the market principle, at least some member of every primary group must sell one of the factors of production or else the produce of his work and land (which amounts to the same thing) in order that his family may be provisioned. The exact opposite is usually called a "subsistence economy," which means no more than that the basic provisions of the members of the society are gained some way other than through market exchange, and that ultimately the factors of production, particularly land and labor, do not enter the market (albeit they are no less necessary to production).

The word "subsistence" is tricky in English because it means two things at once. It is associated with the word "level" on the one hand, to indicate poverty and life on the thin edge between existing and perishing—"bare existence." A subsistence economy is different; it must not be confused with subsistence level. The only link between them is the ambiguity in the word subsistence. There is no reason that a subsistence economy must always or even commonly be found to hover at the subsistence level. A subsistence economy means merely the absence of factor markets or a comprehensive political substitute for them.

Poverty, obviously, need not accompany the absence of a factor market and may, just as obviously, be overwhelming in the presence of factor markets.

Except for hunting and gathering economies of the rapidly disappearing Bushmen and Pygmies, the subsistence level is usually far exceeded by all subsistence economies of Africa. There are some places in which there is a hungry season, but that is of a different nature. The hungry season occurs just before the harvest in some areas: it has to do with the rhythm of agriculture and the difficulties of storage in a tropical climate. Even in the hungry season, people usually eat. They do not eat as much as they would like; in fact, they may regularly lose weight during it. But this period, where it occurs, usually lasts at most six or seven weeks.

In a market society, produce and the products of factories are sold on a more or less controlled market at prices more or less determined by supply and demand. The result is that the market in produce can and does limit and even control the market in factors, because of the workings of supply and demand (or a political equivalent). Such a system is to be found in many parts of the world. However, as far as I can determine, it is unique to modern industrialism that this principle has become the primary organizational principle of society. The uniqueness is not in the market principle, it is rather in the relatively great influence it has in creating the political and social milieu.

Some subsistence economies have extremely highly developed *produce* markets. Throughout West Africa south of the Sahara, and down through the Congo, a highly complex system of markets is to be found. What enters those markets is produce and imported goods.

It was only rarely in indigenous Africa that labor, land, brains, or ability, and that strange thing called capital (difficult to define significantly for economies that are non-industrial), all go into the same market as do the products of their utilization and manipulation. Therefore, production did not reallocate factors to any appreciable degree.

The problem, then, becomes one of realizing how distribution was effected, what was distributed, and how life was organized in the absence of this overwhelming principle, to which modern industrial man has acclimated himself.

MARKETING AND TRADING

Market places can be, and sometimes are, highly developed institutions even in areas in which trade is of secondary importance. The difference is one that was drawn long ago—at least as early as Marx—and which must be repeated specifically in the case of Africa. Marketing is an activity in which the producer takes some of his produce to market, and exchanges it for other produce. This is a difference in degree and social emphasis from producing for the market, where the producer takes his produce to market and exchanges it for the means—money —to acquire from the same market, the major portion of his subsistence. While many subsistence economies are marked by highly developed produce markets, if those markets were to disappear, the societies would not perish. People would be made uncomfortable and they would have to change their style of living, but the society would not fall apart or even change its structure. Were the market to disappear from the American economy, it would either have to be replaced by government planning (a totally controlled market), or American society would perish.

Trade, on the other hand, is an activity in which entrepreneurs buy in cheap markets and sell in dear markets. The fact that marketing and trading often go hand in hand does not mean that they are inseparable. Market places, as we have seen, appear in many parts of Africa in which trade was minimally developed; trade, across the Sahara and along the east coast, often took place in the absence of market places. In preconquest Dahomey, for example, the two were totally separated in their institutionalization.

Much marketing in the West African and Congolese areas was done traditionally by women. In many but not all of these areas where the women were the chief marketers, the men were the chief producers.

There have been for many decades now—the history of the matter is not at all clear—many women who have slipped over from marketing into trade, particularly if they had a social background (as with Yoruba, say) in which men did the major tasks in food producing. By the second and third decades of the twentieth century (and perhaps long before that) the major internal trade in subsistence produce throughout the West African area was in the hands of women. Although their wealth and their activities have sometimes been grossly overestimated by travelers, it is nevertheless true that some women, particularly from the Yoruba and Dahomey areas, built up large empires in trade, and in some cases became the chief outlets for European import and export houses.

Today, that situation is changing. Competition to market women is coming from men who are grasping more and more of the trading opportunities as the market expands and becomes central rather than peripheral to the economy.

The kinship groups of Ibo in Nigeria, for example, as well as new "firms" of Ibo founded on contractual relationships, are taking over much of the long-distance trade. Ibo women grossly resent the fact that their trade and even their marketing is being undercut by men.

Hausa and Dioula kinship groups, which have always provided the most important link in the north–south trade between forest and savanna, are expanding their activities. The telegraph run by the posts and telegraph departments of the government makes it easy to keep in touch. These groups own fleets of trucks. The result is that Ibo and Hausa trading "empires" are spread through Nigeria and across its boundaries into neighboring countries.

With the development of trade and of the communications and transportation network, the market principle has entered more fully into the lives of all Africans, and market places have taken on new emphases.

The individual transaction in most African markets involves a good deal of haggling. Prices may vary with the status of the individuals involved: the richer the customer the more he is expected to pay—and he would be ashamed to pay less. On the other hand, prices in some areas—traditional Dahomean market places, for example—were rigidly controlled by the king's bureaucracy and by guilds of producers.

In a marketing system found in a subsistence economy, labor and time are seldom evaluated in terms of money because these factors of production are not distributed by the market mechanism. I once knew a Nigerian who carried, on his head, sixteen gallons of palm oil almost fifty miles to market. When I asked why he did not take a lorry, he said he did not want to "spoil his money." I suggested that he would "spoil" his body if he did not; his reply was that he would recover. This was not so much an economic choice—although, from the economist's point of view, it can be so considered—as his disregard of the fact that his "labor" might be "sold" at a price.

Thus marketing—as with some do-it-yourself items in America—is not distinguished from living. The economy cannot be distinguished, in such cases, from the domestic economy. Everybody, if we may think of it so, "lives over the store."

MARKET PLACES

Because the main point of this section is the diversity of uses to which Africans put market places, and the vast amount of fun that they have in them, it is well at the beginning to emphasize the fact that market places are primarily regarded as points to do one's marketing and trading. The amount of internal trade in various African countries that goes through the market places is tremendous, but nobody has any idea how much volume or what value of goods may actually be distributed in this way. Weights and measures are more or less absent, although in many parts of the continent standard weights and measures have appeared in the last few decades. The quart beer bottle, the standard-size cigarette tin, the standardized four-gallon kerosene tin, and an empty 30-30 shell casing are all used as measures. There are others. There are also many nonstandardized units of measurement. Moreover, no formal records are kept by individual marketers. Many West African traders do keep books of one sort or another, although most do not. Marketers—even when marketers do a little bit of trading along with their marketing—never separate their marketing or their trading from their domestic activities. Obviously, acquiring any kind of quantitative ideas about the amount or the value of such goods becomes a task in data acquisition that has scarcely been tackled, let alone solved.

It is true, however, that vast quantities of local produce such as food, craft products, livestock, cloth—everything that is the staff of life and the basis for the provisioning of society—may go through these markets in parts of West Africa and the Congo. Yet in relatively few places are people dependent on the markets for the basis of their subsistence.

Markets are vital links—they are the very nodes—in the transportation network. The famous "bush telegraph"—the rapid spread of news by means unknown to Europeans—works in part through the market places. Africa is a country on the move, and it appears that it always has been. However, the peace of the colonial era and the improvement of roads that accompanied it meant that market places increased in number, that the amount of travel to and from marketing increased vastly, and therefore the "bush telegraph" worked with better and better efficiency.

Markets are, throughout that part of the continent to which they are indigenous, organized under political authority. Indeed, in those parts of East and South Africa to which they have been introduced, it was colonial government that introduced them. In some tribal areas of West Africa, chiefs retained direct control over the markets and either themselves or through special deputies maintained the market place and kept the peace within it. In other areas, committees of elders, representative in whatever way was considered important to the community, took it as one of their most serious civic duties to maintain a market place so that their part of the world would be "kept on the map" and prosperity would reign.

All African market places are policed by someone. In many areas, this task has gone to the policemen of the regular local government. In others, however, they are still policed by special appointees or by the kinsmen of the chief, or by special groups designated by the chief or by the elders to carry out the task. These policemen are always subject to the authority of somebody who is the headman (it may be a committee) to whom they can refer wrongdoers and disputes which occur in the market place. Disputes inevitably arise in market places, because people may cheat each other, and because they may meet their enemies and their debtors. For this reason, every ordinary African market has, some place in it, a court in session. It may be no more than a market court concerned with arguments over shortchanging, quality of goods, and petty theft. In other market places, however, the judges of the local government may set up their courts. Courts are a necessary concomitant of market places and of the type of crowds which meet in market places.

In some parts of Africa, the market authorities enforce quality control. They disallow sale of rotten meat or other unsatisfactory goods. The usual mode of treatment is *caveat emptor*, but some control is maintained, the degree varying with the personalities and power of the market officials.

Market administrators are usually rewarded. They may be paid salaries by the local government. They may, on the other hand, be allowed to make a levy on the goods sold in the market. Sometimes entry fees are demanded from marketers who intend to sell goods. The amount of the levy or entrance fee is itself subject to what the market will bear. If the levy is too high, traders and marketers will avoid such market places and establish new ones nearby. The only way to avoid such a situation is for governments to demand control and licensing of market places—a situation that was fairly widespread in colonial Africa and is found in a few of the new African states.

Market places can "die," which means merely that people cease to come to them. They can also be "stolen," which means that one gains popularity at the expense of another. In short, the location of market places, their organization, and their popularity are all highly volatile and subject to quick change. Since it is to the advantage of individuals and government officials to control large popular market places (by so doing they are able to see and to influence large numbers of people), few petty tyrannies can be kept up for long.

In traditional Africa, almost all market places were associated with religious activities. That is to say, the market places were consecrated in one way or another, and to this day, most African market places have shrines associated with them. Such consecration guaranteed that supernatural sanctions would back up the political authorities in their maintenance of peace in the market place. Such supernatural sanctions, and the shrines that were their symbols, varied with the particular tribal religion in question. They may have been no more than a bundle of "medicine." In many areas they were specially consecrated trees. In some, there were special small huts with carved figurines in them. The purpose of these shrines was the maintenance of the market peace. It is well recognized that it is impossible, in even the best-policed market place, to be sure that all who cheat or steal or water their beer or sell bad meat will be caught by the mundane authorities. Therefore, it is best to reinforce their vigilance with supernatural sanctions.

Finally, markets are fun. Each displays an element of the fair or the carnival. In West Africa and the Congo they are major centers of entertainment. Dancers come to the market and display their skill. Work parties, wedding parties, christening parties, and spur-of-the-moment parties come to the market to dance and sing and to announce their good news to enlarged audiences.

In all these regards African market places are reminiscent of those in Europe during the Middle Ages and indeed up into the eighteenth century. Markets in Europe were also fairs that were held in the shadow of the church and were policed by the bishop and the market-master and their officials. They were religious centers as well as important centers of trade and distribution. Market places may be extremely important institutions in almost every phase of human activity. Yet for all that, the fact remains that their *raison d'être* is channeling trade and providing an outlet for the marketing of subsistence farmers.

SYSTEMS OF MARKET PLACES

Different market places specialize in different goods and in different activities. One market is a good place to buy X and sell Y. The next one is a good place to buy Y and sell Z. The next one may be well known for its beer drink, and the one after that for its wise counselors and judges. Such specialization, when combined with another fact—that markets do not meet every day—led to two vital points about the marketing system of Africa, particularly West Africa and the Congo. First of all, every community is at the center of a group of markets which meets every fourth, fifth, or seventh day, depending on the tribal area. There is, therefore, an association of market places with time as well as with special products. In a neighborhood with markets that meet every five days, each community is likely to be either at or near the center of a cycle or a ring of five markets, each of which meets one day of the five-day "market week" that results. These market neighborhoods, or rings, overlap in a chain-mail fashion, and spread across the countryside. Such overlapping rings, with a few gaps, run from Dakar almost to the Nile, and south well into the Congo Basin.

The other major characteristic of the market system is that goods can move through market places and traverse very much greater distances than people themselves. Every different African product that goes through market places follows a route determined by specialization of market places. A large number of "middlemen" add to the price, but the markup is amazingly small, considering the number of intermediary links that may separate a producer from a consumer.

Market places, thus, provide another map, based on a different institution, by means of which space, time, and social structure are coordinated. This trade map or market map permeates different tribes, different cultures, and crosses national and language barriers. If a market place is commonly used by several tribes, the consecrated shrines and the ritual that surrounds them contain the elements from each tribal religion which make it workable in all the cultures. There may be, indeed, very highly original rituals consciously created and especially performed in order to get in the vital elements from several religious systems. Violence can still occur, however. Today weapons are forbidden—and usually were so even before colonial governments reinforced the practice. Moreover, throughout the indigenous market area of Africa, people sit in the position in the market place closest to the path leading to their homes—particularly is this true of women marketers. Such seating arrangements keep the escape routes open. Yet, market places are, at the same time, often legal sanctuaries, because of their position of political neutrality and their consecrated shrines.

THE SPREAD OF THE MARKET PRINCIPLE

One of the first reactions to colonial control was the vast expansion in the number of market places in Africa, and of the goods that went through them. Only later did the market places themselves begin to dwindle as their task was taken over by modern transport systems and expanding firms and thousands of entrepreneurs, some petty, some handling large volume.

In the process of the enlargement of the importance of

market places, the importance of the market principle also became magnified. The "market" in both its senses was spreading.

To Westerners, money, trade, and market are more or less inseparable. Rather, they need not be separated to be understood. European governments therefore encouraged the growth of market places, and by introducing coinage and demanding that taxes be paid in it (and abetting importation of goods that could be bought with it), they actively hastened the enlargement of the social scope for the market principle.

Money is probably the most important single item in the changing of an economy. A monetized economy is, by that very fact, different from a nonmonetized economy. Money is a cultural trait that has been discovered several times in the history of the world, including several places in Africa. However, there is money and money. Money is said by economists to do at least three things: (1) it is a method for evaluating and comparing goods of different kinds; (2) it is a means of payment; (3) it is a means for facilitating exchange. If the authority is old enough, money may also be said to be a means of storing wealth.

The three uses of money must not be confused simply because coinage—a single cultural item—carries out the three tasks in our own society. Money is used in the West to pay fines (while crimes cannot be evaluated) and money is used to pay taxes (which is only by the farthest stretch of analogy an exchange). We have a general purpose money, but we must not therefore assume that a money used for one of these purposes in other cultures is general purpose money.

Africa had some examples of general purpose money—cowrie shells in a few places in West Africa and the Congo were such. Most African money, however, served only one purpose and can be called "special purpose money." For example, the metal "hoes" of the coast of Guinea and Liberia were used primarily for bridewealth: aboriginally, one could not use them to acquire subsistence; during the era of the slave trade, many of the items included in the "sortings" of goods with which slaves were purchased were limited to that money use—payment—and were the prerogative of certain political figures.

To understand the changes occasioned by the introduction of general purpose money into a culture that had lacked it, one must first point out other social factors that lie behind the two monetary systems.

There are three (perhaps more) economic principles on which society can be organized: they are the market principle, the principle of reciprocity, and the principle of redistribution. Taking the American economy as a model, we can think quite correctly that we live in a market economy. Most of the transactions that take place are transactions according to market principles of price determined by supply and demand, with more or less government "interference." However, we pay taxes which is a form of redistribution: wealth moves toward a political center and is redistributed from it.

Redistribution may be (but in our own case is not) the dominant mode of institutionalizing an economy. In some traditional African societies, of which Dahomey is probably the best recorded, what trade or allocation of goods takes place is done primarily within institutions of redistribution. "Tribute" is paid into a center, and the goods are then redistributed in accordance with political principles. In such an economy, generosity must obviously be the greatest virtue, just as in a market economy, cleverness must be the greatest virtue.

The other allocative principle is reciprocity. Mid-twentieth-century Americans have a sort of vestigial reciprocity, confused easily with market because we acquire on the market most of the goods that enter the institutions of reciprocal allocation. Gifts we give at Christmas are usually bought—yet, even there, it was until very recently considered more genteel to make your own Christmas cards and to put personal work and attention into the gifts one gave—only today have we come to prize instead the thoughtfulness and individualization that go into buying a gift to suit the personality of the recipient. It is still bad taste to compute market price on the gifts that are exchanged.

Americans in their own economy have taken the three principles and created a form in which the market is central, in which reciprocity is totally peripheral, and in which redistribution occupies an important but purposefully underplayed part. In Africa and in any other nonmonetized economy, there will be a different sort of emphasis among the three principles. In the subsistence economies of western Africa, the principle of reciprocity or of redistribution is likely to be dominant and the principle of market peripheral: the market exists and products go into it, but it is like gift-giving in the West: it could disappear without chaotic results.

The market in traditional Africa was peripheral in this sense. It works precisely as it does anywhere else; the difference is that it affects the way of life of the people very much less.

The economic change in Africa is the result of the victory of general purpose money and the concomitant spread of the market in both senses. When that economic situation is combined with the kind of polity known as the nationalist state, we see the fundamental three tools that have created the African revolution.

One vivid example of the spread of the market principle in Africa must suffice. In many parts of the continent, a man had to purchase rights in his bride. Those rights could be *paid* for *only* in a special purpose money—if such were not the case, the transaction would amount to a monetary *evaluation* of the bride, a situation which Africans both joke about and seriously deny. Bridewealth in East Africa was paid in cattle; in central Africa in spears;

in West Africa in cowries, metal rods, or some other special purpose money.

When the special purpose moneys were undermined by government introduction of general purpose money, it often happened that coinage came to be used to pay bridewealth. For the first time, brides "entered the market"—one could work, or trade, or sell produce; then save coinage and buy a wife. Wives traditionally never entered the same market as farm produce, because there was no "money" which could evaluate both. The spread of the market, here and in many other branches of life, has thus created tremendous moral problems.

In rural Africa, the noisy, colorful market place is a growing phenomenon. But a reverse trend has also set in: in urban centers, the market principle and its institutionalization in the firm have begun the process of taking over. The market principle is becoming dominant, and the market place is being turned into the supermarket.

Chapter 14

African Religion

The myths in the West concerning African religion so distort the facts, let alone the quickening ideas that lie behind the facts, that it becomes difficult to present these ideas without opening oneself to the charge of being a "see-no-evil" optimist who is trying to get away with a whitewash job. Yet the facts have to be stated, at the same time that one declares oneself not to be a do-gooder setting out to erase the differences among people in the name of a sentimental reinterpretation of the doctrine of the psychic unity of mankind.

All African religions are monotheistic in the sense that there is a single High God, who is said to be the creator of the world and of mankind, and a central source of order and of whatever sense is to be found. Many African religions are also polytheistic in that either pantheons of gods or large numbers of spirits or ancestors or some other kind of divinities may stand between man and the ultimate God.

African religions also tend to be tribal religions, which is to say that they have a precise, one-to-one association with a particular form of social group. In this characteristic they are unlike the international religions, which are supple enough to subserve many forms of social structure. Tribal religion and tribal society are different ways of viewing the same universe, for God and the spirits are, even to the skeptical, members of the same society as enfolds living human beings.

Prayer and sacrifice are to be found in all the religions on the continent. Prayers, however, are likely to be generalized requests for health and well-being, and to include statements of innocence of any evil intention. Sacrifices are used not so much for purposes of cleansing (although such may be dominant, as in Kikuyu religion) as to provide paths of communication between the human beings and divinity. To oversimplify, it can be said that in all parts of the continent, life is the supreme value, and that sacrifice takes life (usually goats or chickens) as a means of getting in touch with the source of life and enhancing human life.

Perhaps the most characteristic quality of African religion is that there are many strings to the bow: the late S. F. Nadel, an anthropologist with wide experience in Africa, was the first, so far as I am aware, to point out (for Nupe religion) that for each purpose to be achieved there were several ritual and moral ways of doing it. African religion does not in most places have undeniable orthodoxy (the exceptions are those such as Dahomey in which an established priesthood exists). Therefore it has no heterodoxy. It must be understood rather as a set of goals, a dogma of the nature of God and man, and a more or less experimental (and therefore constantly and rapidly changing) set of rituals for achieving those goals within that conceptual framework of dogma. To study African religion, therefore, means to study the ritual and the stated dogma behind it, and the goals to be achieved by it.

Ritual occupies an important place in Africa. Passage through the life cycle tends to be marked with religious ritual—at least, there is the idea that it should be, and if a man gets ill the reason may be found in the fact that a vital rite was omitted. Christenings, initiations, weddings, burials—moreover, the seasons and the annual schedule—are usually marked by religious rites. The world must be constantly renewed by the ritual activities of man, so that man may prosper as the world prospers. Most importantly, perhaps, ritual occurs in association with medicine as a means of curing the infirm and postponing death.

Africans have, however, a tendency to neglect ritual until it is demanded by the divinities—the demands take the form, they say, of illness or crop failure among the living members of the societies. The immediate reaction to misfortune is always to ask "Why?" and to consult a diviner about those aspects which are beyond the reach of the human senses, then to repair the ritual breach and treat the difficulty.

Perhaps most impressive of all to a European visitor is the casualness of African religious activities. This casualness does not mean that Africans do not take their religions seriously, but only that they do not consider the divinities either prudish or unsolicitous.

A *RUBRIC FOR AFRICAN RELIGION*

The absence of orthodoxy in African religion means that there are many "literary" versions of its substantiating myth to be collected from any single society, and that the "truth" must be extracted from the common motifs of the many versions. In Dahomey, priests can give fairly congruent versions of views concerning the nature of man and divinity and the establishment of the social and divine order. In stateless societies such as the Tiv, every man is his own expert—in religious matters as in everything else. What specialists there are maintain their position by social criteria and not by priestly ones, even as they use ritual knowledge for political ends.

Underneath the wild diversity of African religious practice runs a common set of themes and occurrences which an investigator can pick out and turn into a story. He must, as he does so, warn his readers that if they read such a story as a connected version of African statements, they will be wrong. Rather, a story is the most economical means by which to interrelate beliefs and practices. Unlike the myths that we have tried so far to expose—untrue but widely stated—this story is true but never stated.

In the beginning, the story behind African religion might run, God created the Heavens and the Earth. And he created them without regard for good and evil. They existed and, like God himself, were morally neutral. God, having accomplished his task, withdrew. The extent of his withdrawal varies from one tribe to the next—from the truly "otiose" or removed God, who is not available to human beings, to a God almost as personalized as the Judaeo-Christian Divinity. In all places, however, the created universe was a mechanically or organically perfect system (both analogies misinterpret the African view to some extent, but allow Westerners to see the interconnectedness in it). It lacked only one thing: energy (again, to use a non-African metaphor). The power had to be supplied by the human creatures and their ancestors and the lower spirits that God had created. Human effort and spiritual energy (which often had to be primed by human effort) were the driving forces.

The nature of the creatures that lie between men and God is everywhere said to be unknown, but everywhere described by local people. There are usually at least two levels in the hierarchy—in the "channels," to use a bureaucratic analogy. One is the ancestors, the other is a set of aspects of God or more straightforward, personalized godlings. The will of God (which may be fixed, and therefore unwilled in any specific instance) is made known down through the channels; it is satisfied by ritual, sacrifice, and the protestations of prayer, which carry up through the same channels.

Good and evil enter such a system by two possible routes, and African religions may use either or both: the evil is inherent in human selfishness, which leads men to pervert the ritual that is the means for supplying the force. This (one might almost say "Protestant") notion is commonly found among such peoples as do not have states; here it is human selfishness in its individual manifestations that create misfortune and cause death. Man's weakness and selfishness throw a spanner into the works.

The other source of evil is the "joker," played wild. The joker is a widespread religious phenomenon—the Judaeo-Christian devil is, in fact, a joker who perverts all the rules and hence accounts for evil. Legba of Dahomean religion can be seen as the archetype of the joker whose ineptitudes, carelessness, and malice have allowed misfortune, death, and the threat of dissolution of society to enter the firmament. "Fate," as the joker is often called, must be invoked to explain catastrophe in the absence of selfishness and weakness.

The task of man is, through worship and sacrifice, to hold up his end of the process by supplying the motive force for the universe. Even more important, it is up to man through right and generous living to avoid creating the antisocial and anticosmic situations that bring about disaster. Whoever says that African religion has no moral content (and it has often been said) does not know an African religion—or else he is saying that African religion does not much concern itself with the sexual conduct of human beings and does not set forth its moral precepts as ten imperatives.

If I be charged with creating a myth for African religion in these paragraphs, my defense is that the line between myth and theory is still vague in the study of comparative religion. A myth organizes data as narrative in order to condense mountains of facts or beliefs into recognizable form; a theory is not a story, but does the same thing. Myths and theories are also subject to different canons of proof: theories must stand up to experiment and ratiocination. Myths must stand up to the abrasions of social life. In that sense, this organization of the data is a theory—it allows the exposition of the concepts. But it cannot be gathered, in this form, from any informant.

DOGMA

Like most religious practitioners, Africans start at the opposite end of the chain of events from theologians or social scientists. They begin with the situation that calls for explanation and perhaps intervention between God and his emissaries. In Africa, that situation is most commonly individual or community misfortune: disease or sterility, misgovernment or plague.

Twentieth-century Europeans often fail to remember that it is only about three hundred years ago that William Harvey discovered the circulation of the blood, and that scarcely a century has passed since bacteria were discovered to be the carriers of some diseases; that only a few decades have passed since we have discovered viruses, and only a few years since we have discovered a few hints about the etiology of diseases created by chromosomal malformation. Scientific information of this sort filters, via the press and the educational system, so rapidly into the general knowledge of the educated public that it becomes difficult to appreciate ideas about the nature of disease and its causation held by peoples who lack such scientific knowledge. Science has, if we may put it so, mainly "dominant genes," and the cultural gene loss that accompanies the achievement of scientific progress is surely as vast as the gene loss involved in the hybridization of corn.

Most traditional African religions state the opinion that were it not for the workings of the forces of evil, human beings would live forever in health and happiness. Therefore, when disease and misery strike, the source must be rooted out. That source contains two elements: there is, on the one hand, the cause of the difficulty—Africans, within their knowledge, are as sensible about cause as anyone else, and most of them know that some diseases are communicable, and that droughts appear in recurring cycles. Cause in this sense, however, leaves certain questions unanswered—all the "why" questions. Therefore, misfortune must have not only a cause but it must have a source of motivation (like the running of the world itself must have motive energy).

Therefore the very fact that misfortune strikes is in itself an indication that all is not well in the world and in the cosmos. The cause and motivation must be discovered. It is possible from a Western point of view to realize that motivation cannot be determined by what we would consider to be rational means. Westerners have, in fact, been rigorously trained not to ask "why" questions about misfortune. When a doctor tells us that we have a rare disease we do not immediately say "Why me?"—at least we do not say it to the doctor. We have become a statistic, for better or for worse. It is, however, exactly the "Why me?" question that Africans ask, and to which they seek an answer. In answer, they link social problems to divine action. In so doing, they air and often solve the social problems in the course of seeking to counter the divine manifestations.

When misfortune strikes, the first thing one must do is go to a diviner to discover the device which was used to bring it about and perhaps also to discern the author of it. That author may be a spirit to whom insufficient attention has been paid. It may be an ancestor who is punishing a descendant—perhaps an innocent one—for social, moral, or spiritual shortcomings of the group of his descendants. Or it may, indeed, be a "witch," who is a human author of evil, venting his anger, his envy, or his selfishness.

African diviners use many modes of carrying out their task. They may throw palm nuts and read answers to their queries in the juxtaposition of the fallen kernels. They may toss chains of snake bones. They may rub carved oracle boards together. They may become possessed, and receive their answers through a spiritual intermediary. They may administer to chickens a poison that is sometimes lethal and sometimes not, and then judge by the results. They may examine the entrails of sacrificed beasts. In short, when one is seeking to establish a connection which is in scientific fact a *non sequitur*, any means save a scientific one can be brought into play.

Divination in African religion is vital because it tells priests, patients, and the entire community what ritual they must perform. Successful diviners are, in my experience, all highly intelligent, and often high-strung men or (occasionally) women. They are often also physically handicapped. Divination is one of the specialities most likely to attract the person with an intellectual bent. Diviners must have an excellent intuitive knowledge of the societies in which they live—and often the knowledge is not merely intuitive but can be made explicit, so that diviners sometimes make excellent informants for anthropologists. They must also be men of courage. It is they who are putting their fingers on, and bringing into the open, the inadequacies and the sore spots in day-to-day living. Unless they are strong and forceful, they can be cowed. Many diviners who complete their training never practice, specifically because they cannot stand the heat in the kitchen.

Once divination has been carried out, two steps remain. One of these is ritual, the other medical—or in the case of community misfortune, legal. Indigenous African practice was first to carry out the ritual so that the motivation for the misfortune could be counteracted. Only then could medical curing be undertaken, for to do so before ritual counteraction of the motive force would be fruitless.

RITUAL

All African ritual—perhaps, indeed, all ritual—involves putting a person, or the representatives of a community, into touch with God or his representatives, in order that communication can be made. The person must then also be safely returned from the state of sacred contact. There are two main components of most African rituals: sacrifice and prayer. There are many lesser elements: magical gesture, a social demand that ritual must be carried out by certain people in the presence of certain other people; prayers must be supported by communities—the congregation—and the sacrifices must be consumed by the beneficiaries, past and present, of such ritual.

Most sacrifices in African religion involve the taking of life—there are a few offerings of food, tobacco, or kola nuts that are of a different nature and are sometimes called sacrifice by Westerners. For major purposes, however, sacrifice takes life. The common sacrificial animal is the chicken, although every kind of domesticated animal that one can think of has probably been sacrificed. In West Africa, and indeed throughout most of the continent, the blood of the sacrificed animals is smeared onto the beneficiary of the sacrifice and onto the emblems of divinity, whatever they may be. There are, however, some areas in East Africa in which the cheam of cattle or goats —that substance contained in their first stomach—replaces blood. The point is that the taking of life and the smearing of the symbol of life onto the person and the divine emblems establishes a contact between the two. While thus exposed, one is in a state of extreme jeopardy. However, only through such exposure is curing and reparation possible.

Either as a part of the ritual, or at the completion of the ritual, the sacrificial animal is eaten. It is cooked and consumed by the congregation of the persons who have benefited from the specific ritual in question. The ingestion of the ritual animal redoubles the solidity of the community, and also provides symbols of status.

A good deal of nonsense has been written about human sacrifice in Africa. Human sacrifice has been witnessed and reported by European travelers in several parts of the continent during the nineteenth century; it has occurred secretly (occasionally exposed by government police and courts) on a small scale into the twentieth. Human sacrifice is, in almost all cases (but there may have been a few exceptions), an act of desperation: since human life is the dearest life, it is therefore the most powerful when taken in sacrifice. The idea of human sacrifice is not unknown in modern international religions—it is merely that most of them have devised symbolic means by which the sacrifice, once made, can have permanent effect and need never be repeated. Africans too have devised many means of maintaining the idiom of human sacrifice while not actually carrying it out. One is outright symbolic association of an animal (commonly the dog) with the human being; another is to treat the corpses of those that died natural deaths in such a way that they count for sacrifices and hence for the greatest good of the community.

Although there are vast quantities of texts of prayers from African religious services preserved in the literature, there has not, so far as I know, been any systematic examination of them. Only very broad generalizations can be made. They often protest the innocence from evil of all those present, particularly the ritual participants; often such protests involve oaths—"May I die if . . ." or some equivalent form. The request is usually uttered in very broad terms: for health, welfare, and fertility of entire communities. There are also private prayers in African religion, but it is difficult to say whether the general opinion that they are of considerably lesser importance than the prayers uttered in public ritual is the actual case, or whether it is just that the public prayers are overwhelmingly easier to observe and discuss.

WITCHCRAFT: THE PARASITE OF RELIGION

Witchcraft has to a greater or lesser extent been a parasite on religion in widely scattered areas of the world for the simple reason that it answers many of the same questions about misfortune that religious dogma sets out to answer. There are deep psychic bases for setting the cause of one's troubles outside one's self—the defense mechanism that Anna Freud called "projection." Western history is rife with witchcraft: accusations, trials, and executions of people who were necessarily innocent of the charges made against them for the simple reason that there were no human means to encompass such acts. African history displays the same phenomenon; the same subject/object confusion, the same charges, trials, and executions. Witch-hunts go in waves, whether in Calvin's Geneva, in Adoula's Congo, or in McCarthy's Washington.

Most telling of all, witchcraft is a faulty logical device. Its fault lies in its premise. The premise is that human disease and death can be caused by the ill will of other human beings. Often a vast lore surrounds the necessarily secret (because they are nonexistent) devices by means of which malice is converted into misfortune. It may be the "Evil Eye," so that even a glance can be lethal. There may be mysterious ways of introducing foreign substances beneath the surface of the skin. "Black magic," even Black Masses, may be said or performed in order that good can by inversion be turned to evil. In this realm of imaginative activity—if it occurs it is called "black magic"—there can be no limit on the ways in which people think that evil can be done. Somebody, evil through and through, can always invent a new one.

Witchcraft under some conditions has some positive benefits, although such a view can be quickly overworked. It is a means in most places by which the tensions in families and within communities can be brought into the open and treated. It is nevertheless also true that witchcraft is usually more upsetting than it is soothing to a community. Africans are not, however, constantly afraid of witches, nor do they lead their lives in terror of black magic, as some nineteenth-century writers would have us believe. To a community that believes in it, the occurrence of witchcraft is rather like an accident rate to a community that uses automobiles. One deplores both accident rate and witchcraft, but learns to live with it and is not really convinced that it will strike one's self, so long as one conducts one's own affairs sensibly, morally, and with caution.

It takes a very high degree of education and training to stamp out witchcraft from a community which has known it. It also takes good government and good welfare. The reason is that witchcraft is one of the most suitable answers to the question "Why me?" "Those nasty people" have brought about my misfortune. The world is always full of nasty people and misfortunes. The *non sequitur* is apparent only to the most sophisticated and to those who lack a dogmatic faith that evil spirits may indeed possess persons and turn them into their own evil instruments.

ISLAM AND CHRISTIANITY

Christianity has impinged on Africa for centuries. Ethiopia is a Christian nation, and has been so for centuries. The Coptic church found there and in Egypt is one of the basic forms of Christianity. Christianity in northeast Africa, however, has lost ground to Islam, which has spread widely across the sudanic lands and down the eastern coast of the continent. Many African nations today regard themselves as Muslim; and most others regard themselves as Christian.

Islam and Christianity, although in one sense they have

divided the continent between them, in another sense are both only marginally in control. It is the opinion of both Muslims and Christians that both religions will continue to spread in Africa during the coming decades. They are probably right. It is the opinion of Muslims and some Christians that Islam demands less cultural change than does Christianity when it is embraced, and that therefore it will expand more rapidly. Christianity, however, has a pronounced lead in another respect: it is the Christians who created, manned, and financed most of the schools in Africa. Therefore the educated elites have, with a few exceptions, been educated primarily in Christian schools. Thus, in much of the continent, the new national leaders profess Christianity.

One thing can be certain. With development and industrialization, the tribal religions will dwindle in importance. It is unlikely, however, that they will disappear for many decades to come. The reason is that they are both tough-minded and have been found to work in the tribal situation; they also answer that nagging question, "Why me?" Christians and Muslims fall back on a doctrine of the Will of God, or else back on the explanations garnered from tribal religions.

In most other points, however, there is an amazingly close overlap between the basic ideas of Islam and Christianity, and of the African religions. Neither Islam nor Christianity is foreign in its essence to African religious ideas. And once they are stripped of some of their specific modes of expression, African religious ideas are not foreign to the Christian or the Muslim either.

It is impossible to overemphasize the influence that missionaries, particularly Christian missionaries, have had in Africa. It should at the same time be pointed out and recognized that much of their influence was of a cultural nature rather than merely of a theological nature. They have indeed taught new theologies, but they have also taught literacy, new ways of expressing basic theological notions, new moral precepts, and the principles of bureaucracy. Christianity and Islam both bring the morality of the individual into the religion in a way that is not done in African religion itself, and that has in the past often led Christian and Muslim observers to say that African religion had no moral dimension. The great debt that Africa owes to missionaries is that in a situation in which the forces of trade, colonial government, and the missions themselves were creating cultural havoc, it was only the missions that began to rebuild, and gave them a chance to rebuild. Whatever any individual Westerner may think of the missionary edifice, every African knows that it is to missionaries that they owe the beginning of the African educational system.

Part IV
AFRICA AND THE MODERN WORLD

Chapter 15

The Scrambles for Africa

As this chapter is being written—in late May of 1963—the leaders of thirty-one independent African states, meeting in Addis Ababa, have pledged military support and (in some cases) 1 percent of their national budgets to complete the job of wiping colonialism from the face of the continent: to erase Portuguese colonialism in Angola and Mozambique, and end apartheid in South Africa and Southern Rhodesia. If the late nineteenth century saw a European struggle for Africa, the middle and late twentieth century is seeing an African struggle for Africa.

The scramble for Africa in the years centering around 1885 was a struggle among expanding European powers; like the colonization of the Americas and Australia, it was an integral part of the population explosion and widening technical horizons of the European peoples. The African scramble for Africa in the years centering around 1960 is a struggle for *uhuru* or freedom, and the right to create African nations; it is an integral part of the expansion of population and technical horizons of African peoples.

The African struggle for Africa has, in one sense, continued since the earliest history of mankind. That struggle was, for a few decades, slowed to a crawl by the treaties and the colonial governments that were established in Africa at the turn of the century. The illusion of stability in Africa and the European concept of "progress" (based as it was on the rate of material and scientific change) gave rise to the idea of a "traditional" and static African culture. Anthropologists, in search of a "base-line of change" which allowed them to isolate for study certain aspects of the impact of the colonizer's culture on African culture, added a pseudoscientific dimension to the idea of the "traditional" African culture.

"Traditional" African culture was African culture as it appeared between about 1880 and 1945; it had deep roots in the millennia that preceded it, and it furnished much of the substance and the idiom of the new Africa. But it is not static now, and it never was.

THE NEWEST SCRAMBLE

The national revolution in Africa took place in an idiom of polity and economy. Such a fact reflects not merely the truism that revolutions are concerned with power and control of the necessities of life, but another and more fundamental truth: the colonial era worked changes in all aspects of African life, but it was only in the realms of polity and economy that those changes were made with other than African insistence and cooperation. Africans changed their own arts, their own families, their own religions—often with help from Europeans, often not. But "traditional culture" in nonpolitical, noneconomic spheres was undergoing a sea change from immersion in colonial society.

The newest scramble for Africa—one that is just now emerging—is a struggle of ideology. It overlaps with the struggle for national independence. Both gained momentum after World War II, but the struggle for ideas—unlike that for independence—has not yet been won. It has only in fact begun to focus sharply. Fuzzy ideas such as "*negritude*" (which means merely "blackness" in French, but which a group of West African poets, writing in French, have given a pregnant sentimental and nationalistic connotation) and the "African personality" are beginning to give way to real cooperation and to purpose shared by the whole continent. "Negritude" will become unnec-

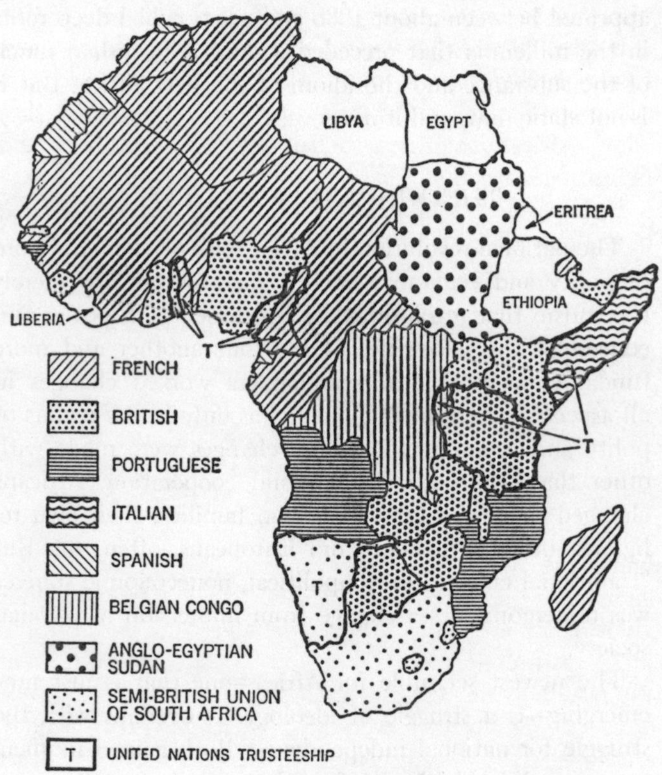

FIG. 10. Africa at the end of World War II.

essary because it has done its job—along with a lot of other forces, it is bringing Africans together.

The ideological struggle is not merely part of the Cold War as it appeared (to both Westerners and Communists) to be in the 1950s—although it is that too. Rather it is a search and a struggle for new forms of society, new forms of religion, new forms of culture that preserve African moralities and sensibilities at the same time that they allow African countries to drive toward economic and political leadership.

Perhaps most telling of all is the search for the form of the new African state—a search that must take place in an age of specialization undreamed of by the largely nonspecialized men who created the American state in the late eighteenth century. The task of Nkrumah, Touré, Nyerere, and Kaunda is very different from that of Jefferson and Franklin—and the results will show not merely the differences in cultural experience, but the results of the change in the temper of the world that have occurred in those two centuries.

Americans today have no more right to think that they know the nature of the state than Europeans, in the eighteenth century, had to think that they and they alone knew its nature. Philosophical, moral, and cultural problems must be coped with in order to determine what the nature of the African state is going to be. The people are going to interpret everything that happens in accordance with the cultural genius of the "traditional" culture with which they grew up. No matter how rapidly education progresses, more time is needed for re-habituation —the changing of habits and views that people scarcely know they have. It will not take as long to change as colonial administrators thought a few years ago. Not "generations." But some time.

The ideas, the values which motivate these states will be found in many cases to be some of the forms of the colonial era, almost always leavened by the ways and ideas that are deeply and anciently African. When African apologists for one-party rule say that it is the African legal genius to "beat things out" and then to present a united front, they are absolutely right. This does not mean that they did not learn many of the forms in which to do so from the colonial powers. It is not to say that any particular kind of "traditional" sentimentality cannot be used to cover up most of the sins of African leaders—of course it can. People cover sins with whatever is handy. It is rather to say that the most vital evaluations of African governments will be African evaluations.

In summary, what we have is a group of people who are now suddenly faced with a changed task, and have come into a modern world largely unopposed, so that their revolutionary organizations were not tightly and effectively organized. They did not work up a big organization, because their primary aims were achieved without one. Their problem is to create the organization to run the governments that were created by the relatively painless revolution.

Africans are searching for—and finding—an identity in the modern world. They are asking who they are, and in the process of finding the answers they are creating the new myths to back up whatever it is that they are becoming.

AFRICA AND THE UNITED STATES

From the outside, this newest struggle for Africa takes on a different form. It is a scramble for African allies. The weapons are development programs, technologists, and UN support. The adversaries are natural forces, climates and soils, outmoded cultural values, and inadequate social organizations that thwart assistance in carrying out the drive to the new societies which Africans envisage and Europeans and Americans have pledged themselves to assist in building.

What do Americans do when they are face to face with this reality: do they react as *Time* magazine reacted in the summer of 1962 and wear the ethnocentric blinders and mouth the platitudes that are both uncomprehending and rude to new allies? Or, do we go out and learn something about it? Learn something about the nature of the new Africa even as Africans are creating it? We can cope with it only if we know what it is. If we are going to call it "savagery" as *Time* did, or if we are going to pervert the image to our own old-fashioned forms, we cannot cope with it. "Savagery" cannot be coped with save by force and paternalism. The day of colonialism is gone. So are the days of savagery. It is not necessary for Westerners—or Communists—to like what they see. It is, however, necessary to understand it. And the blockage to understanding it is monumental; it permeates the American press. A handful of good correspondents is at the mercy of the old myths in the hands of the rewrite men who recast their material for much of the daily press, as well as for *Time*.

The attitude of European powers and America has changed a great deal over the years. Until the early nineteenth century, most European powers still contacted the chiefs of African governments more or less as equals. They "treated" with them. It may have been a narrow equality, but it was an equality. With the expansion of European colonialism rather than mere trade—when the white man's burden began to take on weight—the duty to "raise the level" became more intense. It cannot be overemphasized that early colonial officials—the empire builders—were not wicked people, as many Africans would necessarily have us believe. It was only later that it became evident that paternalism is as unbearable as any other form of tyranny.

After World War II, the white man's burden shifted to the black man. Europeans had to convince themselves that they had intended all the time to hand over the reins just as soon as there were people capable of taking them. Many have still to convince themselves that they stand in the presence of political equals.

Since the independence, there is no doubt that the standards of government have "deteriorated" from a European point of view. There is no doubt that standards have been lowered in all but three or four African universities, and will be lowered farther still. There is no doubt that the parliaments have failed to "live up to" the ideals of the mother of Parliaments.

But there is also no doubt that literacy figures have risen startlingly faster than they did under colonialism. There is no doubt that medical care has increased and been improved, that a new literature and art are in the making. The list could be almost endlessly extended.

The point is that no one can hold back the spread of new culture in order simply to maintain exteriorly defined standards. Europeans may deplore the falling of standards; but they must see such a reduction in context and see it as a whole. Spreading education is good politics, and good developmental policy. If it be spread fast enough and whole enough and widely enough, tyranny must of necessity be temporary.

The problems of the African states are deep problems. All outsiders can do is look at them, examine them, learn from Africans, and try to be sympathetic. The days in which Europeans can do very much about it are finished. Technical aid and the Peace Corps, perhaps. But they scarcely scratch the surface. The good that the Peace Corps and AID programs perform are ultimately good for America—which does not mean that they are bad for Africa. Let us go on helping: American generosity is one of our most prized characteristics. Unfortunately, so is sentimentalizing that generosity.

But let us not forget meanwhile that a new breed of cat is emerging in Africa—and it is going to change the look of the world, no matter from what place one takes up a stand.

THE NEW AFRICANS

More and more modern African politicians, civil servants, students, and businessmen are visiting Europe and America, talking to their opposite numbers and to various American audiences, from national television interviews to church suppers. They are impressing those Europeans and Americans on two very important points. First of all, they themselves are men of very broad cultural competence and understanding. The wide range of cultural aptitude that most of them demonstrate is little short of amazing. Commonly they are able to participate with understanding in a tribal culture, in political parties, in national cultures, and in the new milieu of international culture.

The second point is a dependent factor because it is obviously this range of culture which makes these African leaders so astoundingly humane and tolerant. It is surprising to many Westerners that there is so little vindictiveness, so few attempts at reprisal. In exactly the same way Americans did not understand and still do not understand the ways in which the Japanese reacted to the American conquest after World War II, many fail to understand the African desire to share rather than to get even.

It is also evident that with these two qualities—broad cultural capacities and a genuine humaneness—many of these African leaders have achieved much, and will achieve more.

Such leaders, however, present two serious problems to Westerners as well as to themselves. The first is primarily a Western problem; it is one of how Westerners too can produce more of this wide-ranging type of man whose art of culture covers a very great range and can still be handled with ease. The second problem is of greater importance to African leaders but is a similar problem. As they organize their new countries, they are finding it necessary to call upon men very much less well qualified than themselves, men not so well educated and with a more modest range of experience. The problem is whether the humane quality can be maintained.

Fundamentally, it is a matter of education. Modern African leaders are educated in a very broad sense. They were educated in their various tribal societies or in small African subcultures not so far removed from tribal societies. Most of them were further educated by missionaries. They received as a result of this training a profound respect for the Christian, or sometimes the Islamic, tradition. Almost all of them have been further educated in Europe or in America. Occasionally one even finds those educated in Moscow, in India, or even farther afield. It is obviously a wide and broad education which has created in them the capacity to master such a wide range of culture and, at the same time, the humane quality that springs from genuine understanding that merely because different peoples do things in different ways, they are not necessarily suspect.

The ultimate success of the African revolution will depend on whether or not men of the caliber of those who are now leading that revolution can be maintained or even improved. The question is very simply one of whether or not enough liberally educated humane people can be turned out to run rapidly expanding institutions which are in line with the visions of the present leaders.

The Western problem is a similar one, but must be seen from the other side of the screen. The ultimate success of Europe and America in the world—a world in which the United Nations can be dominated by Asian and African powers—will depend upon their capacity to cooperate with and to esteem these people. Westerners start at a considerable disadvantage, for they know that these people have much to forgive. When Europe and America expanded, they expanded against these people; today these people in their turn are expanding, and there is no place for them to expand save back against Europe and America. Europe and America can ultimately best preserve themselves by inviting these people in and sharing what they have with them. Such is the background of AID and the similar efforts of other Western—and Eastern—countries.

And yet doing this very thing demands more self-control than ever did the expansion of the West. It demands more political and social acumen than any people has ever before been called upon to produce. Paradoxically enough, twentieth-century Europeans and Americans can find a pattern in the modern African leaders who are visiting their countries today. These Africans are people who are rooted firmly in their own societies, with broad traditional and equally broad developing aspects. A wide range of education has given them a humanity and a tolerance which they are finding necessary to the challenge which the withdrawal of the colonial powers from Africa has created. Today, Westerners as well as Africans find education for the coming type of twentieth-century man to be one of the major social problems. Any education is a systematic increase of the range of culture which a person is capable of handling. But as technology grows, education and the analysis of the coming society for which educated persons are being produced become more and more important. A major dimension is that education must allow peoples of different specialities, different nationalities, different traditions, whether they be within our own society and culture or of the varied societies of Europe, Asia, or Africa, to discern one another's problems and to be fully aware of the quality of cross-cultural barriers.

ENVOI

Africa is a part of the world about which we all realize that we can no longer afford to be ignorant. We can no longer afford—we, the human species can no longer afford—to have large areas of the globe agriculturally and technically backward. Human and natural resources can no longer be wasted in the struggle for survival, meaning, and prosperity. The "oldest continent" has produced the "newest" nations. The ferment for development and search of character within those new nations has made it necessary for the rest of the world to examine itself again. The new Africa sometimes appears to Europe to be a counterexpansion against European culture and polity; to some few it appears as a threatening force to be resisted. It has, in fact, been one of the factors unleashing the Negro revolution in America—since late in the nineteenth century, African and American Negroes have been linked, no matter how tenuously, in Pan-African movements.

It is fortunate that for most of the Western world, the new Africa does not constitute a threat—unless the job of creating smooth relationships with Africans be botched. European, Asian, and American nations are all sending development missions to Africa. African leaders are spending vast proportions of their admittedly still small national budgets on education. But Africa is no longer a mere theater of activities—a mere laboratory. Africans are now writing the drama and performing bold experiments. Within the European and American nations, vast new struggles in practical politics and scholarship are opening up, because both the arts of diplomacy and the science of human interaction have found in Africa a new challenge.

Perhaps most important of all is the realization of how much the West has to learn from Africa. Such realization is made the more difficult by the fact that Westerners tend to think (correctly enough) that Africans have much to learn from them. And both Africans and Westerners stand a little amazed to find that each is in the presence of an equal.

Further Reading

The literature on Africa is large and of uneven quality. Much is superficial; some is wrong. Below are a few bibliographies, a select group of periodicals written by specialists (though not in specialese), and a number of books that are good in themselves, most of which also contain more or less extensive reference lists.

Bibliographies

The International African Institute of London has issued several volumes of bibliographies, by area and tribe; some by country and a few by topics, such as maps and labor. Probably the best single source for general bibliography on Africa is the published version of the catalogue of Northwestern University's collection of African books. Northwestern also publishes quarterly a consolidated list of accessions by several libraries specializing in African matters.

Periodicals

Periodicals such as *Africa Report* (African American Institute) and *Africa Today* (American Committee on Africa) are written to keep those interested in African affairs abreast of what is going on there. *The Journal of Modern African Studies* (Cambridge University Press) is somewhat more technical, its special fields being international relations, political science, and economics. *The Journal of African History* (Cambridge University Press) is a scholarly publication covering the area implied by its name. *Africa* (International African Institute) actually covers primarily the fields of social anthropology (including linguistics) and education, although sometimes it publishes a professional article in other fields. *West Africa* (published in London) is a news magazine that covers thoroughly and well its area of concern. *Drum* is a magazine published for and by Bantu South Africans.

General Books

General books about Africa—like those about anything else—fall into two sorts: those that provide background for current events, and those that provide background for more comprehensive study. The former soon date: John Gunther's *Inside Africa* (New York: Harper & Brothers, 1955) was, in its day, a useful compendium, but the world to which it referred no longer exists.

Of the latter sort, three books can be recommended: Vernon McKay's *Africa in World Politics* (New York: Harper & Row, 1963) contains a thoughtful and well-described summary by a historian who is one of the acknowledged American experts on Africa. Another is also a book by a leading American authority: the late M. J. Herskovits' *The Human Factor in Changing Africa* (New York: Alfred A. Knopf, 1962). Its facts and technical interpretations are sound throughout; the reception of the book was mixed only because Professor Herskovits stood also for a liberal moral position (best explained in H. K. Schneider's thoughtful review of the book in the March 1963 issue of *Africa Report*) that proved unacceptable to some reviewers. G. P. Murdock's *Africa: Its Peoples and their Culture History* (New York: McGraw-Hill Book Co., 1959) is written by an anthropologist who is frankly not a specialist on Africa, but who has nevertheless combed the literature more finely than any student before him. His book has been widely influential, though its historical formulations and some of its ethnological groupings have been challenged (a statement that would have to be made of any book on the continent).

Specialized Books

Geography: There are two standard works that cover the continent: L. Dudley Stamp, *Africa, a Study in Tropical Development* (New York: John Wiley & Sons, 1953, with new editions every few years), and Walter Fitzgerald, *Africa, A Social, Economic and Political Geography of its Major Regions* (New York: Dutton, 1957, 8th edition revised by W. C. Brice). The first volume of George H. T. Kimble's *Tropical Africa* (New York: Twentieth Century Fund, 1960 and Doubleday Anchor Books, 1962) concerns geography (the second volume, on social problems and social environment, has not been well received). A regional geography of prime quality is R. J. Harrison Church, *West Africa* (London and New York: Longmans, Green & Co., third edition, 1961).

History: A Short History of Africa by Roland Oliver and J. D. Fage (Harmondsworth, England and Baltimore: Penguin Books, 1962) is readable and amazingly complete, though some critics claim they have overemphasized the importance of Egypt and Meroë. These men are at work on a history of Africa in several volumes. Basil Davidson's *The Lost Cities of Africa* (Boston: Little, Brown & Co., 1959, originally published in London by Victor Gollancz, Ltd., 1959, as *Old Africa Rediscovered*) is a popularized account that maintains high standards of scholarship. A forthcoming book by Philip D. Curtin, *The Image of Africa* (Madison: University of Wisconsin Press, 1964) promises to cover large amounts of detail that are not presently to be found in any except the most recondite sources.

Polity: Two general books can be highly recommended: Immanuel Wallerstein, *Africa, the Politics of Independence* (New York: Vintage Books, 1961) and Rupert Emerson, *From Empire to Nation* (Cambridge: Harvard University Press, 1960). Pioneering studies about individual countries on which such books must be based are best represented by James S. Coleman, *Nigeria: Background to Nationalism* (Berkeley: University of California Press, 1958) and David E. Apter, *The Gold Coast in Transition* (Princeton: Princeton University Press, 1955). Thomas Hodgkin has written a short and fine account of *African Political Parties* (Harmondsworth, England and Baltimore: Penguin Books, 1961). Accounts of "traditional" African polity can be found in two well-known collections: *African Political Systems,* edited by

Meyer Fortes and E. E. Evans-Pritchard (London: Oxford University Press for International African Institute, 1940) and *Tribes without Rulers,* edited by John Middleton and David Tait (London: Routledge & Kegan Paul, 1958).

Economy: The publications of the United Nations cover this area of African studies more fully than any other. The key paper is E/2557 ST/ECA/23 (Sales No: 1954, II. C. 4) called *Enlargement of the Exchange Economy in Tropical Africa.* The World Bank has also published many special studies of the economies of African countries. *African Labor Survey,* compiled by the International Labor Office (Geneva, 1958, Studies and Reports, New Series No. 48) is a basic reference work. The material on African indigenous economy is found almost entirely in ethnographic reports such as William Watson's *Tribal Cohesion in a Money Economy* (Manchester: Manchester University Press, 1959), S. F. Nadel's *A Black Byzantium* (London: Oxford University Press, 1942), and P. H. Gulliver's *The Family Herds* (London: Routledge & Kegan Paul, 1955). A collection of essays about market places and the expansion of the market principle is to be found in *Markets in Africa* (Evanston: Northwestern University Press, 1962), Paul Bohannan and George Dalton, editors.

Art: There are many attractive picture books that deal with African art. Of special importance are Denise Paulme, *African Sculpture* (London: Elek Books, 1962) and Eliot Elisofon and William Fagg, *The Sculpture of Africa* (New York: Frederick A. Praeger, 1958). Roy Sieber, the art historian at Indiana University, is preparing a forthcoming Pelican book on African art that will be of high caliber.

Religion: This subject is particularly difficult because the information is scattered, primarily in such ethnographic monographs as E. E. Evans-Pritchard, *Nuer Religion* (London: Oxford University Press [Clarendon Press], 1956), S. F. Nadel, *Nupe Religion* (London: Routledge & Kegan Paul, 1954), M. J. Herskovits, *Dahomey, an Ancient West African Kingdom* (New York: J. J. Augustin, 1938), Godfrey Lienhardt, *Divinity and Experience, the Religion of the Dinka* (London: Oxford University Press [Clarendon Press], 1961),

John Middleton, *Lugbara Religion* (London and New York: Oxford University Press for International African Institute, 1960).

Missionary activity is well documented, but again the material has not been brought together in most instances. Roland Oliver's *Missionary Factor in East Africa* (London and New York: Longmans, Green, 1952) is among the best pieces of missionary history. It is safe to say that this field will be vastly better studied within the next few years. The best book on African separatist churches is Bengt Sundkler, *Bantu Prophets in South Africa* (London and New York: Oxford University Press for International African Institute, second edition, 1961). Finally, world view is discussed in one symposium edited by an anthropologist (Daryll Forde, editor, *African Worlds*, London and New York: Oxford University Press, 1954), and in another by a missionary who also made an extensive and vital contribution to anthropology, Edwin W. Smith, editor, *African Ideas of God* (London: Edinburgh House Press, 1950, second edition, 1961).

Index

Aesthetics, 150–52, 153–54
Africa companies, 112, 121
African Studies Association, 2
Afrikaans, 113
Agriculture, 135, 136 ff
  discovery of, 80–81
  spread of, 81, 84 ff
Apes, 49 ff
  early, 51
Apter, David, 2
Arabs, 95, 99–100
Ardrey, Robert, 52, 56, 57
Art, associated with religion, 149–50
Australopithecene, 53–54, 55
Authority, 191–93

Bananas, 138
Barth, Heinrich, 114
Baumann, Hermann, 127
Beer, 139
Beggars, 139
Benin, 147–48
Birth rates, 161–62
Blood, 67
Blumenbach, Johann F., 63
Bond servants, 107–8
Boundary, 18–19, 124
Bridewealth, 158, 166 ff, 220–21
British, 14 ff
Bronzes, 145
Broom, Robert, 53–54
Bureaucracy, 189, 191–92, 197
Business men, 4

Cash crops, 21
Census, 77–78
"Chain of being," 4–5, 71, 72
Change, 24 ff
  resistance to, 6
Childrearing, 170–71
Chinese trade in East Africa, 96–97
Christianity, 233–35
Churches, separatist, 26 ff
Clan, 169
Climates, 35 ff
Climatic theory of race, 77
Cold War, 9, 241
Coleman, James S., 2
Colonialism, 238, 243
  aftermath of, 241–42
  defined, 11 ff
  social structure of, 14–18
Communal ownership, 179
Communication, 13, 141
Concubines, 167
Congo Free State, 121–22
Constitutions, 16–17
Contest, 203–4
Contract, 18, 20, 185
Cooking, 137, 138

Copper, 43, 44
Courts of law, 15, 199–200, 202
Co-wife, 160–63
Cowrie shells, 4–5, 100, 218–19
Critics, 142, 150–52
Culture areas, 126–28
Curtin, Philip, 68 ff
Cush, 87 ff

Dancing, 142–43, 215
Dark Continent, 1, 4, 97, 98 ff, 102
Dart, Raymond, 48, 53, 55
Darwin, Charles, 72, 73
Dates, 138
Degeneration theory, 63–64
Denmark, 112
Deprived people, 24–25
Descent groups, 169–70
Diamonds, 44
Diet, 133, 135–36, 139
Disease, 6, 42, 45 ff, 78, 227, 232
Divination, 228–29
Divorce, 162–63
Dogma, 227–29
Dominance, 174
Drink, 138–39
Dutch, 111, 112–13

Economic development, 182, 185–86
Economy, 174, 239
Education, 23, 29, 122, 244, 247
Egypt, 81–82, 85 ff, 145
Egyptian influence in Africa, 86 ff

Equivalence, 196–97
Evolution, cultural, 50

Fagg, William, 148
Family, 159 ff, 183, 201, 232–33
Farmers, 135–36
Farm tenure, 176–77, 178
Feudalism, 95 ff
Figurines, 144, 149–50
Fiji, 16, 118
Fire, 79–80
Firms, 185
Fishermen, 83–84, 133–35
France, 113
Frobenius, Leo, 146

Genetics, 7
Geography, 32
  early study of, 103–4
Geology of Africa, 32–34
Germany, 116 ff
Ghana, ancient empire of, 92–93
God, 222, 225
Gold, 42–43, 104
Grain belt, 136–38
Greenberg, Joseph H., 129, 131

Haggling, 211
Hamites, 65 ff
Hand axe, 57–58
Hawkins, Sir John, 112
Henry the Navigator, 101, 103 ff
Herding, 41–42, 135–36
Herskovits, Melville J., 126–27
Heterodoxy, 224

Ife heads, 146
Income, 21
Indian Ocean, trade in, 96–97
Indirect rule, 17
International African Institute, 2
International law, 196, 198
International relations, 188
Irish, 69
Iron, 43, 89 ff
Islam, 233–35

Joker, 226

Kanem, ancient empire of, 93
Kings, divine, 191–92
Kingship, 86–87, 93–95
Kinship, 159–60, 171–73, 195
  sanctions of, 171–72

Labor, 182 ff, 211–12
  migration of, 186–87
  sexual division of, 137–38
Land, 175 ff
Land tenure, 180–82
Language, 76–77
Languages of Africa, 128 ff
Law, 188–89, 197, 199 ff
  writing of, 16
  sureness of, 16–17, 20
Leakey, L. S. B., 49, 51–53, 55, 57
Le Gros Clark, Sir Wilfred, 54–55
Leopold, King of the Belgians, 116, 120–21
Levirate, 168
Lingua franca, 132–33
Linnaeus, 70–71
Livingstone, David, 102, 109, 114
Love, 165

Madagascar, 97
Malays, 97
Malaysian crops, 84–85, 91, 138
Mali, ancient empire of, 93
Man, definition of, 48 ff
  early, 48, 50
    reconstruction of, 56
Maps, 175–76, 217
  ethnic, 176, 177–78
  tribal, 124, 126, 128
Market, 184
  administration of, 213–14
  expansion of, 118–20
  labor, 184–85
  places, 206–7, 209–10, 212 ff
Market places, systems of, 216 ff
Market principle, 207–9, 211, 217 ff
Market system, 187
Marketing, 209–10
Markets, 206 ff
  factor, 208–9
Masks, 144, 149
Mau-Mau, 26 ff
Meroë, 88 ff
Metallurgy, 84, 88 ff
Misfortune, 224, 228
Missionaries, 1–2, 3–4, 22–23, 116, 235
Misunderstanding, working, 11 ff, 24

Mobility, 18, 176–77
Money, 18, 20, 21, 218–21
Moot, 202
Moslems, 92–93
Mosquitos, 45–46
Murdock, George P., 67, 91, 97, 124
Music, 142
Myth, 1 ff, 222, 224–26

Nationalism, 25 ff, 239
Nativistic movements, 25 ff
Negritude, 8, 239–41
Negroes, American, 7 ff, 30, 106–7
  origin of, 67, 82 ff
Nile valley, population of, 85–86
"Noble Savage," 4–5, 69–70
Nok culture, 145–46
Nurse, 170–71

Old World culture area, 83
Oracles, 193–94, 203
Orthodoxy, 224

Painting, 145
Paleontology, 52
Pan-Africanism, 7–8
Park, Mungo, 74–75, 102, 114
Paternalism, 24
Peace, 19
Peace Corps, 3, 244
Perham, Marjorie, 29
Phrenology, 73, 75
Piltdown "man," 50
Politics, 174, 188 ff, 239
Polygyny, 158, 160 ff
Polytheism, 222
Population explosion, 77–78, 81, 86
Portugal, expansion of, 100 ff
Portuguese, 147, 238
Prayer, 222–23, 231
Prejudice, 69, 71–72
Prester John, 104
Price, 211
Pritchard, James, 72–73
Proconsul, 52–53
Property, 179–80

Race, 6–7, 60 ff
  as a social referent, 62–64
  biological definition of, 62
  geographical, 61–62
Rainfall, 38–39
Reciprocity, 219–20
Redfield, Robert, 98
Redistribution, 219–20
Religion, 170–215
  association with art, 149–50
Resources, 42 ff
Responsibility, 15–16
Rift Valley, 34
Rights in women, 167–68
Ritual, 223–24, 229–31
Root crops, area of, 138–39

Sacrifice, 222, 226, 230–31
Sahara Desert, desiccation of, 82, 85–86, 98
Sculpture, 144 ff, 152–53
Self-help, 204
Seligman, Charles G., 65 ff, 126
Settlers, European, 27
Shifting cultivation, 40–41

Slave trade, 107–8
  abolition of, 110–11
  Arab, 109
  East African, 108–9
Slavery, 101, 104, 105 ff
  African and European contrasted, 105–8
  failure of, among American Indians, 110
Slaves, 100–1, 104
Sleeping sickness, 46
Soils of Africa, 39 ff
Southeast Asia, 85
Sovereign, absentee, 11, 13–14
Space, geographical, 174 ff, 188
Sphere of influence, 118
Stanley, Henry M., 116
State, 189, 190 ff, 194–95
  new forms of, 244
Stateless society, 189–90, 194 ff, 201
Stone Age, 57 ff
Storage of food, 137
Subsistence areas, 133 ff
Subsistence economy, 207–8
Subsistence farmers, 139
Sudanic empires, 89, 90, 91 ff
Sundkler, Bengt, 26
Swahili, 132–33

Tales, 143–44
Target workers, 187
Taxes, 21
Territoriality, 174 ff
Time magazine, 243
Tool making, 48–49
Tools, 79
Touré, Sekou, 29
Town meeting, 202
Trade, 19–20, 133, 210–11
  across the Sahara, 4–5, 100–1
Tradition, 239
  Tradition, Great and Little, 98 ff
Tribe, 124–25
Tribute, 193, 219
Tucker, A. N., 131
Tyranny, 24–25

Unemployment, 187
UNESCO, 3
UNICEF, 46
Unity of culture, African and European, 5–6

Vansina, Jan, 191, 193, 202

War, 19, 194, 197, 199
Water, 44–45
Weights and measures, 212–13
Westermann, Diedrich, 91
Wheeler, Sir Mortimer, 96
Widows, 168
Wilberforce, William, 71–72, 110
Witchcraft, 232–33
Women, as marketers, 210–11
  position of, 163–64
Work, 133, 182, 183, 215

Zinjanthropus, 51, 55–56, 57